Making Justice Work

THE REPORT OF THE CENTURY FOUNDATION/ TWENTIETH CENTURY FUND TASK FORCE ON APPREHENDING INDICTED WAR CRIMINALS

MAKING JUSTICE WORK

With background papers by

MARSHALL FREEMAN HARRIS, R. BRUCE HITCHNER, MICHAEL P. SCHARF, AND PAUL R. WILLIAMS

and

DIANE F. ORENTLICHER

1998 ◆ THE CENTURY FOUNDATION PRESS ◆ NEW YORK

The Century Foundation/Twentieth Century Fund sponsors and supervises timely analyses of economic policy, foreign affairs, and domestic political issues. Not-for-profit and nonpartisan, the Fund was founded in 1919 and endowed by Edward A. Filene.

Library of Congress Cataloging in Publication Data

The Century Foundation/Twentieth Century Fund Task Force on Apprehending Indicted War Criminals.

Making justice work: the report of The Century Foundation/Twentieth Century Fund Task Force on Apprehending Indicted War Criminals / with background papers by Marshall Freeman Harris, R. Bruce Hitchner, Michael P. Scharf, Paul R. Williams, Diane F. Orentlicher.

p. cm.

ISBN 0-87078-421-8

1. International Tribunal for the Prosecution of Persons Responsible for Serious Violations of International Humanitarian Law Committed in the Territory of the Former Yugoslavia since 1991. 2. International criminal courts. 3. Arrest. I. Harris, Marshall Freeman. II. Hitchner, R. Bruce. III. Scharf, Michael P., 1963– . IV. Williams, Paul R. V. Orentlicher, Diane F. VI. Title.

KZ1203.A2074 1998 98–5924
341.7'7–DC21 CIP

Cover Design: Claude Goodwin
Manufactured in the United States of America.

Foreword

In the realm of commerce, the construction of an international legal order has been the work of centuries. While the effort has been aided in recent decades by the triumph of capitalism over its economic rivals, the existing framework is still a long way from a finished project. Perhaps, then, it is no surprise that the much more difficult task of building an international rule of law applicable to political and military behavior remains very much a work in progress.

Since Nuremberg, the concept of accountability for war crimes has evoked widespread support in many nations. The cold war, however, effectively made impractical virtually all efforts to reach agreement in this area. More recently, the possibility of enforcing international standards and an expanded respect for human rights has become a more realistic prospect. The most important steps in this direction were taken in 1993 and 1994 when the United Nations established two ad hoc war crimes tribunals to investigate and, where appropriate, indict individuals suspected of breaching the Geneva Conventions either in the former Yugoslavia or in Rwanda.

However, while the tribunal for the former Yugoslavia has publicly indicted more than seventy individuals for war crimes, only about one-third have been detained; and the two most notorious—Serb party leader Radovan Karadzic and army commander Ratko Mladic—remain free. Despite this fact and the continuing tensions in the former Yugoslavia, there have been only three attempts to apprehend indicted Bosnian war criminals. Yet, the

U.N. resolution that established the tribunal obligated all members of the international community to comply "without undue delay" in "the arrest or detention of persons" indicted for war crimes and "the surrender or transfer of the accused to the International Tribunal."

In this context, the Twentieth Century Fund established a distinguished international Task Force—chaired by Richard Goldstone, the first Chief Prosecutor for the International Criminal Tribunals for the former Yugoslavia and Rwanda—to examine what steps the world community should take to bring a stable peace to war-ravaged Bosnia and maintain the international rule of law. Finding that there can be no lasting peace or end to the Bosnian nightmare until "all war criminals are arrested and brought to justice," the Task Force concluded that nations—with the United States and European Union in the lead—must use military force where necessary to apprehend indicted war criminals, enact U.N. sanctions against states harboring indicted war criminals, and freeze the assets of individuals indicted for war crimes or fail "a profound test of their moral, ethical, political and military leadership in the world."

These conclusions were reached after serious deliberation by the members of the international Task Force, including Morris Abram, chairman of the United Nations Watch, Geneva; Gianfranco Dell'Alba, a member of Italy's Transnational Radical party; Patricia Derian, former U.S. assistant secretary of state for human rights and humanitarian affairs; Benjamin Ferencz, former war crimes prosecutor at Nuremberg; Shirley Williams, cofounder of the Social Democratic Party (UK); and Nobel Peace Prize winner and noted author Elie Wiesel. Others have endorsed the Task Force's conclusions, including former president of Costa Rica and Nobel Peace Prize winner Oscar Arias; noted authors Bette Bao Lord and Susan Sontag; former senator Paul Simon; Lieutenant General DeWitt C. Smith, Jr. USA (Ret.); former U.S. deputy secretary of defense William H. Taft, IV; and former secretary of state Cyrus Vance. Morton H. Halperin, senior vice president of the Fund, coordinated the work of the Task Force.

The deliberations of the members of the Task Force benefited from the work of several international law experts. First, Paul R. Williams, senior associate at the Carnegie Endowment for International Peace and executive director of the Public International

Law and Policy Program, and Michael P. Scharf, professor and director of the Center for International Law and Policy at the New England School of Law, assisted in drafting the statement of the Task Force; they—along with Marshall Freeman Harris, vice president of Freedom House, and R. Bruce Hitchner, professor and director of the Center for International Programs at the University of Dayton—also provided the important analysis of the legal, moral, and practical obligations and options of the international community in bringing war criminals to justice that appears in the background materials in this volume. Second, Diane F. Orentlicher, professor at the Washington College of Law, provided the Task Force an examination of these responsibilities, focusing on the specific issue of arresting indicted individuals, which also appears in this volume. The Fund would also like to thank the Coalition for International Justice, and specifically, John Heffernan, executive director; Nina Bang-Jensen, special counsel and director of advocacy; and Kathy Ward, consultant, for directing this effort; and Steve Rabinowitz and Hadass Tesher of Rabinowitz Media for assisting in communicating the Task Force's conclusions to U.S. government officials and the public.

The Twentieth Century Fund has a long history of supporting work in the area of human rights and international law, including the recently released *Unwinnable Wars: American Power and Ethnic Conflict* by David Callahan and Rosemary Righter's *Utopia Lost: The United Nations and World Order*. In addition, we have two ongoing projects: Harold Hongju Koh's analysis of why nations obey international law and Kathryn Sikkink's examination of the origins and effectiveness of U.S. human rights policies. The Fund has also supported work addressing the issue of building peace in Europe, including Steven Burg's *War or Peace? Nationalism, Democracy, and American Foreign Policy in Post-Communist Europe*, John Gerard Ruggie's *Winning the Peace: America and World Order in the New Era*, Michael Mandelbaum's *The Dawn of Peace in Europe*, and Jonathan Dean's *Ending Europe's Wars: The Continuing Search for Peace and Security*.

When future historians look back on our time, the most profound question that they are likely to ask is, How did we react to the great international opportunities presented by the end of the cold war? Clearly, they will find that many nations and international organizations seized the vast economic opportunities offered by the collapse of restrictive ideologies and dangerous rivalries. The more difficult question, but the one that is likely to count for the most in the long run, is, What did we do to create a new world order founded on peace, law, and justice?

In this context, the United States, so strikingly the world's most powerful nation, has a special responsibility to lead. Therefore, we at the Fund believe that this Task Force's conclusions on the importance of arresting those who have breached international standards of law and human rights could not be more timely and important. Again, we thank all those who assisted in this effort and take special note of the leadership provided by Justice Goldstone.

Richard C. Leone, President
The Century Foundation/Twentieth Century Fund
March 1998

CONTENTS

Members of the Task Force

Richard Goldstone, *Chairman,* was the first Chief Prosecutor for the International Criminal Tribunals for the former Yugoslavia and Rwanda. He is currently a member of the South African Constitutional Court.

Morris B. Abram, Chairman of United Nations Watch, Geneva, is former Ambassador to the United States Mission to the United Nations, Geneva.

Robert Badinter is Professor Emeritus at the University of Paris and President Emeritus of the Constitutional Council of France. He is former French Minister of Justice and a member of No Peace Without Justice.

Gianfranco Dell'Alba is a member of the European Parliament, No Peace Without Justice, and Italy's Transnational Radical Party. He is also a member of the Executive Committee of the International Crisis Group.

Patricia Derian is former U.S. Assistant Secretary of State for Human Rights and Humanitarian Affairs in the Carter administration.

Uffe Ellemann-Jensen is the President of the European Liberal Party (ELDR), and a member of the Danish Parliament. He served as the Danish Minster of Foreign Affairs (1982–93) and was National Chairman of the Liberal Party "Venstre" (1984–98).

Benjamin B. Ferencz served as a war crimes prosecutor at Nuremberg. Now a retired professor of international law, he is an author and lecturer on problems of world peace.

Richard Gardner is the Henry L. Moses Professor of Law and International Organization at the Columbia University School of Law. He is also a practicing lawyer with the firm of Morgan, Lewis and Bockius. He formerly served as the U.S. Ambassador to both Italy and Spain.

Bianca Jagger is a member of the Executive Director's Leadership Council of Amnesty International. She also serves as an advisory board member for Human Rights Watch and the Coalition for International Justice.

Theodor Meron[*] is the Charles L. Denison Professor of Law at New York University Law School. He is a leading scholar in the field of international law and the author of numerous publications.

Aryeh Neier is President of the Open Society Institute and former Executive Director of Human Rights Watch.

Herbert S. Okun served as the Deputy Cochair of the International Conference on the Former Yugoslavia, as a mediator of the Greek-Macedonian dispute, and as U.S. Ambassador to the German Democratic Republic and to the UN. He is currently a visiting lecturer at Yale Law School and U.S. member of the UN International Narcotics Control Board.

John Roper is a Fellow of the Royal Institute of International Affairs and a member of The International Commission on the Balkans. He is also a former Director of the Institute for Security Studies of the Western European Union and a former member of the British Parliament.

Anibal Cavaco Silva was Prime Minister of Portugal from 1985 to 1995.

---

[*] Professor Meron, acting in his personal capacity, agreed to a draft of this statement in February 1998, prior to his appointment to the U.S. delegation to the ICC conferences.

Stephen J. Solarz is a former member of the U.S. Congress, where he served as a senior member of the House Foreign Affairs Committee. During his eighteen-year tenure on the committee, Mr. Solarz, who traveled widely and met with dozens of world leaders, emerged as a leading spokesman on behalf of democracy and human rights.

George Soros is a philanthropist, international financier, and Chairman of the Open Society Institute, a private operating and grant-making foundation that promotes the development of open society around the world.

John W. Vessey,* General, U.S. Army (Ret.), former Chairman of the Joint Chiefs of Staff, is currently Chair of the Advisory Board of the Center for Preventive Action at the Council on Foreign Relations.

Elie Wiesel, 1986 Nobel Peace Laureate, is the Andrew W. Mellon Professor in the Humanities at Boston University and the author of more than forty books. He was Founding President of the Elie Wiesel Foundation for Humanity, and Founding Chairman of the U.S. Holocaust Memorial Council.

Shirley Williams is the Right Honorable Baroness Williams of Crosby, a Privy Councilor, and the cofounder of the Social Democratic Party (UK).

---

* General Vessey was unable to review and approve the Task Force Statement prior to its release.

Statement of the Task Force

Meeting the Obligations of Justice[1]

We have an obligation to carry forward the lessons of Nuremberg. . . . Those accused of war crimes, crimes against humanity and genocide must be brought to justice. . . . There must be peace for justice to prevail, but there must be justice when peace prevails.

U.S. President William Jefferson Clinton[2]

International military forces have engaged in only three attempts to aggressively apprehend indicted war criminals in Bosnia in the two-plus years since the signing of the Dayton Peace Accords and four years after UN Security Council Resolution 827 bound all members of the international community to comply "without undue delay" in "the arrest or detention of persons" indicted for war crimes and "the surrender or transfer of the accused to the International Tribunal."

In late June and early July 1997, international military forces engaged in two actions that resulted in the arrest of Milan Kovacevic and Slavko Dokmanovic, and the death of Simo Drljaca. In October of the same year, the United States and the European Union successfully pressured the Croatian government into facilitating the voluntary surrender of ten Croatian nationals and Bosnian Croats indicted by the International Criminal Tribunal for the former Yugoslavia. On December 18, Dutch NATO forces captured two Bosnian Croats, Vlatko Kupreskic and Anto Furundzija.

Despite these efforts, there are no clear signs that the international community, in particular, the United States and European Union, intends to engage in further military action or the imposition of economic pressure against the Bosnian substate entity of the Republika Srpska, which harbors forty-seven publicly indicted war criminals, or against the Federal Republic of Yugoslavia (Serbia/Montenegro), which harbors three indicted Yugoslav

National Army officers and intermittently hosts indicted Bosnian Serbs such as General Ratko Mladic as well a number of Serbian paramilitary leaders who are widely assumed to be secretly indicted. Similarly, there are no further signs that the United States and the European Union intend to continue their economic pressure on Croatia to encourage it to facilitate the transfer of the remaining two indicted Bosnian Croats, who are presumably subject to its control.

The failure of the international community to apprehend or ensure the apprehension by local forces of the remaining fifty-two publicly indicted war criminals, including the notorious Radovan Karadzic and Ratko Mladic, a full two years after the signing of the Dayton Accords has helped consolidate Bosnia's ethnic partition, exacerbated the political and economic tensions in the country, poisoned its social and cultural institutions, and entrenched its ultranationalist and ethnic-supremacist forces.

The Merits of Justice

The tribunal represents a chance not only for Bosnia . . . but for the world. We can presume to forget what only God and the victims have standing to forgive, or we can heed the most searing lesson of this century, which is that evil—when unopposed—will spawn more evil.

U.S. Secretary of State Madeleine Albright[3]

When the international community created the International Criminal Tribunal for the former Yugoslavia in 1993, it did so because it believed the only way to halt the atrocities in Bosnia and Croatia was to expose the individuals responsible for those atrocities and to hold them directly accountable with the prospect of a public hearing on their atrocities and commensurate punishment.

In preparing the Dayton Accords, the international community recognized that the only way to secure the implementation of the provisions of the accords for free and fair elections, the return of refugees, freedom of movement, and the protection of human rights was to ensure that individuals responsible for war crimes were extradited to The Hague and thus removed from positions of power from which they could thwart the implementation of the accords, the growth of democracy, and the reunification of Bosnia.

To create a lasting peace in the territory of the former Yugoslavia, the international community further recognized the need to establish an accurate historical record and acknowledge the victims as well as provide a process to assign specific guilt to individual perpetrators. In assigning individual criminal responsibility for specific acts, it was hoped that the assumption of collective guilt that characterized the years following World War II and in part laid the foundation for the commission of atrocities during the most recent conflict could be avoided.

More broadly, it has become apparent that the Yugoslav and Rwandan international tribunals are serving as a test case for the effective and meaningful operation of a permanent International

Criminal Court. The perceived effectiveness of both tribunals will affect international support for and acceptance of the establishment of a permanent International Criminal Court.

Given the scale of the atrocities in the former Yugoslavia, if the international community is perceived to have granted a de facto amnesty for the major perpetrators, it will send a signal to future rogue regimes throughout the world that they have nothing to lose by engaging in such criminal acts, regardless of whether the international community creates a standing International Criminal Court.

The Obligations of Justice

The establishment of the International Tribunal on the basis of a Chapter VII decision creates a binding obligation on all states to take whatever steps are required to implement the decision.

Former UN Secretary-General Boutros Boutros-Ghali[4]

The obligation of states to provide the necessary cooperation and assistance to an International Tribunal stems directly from its establishment by a UN Security Council decision under Chapter VII, which creates binding obligations on all states. Specifically, UN Security Council Resolution 827 requires all states to "cooperate fully with the International Tribunal and its organs in accordance with the present resolution and the Statute of the International Tribunal."

The obligation of all states to cooperate with the International Criminal Tribunal for the former Yugoslavia is further set forth in Article 29 of the tribunal's statute, which provides for (1) the general obligation to furnish any cooperation that may be required to facilitate the investigation or prosecution of alleged perpetrators by the International Tribunal and (2) the obligation to comply without undue delay with a specific request or order issued by a trial chamber, including arrest warrants.

Although some states and substate entities, such as Serbia/Montenegro and the "Republika Srpska," assert they lack the necessary domestic legislation to comply with the indictments and orders issued by the International Tribunal, Resolution 827 explicitly requires all states to take any measures necessary under their domestic law to implement the provisions of the resolution. Under international law, a state has a duty to comply with its international legal obligations, including binding Chapter VII UN Security Council resolutions, which take precedence over all domestic legal obligations. A state may not therefore assert it is unable to fulfill its international legal obligations on the basis that it is prohibited from doing so by domestic legislation, or that it lacks the necessary domestic authority.[5]

To ensure that all parties to the Yugoslav conflict understood their obligation to apprehend indicted war criminals, the international community included in the Dayton Accords provisions that require all the parties "to cooperate in the investigation and prosecution of war crimes and other violations of international humanitarian law,"[6] and stipulated that "no person who is serving a sentence imposed by the [International Tribunal], and no person who is under indictment by the [International Tribunal] . . . may stand as a candidate or hold any appointive, elective, or other public office in the territory of Bosnia and Herzegovina."[7]

The Bosnian delegation to the Dayton Accords also extracted an explicit promise from the NATO representatives that IFOR (the international peacekeeping force) would neither interact with indicted war criminals nor tolerate their presence in NATO's area of operation. The Bosnian delegation took this promise to mean that NATO forces would actively participate in the apprehension of indicted war criminals.

Means to Promoting Justice

Use Military Force to Apprehend Indicted War Criminals

As demonstrated by the apprehension of Milan Kovacevic, Slavko Dokmanovic, Vlatko Kupreskic, and Anto Furundzija, NATO troops are capable of using military force to aggressively apprehend indicted war criminals and defend themselves against those who attempt to resist apprehension by means of arms. The political leadership of the nations overseeing military operations in Bosnia, that is, the United States, France, Britain, and the other countries with troops in Bosnia, should direct forces under their control to continue to carry out such operations in Bosnia.[8]

Despite the pronouncements to the contrary of various military officials, unequivocal legal authority does exist for NATO military personnel to engage in operations in Bosnia to apprehend indicted war criminals. This authority may be derived from the Geneva Conventions, at least two UN Security Council resolutions, the consent of the Bosnian government, the Dayton Accords, and the Security Council resolution providing for their implementation. A strong legal case can be made that the United States and other countries with troops in Bosnia have a legal obligation to arrest indicted war criminals.[9] This obligation is derived from the Geneva Conventions, UN Security Council resolutions, and the Genocide Convention.

To date, the major objection in the United States and Europe to the more widespread use of force to apprehend indicted war criminals is the fear of casualties, either during the arrests or as a result of retaliation. In the United States, the public reaction to the deaths of American soldiers during the failed attempts to arrest General Mohammed Farah Aideed in Somalia has added to the caution of leaders.

A concern has also been expressed that Serbia/Montenegro, Croatia, and/or their proxies in Bosnia will withdraw their support for the peace implementation process if military force is used. Each of these entities' support, however, has been minimal to date.

While there are clearly risks in any military operation of this type, and those must be acknowledged by political leaders, the risk of not apprehending the indicted and of allowing them to continue to wield political and financial power in Bosnia and to undermine the peace process is far greater.

The Bosnian Serbs regularly used such intimidation tactics during the war but desisted from employing them when overwhelming force was brought against them. The risk of eventual Serb action against NATO troops is equally small, yet to ensure the safety of NATO personnel, any action to apprehend war criminals must be characterized by the readiness of NATO forces to use retaliatory force in the most decisive manner.

Given the inherent risks to NATO personnel associated with the use of military force to apprehend indicted war criminals, once such action is taken, it will be particularly critical for the political elements of the international community to utilize the opportunity of the removal of the enemies of reconciliation to implement the Dayton Accords and provide a real basis for the reunification of Bosnia and lasting peace in the territory of the former Yugoslavia.

Enact UN Sanctions against States Harboring Indicted War Criminals

Through the adoption of Resolutions 757, 787, and 820, the UN Security Council imposed sweeping trade sanctions on Serbia/Montenegro and the Bosnian Serb entity. The sanctions included an embargo on exports to and imports from Serbia/Montenegro and the "Republika Srpska," the freezing of all their government assets, the impounding of all the vessels they own, and the prohibition of their participation in international sporting events.

In November 1995, the Security Council adopted Resolution 1022, conditionally lifting the trade sanctions on Serbia/Montenegro and the Bosnian Serb entity. In that resolution, the Security Council reiterated that compliance with the orders of the International Tribunal was obligatory for Serbia/Montenegro and the "Republika Srpska" under the Dayton Accords. The resolution provided that if either the commander of IFOR or the United Nations high representative reported that those governments had significantly failed to carry out their obligations, then the sanctions were to be automatically reimposed. Yet no such action was taken when tribunal president Antonio Cassese called for the reimposition of sanctions against Serbia/Montenegro for failing to execute arrest warrants. The UN Security Council responded with a statement that it "deplores the failure to date of the Federal Republic of Yugoslavia (Serbia and Montenegro) to execute the arrest warrants," but it neither threatened nor took any further action.[10] The Security Council later permanently lifted the trade sanctions in Resolution 1074, thereby eliminating any inducement to cooperate with the International Tribunal.

The Security Council, acting under Chapter VII, should impose phased economic sanctions on any state or entity that has failed to comply with its obligations to arrest and extradite to The Hague the indicted war criminals living with impunity on its territory. Individual member states of the international community should also impose economic sanctions under their domestic authority on both Serbia/Montenegro and the "Republika Srpska."

Freeze the Assets of Individuals Indicted for War Crimes

In the context of the United Nations' efforts to dislodge the military regime from Haiti in 1993, the Security Council adopted Resolution 841, which required UN member states to freeze the assets located within their jurisdiction of known supporters of the military regime. This was the first time the Security Council acted under Article 41 of the UN Charter to freeze the assets of private individuals rather than of a government. Drawing upon this precedent, the Security Council should pass a resolution requiring states to seize and freeze the assets of any person indicted by the International Criminal Tribunal for the former

Yugoslavia. Such actions would (1) further isolate persons indicted by the tribunal, (2) serve as an effective penalty even if such persons evade justice, and (3) induce such persons to surrender themselves to the tribunal since their assets would be unfrozen (released) upon their acquittal.

As with the case of state-targeted economic sanctions, individual member governments of the international community could act under domestic authority, such as the U.S. International Emergency Economic Powers Act, to seize the assets of indicted war criminals.

Other Potential Mechanisms for Promoting Peace and Reconciliation in the Former Yugoslavia

To promote peace and reconciliation in the former Yugoslavia, consideration should be given to the creation of additional mechanisms, which may include the establishment of a nonamnesty-based truth commission, the adoption of a process for vetting suspected war criminals from military and police forces, and the creation of a victims' compensation commission. The purpose of a truth commission would be to complement the criminal prosecutions before the tribunal and to promote reconciliation by creating an accurate historical record and providing the victims of the conflict with catharsis. A vetting mechanism for the military and police forces and for public officeholders would ensure that those responsible for or reasonably suspected of committing war crimes would be removed from positions of influence. A victim compensation program would assist victims of human rights abuses in exercising their international legal right to receive compensation for their injury.

CONCLUSION

There can be neither lasting peace nor an end to the long national nightmare of Bosnia until all war criminals are arrested and brought to justice. Neither Croatia nor Serbia/Montenegro will be able to join the community of nations with all the rights and privileges that entails, until they honor their obligations to the International Criminal Tribunal for the former Yugoslavia. NATO will have undermined its raison d'être—the freedom and security of Europe—if it does not execute fully its authority to arrest indicted war criminals. Furthermore, the tribunal will not have accomplished its mission if it does not move more efficiently and effectively in its pursuit and prosecution of those who have committed war crimes in Bosnia and Croatia. Finally, the United States and the European Union will have failed a profound test of their moral, ethical, political, and military leadership in the world if they do not act decisively to end the illegitimate freedom of men who have committed and condoned grave and heinous crimes against humanity.

NOTES

1. Prepared by Paul R. Williams and Michael P. Scharf of the Public International Law and Policy Group for the Twentieth Century Fund's Task Force on Apprehending Indicted War Criminals. Mr. Williams is senior associate, Carnegie Endowment for International Peace and an assistant professor of law and international relations at the American University; former legal adviser to the Bosnian Delegation to the Dayton Peace Negotiations; and former attorney-adviser in the Office of Legal Adviser for European and Canadian Affairs, U.S. Department of State. Mr. Scharf is a professor of law, New England School of Law; director of the New England Center for International Law and Policy; and former attorney-adviser in the Office of Legal Adviser for UN Affairs, U.S. Department of State.

2. Remarks by President Clinton at the University of Connecticut, Storrs, October 15, 1995; White House press release.

3. *New York Times*, June 6, 1997.

4. Report to the United Nations Security Council, UN Doc. A/49/342, S/1994/1007, p. 31.

5. See Articles 25 and 103 of the United Nations Charter and Article 46 of the Vienna Convention on the Law of Treaties (Article 46 is considered to reflect accurately customary international law).

6. *Dayton Peace Accords (November 21, 1995), General Framework Agreement,* Article IX.

7. Article IX of Annex 4 to the *General Framework Agreement.*

8. Nine indicted war criminals are reportedly living in towns in the U.S. sector of Bosnia, twenty-three in the U.K. sector, and eight in the French sector. Radovan Karadzic and Ratko Mladic, two men commonly considered leading architects of ethnic cleansing, systematized rape,

and genocide, are openly living in towns in the French and U.S. sectors respectively, according to the Coalition for International Justice.

9. See, for example, Diane F. Orentlicher's background paper.

10. Statement of the president of the UN Security Council, S/PRST/1996/13, May 8, 1996. In October 1996, the Security Council adopted Resolution 1074, permanently lifting the sanctions imposed on Serbia/Montenegro and the Bosnian Serb entity.

LIST OF ENDORSERS*

Morton I. Abramowitz, Board Member and former President, International Crisis Group

Oscar Arias, former President of Costa Rica; 1987 Nobel Peace Prize Winner

Dr. Michael Berenbaum, President, Survivors of the Shoah Visual History Foundation

Boutros Boutros-Ghali, Secretary-General of the International Organization of the Francophonie; former Secretary-General of the United Nations

Edmond L. Browning, Presiding Bishop (Retired), Episcopal Church USA

Hodding Carter III, President and CEO, John S. and James L. Knight Foundation

Paula Dobriansky, Vice President and Washington Director, Council on Foreign Relations

Monroe Leigh, former legal advisor to the U.S. Department of State

---

* Institutional affiliations are for indentification purposes only.

Bette Bao Lord, Chairperson, Freedom House

José María Mendiluce, Member, European Parliament

Julia Ormond, actress/producer/activist

Rabbi David Saperstein, Director, Religious Action Center of Reform Judaism

John Silber, Chancellor, Boston University

Senator Paul Simon, Director, Public Policy Institute at Southern Illinois University

Lt. General DeWitt C. Smith, Jr., U.S. Army (Ret.)

Helmut Sonnenfeldt, Guest Scholar, The Brookings Institution

Susan Sontag, writer

William H. Taft, IV, former U.S. Deputy Secretary of Defense

Cyrus Vance, former U.S. Secretary of State

Background Papers

Bringing War Criminals to Justice: Obligations, Options, Recommendations

Marshall Freeman Harris, R. Bruce Hitchner, Michael P. Scharf, and Paul R. Williams

Responsibilities of States Participating in Multilateral Operations with Respect to Persons Indicted for War Crimes

Diane F. Orentlicher

Bringing War Criminals to Justice: Obligations, Options, Recommendations

Marshall Freeman Harris, R. Bruce Hitchner, Michael P. Scharf, and Paul R. Williams

Acknowledgments

This report is the product of a workshop entitled "Bringing War Criminals to Justice" held at the University of Dayton on March 19–21, 1997. The workshop was made possible by a generous grant to the University of Dayton Center for International Programs from the David and Lucile Packard Foundation. The workshop was organized by the center, the University of Dayton School of Law, the Public International Law and Policy Group, and the Balkan Institute.

Executive Summary

On July 10, 1997, NATO forces conducted their first aggressive apprehension of two indicted war criminals in Bosnia. This followed eighteen months of inaction by the United States and its allies during which time sixty-seven indicted war criminals freely roamed within Bosnia, Croatia, and Serbia, including the notorious Radovan Karadzic and Ratko Mladic. The time has come to arrest and apprehend these individuals for their grave crimes against humanity in order that peace and reconciliation may prevail over tyranny and injustice in the former Yugoslavia.

This report reviews:

- the moral and practical imperatives for apprehending and prosecuting war criminals;
- the international community's involvement in the war crimes issue in the former Yugoslavia;
- the record of implementation of obligations to apprehend indicted war criminals;
- the consequences of the failure to date to arrest and prosecute more than a handful of indicted individuals.

The report offers a range of political, diplomatic, economic, military, and legal options containing fifty specific recommendations on how the international community might improve the likelihood of arresting and successfully prosecuting indicted war criminals. The main thrust of these recommendations is that:

1. A broad range of political, diplomatic, and economic sanctions should be imposed on Croatia and Serbia until they fulfill their obligations to arrest indicted war criminals resident on their territory or on territories under their de facto control.

2. NATO should continue its new policy of aggressive apprehension of war criminals, and U.S. forces in particular should seek out and apprehend Radovan Karadzic and Ratko Mladic and those responsible for operating concentration camps.

3. The operation of the International Criminal Tribunal for the former Yugoslavia should be significantly modified to improve its effectiveness and efficiency in four areas:

    - prosecution strategy
    - witness protection program
    - authority of the International Tribunal to mandate the arrest of war criminals
    - funding

4. Other nonprosecutorial mechanisms ought to be established to augment the work of the International Tribunal. These include the establishment of truth commissions, mechanisms for vetting police forces for war criminals, and a victim compensation program.

5. Quality and effectiveness of domestic prosecution procedures for war criminals should be improved.

INTRODUCTION

We have an obligation to carry forward the lessons of Nuremberg. Those accused of war crimes against humanity and genocide must be brought to justice. There must be peace for justice to prevail, but there must be justice when peace prevails.

U. S. President William Jefferson Clinton

Almost two years after the end of the war in Bosnia, sixty-seven war criminals publicly indicted by the International Criminal Tribunal for the former Yugoslavia remain at large in Bosnia and Herzegovina, Croatia, and Serbia. The failure of the Western allies to carry out the mandate of the Dayton Accords to apprehend these individuals has unwittingly helped consolidate Bosnia's partition. It has also exacerbated political and economic tensions in the country, poisoned its social and cultural institutions, and entrenched its ultranationalist and ethnic-supremacist forces. Croatia's disinclination to fulfill its responsibilities under the accords and to cooperate fully with the International Tribunal has seriously damaged its efforts to become a full-fledged partner in the European Community and undermined its moral integrity. Furthermore, the complete abdication of Serbia on the issue of war criminals has rendered it virtually a pariah among nation-states.

The logical and necessary first steps to halt or reverse this dangerous process are for NATO troops to aggressively apprehend the sixty-seven publicly indicted individuals who not only are responsible for brutal and destructive acts during the war but also in many cases continue to conduct their war by nonmilitary means and for governments to impose political and economic sanctions on state and substate entities that refuse to assist NATO forces in the apprehension of the indicted criminals or to apprehend them themselves.

This report reviews the obligations of the international community to apprehend and prosecute indicted war criminals in the former Yugoslavia and presents a range of political, diplomatic, economic, military, and legal options, including fifty specific recommendations, that would enhance the prospects of bringing Radovan Karadzic, Ratko Mladic, and other indicted war criminals to justice.

I. The Moral and Practical Imperatives for Apprehending and Prosecuting War Criminals

The purposes of the Tribunal . . . are threefold: to do justice, to deter further crimes and to contribute to the restoration and maintenance of peace.

Antonio Cassese, President of the International Criminal Tribunal for the former Yugoslavia[1]

A. Justice

The apprehension and prosecution of war criminals in the former Yugoslavia will further justice by assigning specific guilt and thereby avoiding collective guilt, by acknowledging the victims, and by establishing an accurate historical record of the nature of and responsibility for the crimes committed.

By exposing the individuals responsible for the atrocities in the former Yugoslavia, the apprehension and prosecution of war criminals avoids an assignation of guilt to an entire people, be they Serbs, Croats, or Bosniacs. Just as a primary purpose of the Nuremberg trials after World War II was to remove the stigma of Nazism from the entire German people by isolating those individuals that were directly responsible for war crimes, a primary purpose of the apprehension and prosecution of war criminals in the former Yugoslavia is to counter the prevailing perception that ethnic groups and not individuals are responsible for the commission of atrocities. The avoidance of collective guilt is particularly important in the case of the former Yugoslavia as the failure to do so after the atrocities of World War II contributed to the more recent desire of individuals to take indiscriminate retribution against whole ethnic groups.

The process for prosecution of war criminals further offers an opportunity for the victims of war crimes to state their injuries publicly. According to David Scheffer, the United States ambassador at large for war crimes matters, the opportunity for victims to testify against their tormentors can "provide victims with a sense of justice and catharsis—a sense that their grievances have been addressed and can more easily be put to rest, rather than smoldering in anticipation of the next round of conflict." Moreover, by acknowledging the suffering of victims and their families, helping to resolve uncertain cases, and allowing victims to tell their story, the prosecution of war criminals can serve as a sort of "historical group therapy session" for an entire country, facilitating national reconciliation and individual rehabilitation and imparting to the citizenry a sense of dignity and empowerment that could help them move beyond the pain of the past.

War crimes prosecutions also establish a historical record of international crimes, thereby "preventing history from being lost or re-written, and allowing a society to learn from its past in order to prevent a repetition of such violence in the future."[2] Justice Robert Jackson of the Supreme Court, the U.S. chief prosecutor at Nuremberg, observed that one of the most important legacies of the Nuremberg trials was that they documented the Nazi atrocities "with such authenticity and in such detail that there can be no responsible denial of these crimes in the future and no tradition of martyrdom of the Nazi leaders can arise among informed people."[3] The problems of accurately assessing blame for war crimes in the former Yugoslavia are especially acute. In Justice Richard Goldstone's words, "It doesn't take hours after human rights violations for the denials to begin. . . . Justice plays a vital role in stopping that fabrication, in stopping that cover-up, which is inevitable."[4]

The historical record created by criminal prosecutions may further promote justice by imposing moral condemnation and laying the groundwork for other sanctions and victim compensation.

B. Deterrence

History records that the international amnesty given to the Turkish officials responsible for the massacre of more than one million Armenians during World War I encouraged Adolf Hitler some twenty years later to conclude that Germany could pursue his genocidal policies with impunity. In a speech to his commanding generals, Hitler dismissed concerns about accountability for acts of aggression and genocide by stating, "Who after all is today speaking about the destruction of the Armenians?"[5] Similarly, the failure of the international community to prosecute Pol Pot, Idi Amin, Saddam Hussein, and Mohammed Aideed, among others, likely encouraged the Serbs to launch their campaign of ethnic cleansing against the Muslims in Bosnia with the expectation that they would not be held accountable for their international crimes.

Given the scale of the atrocities in the former Yugoslavia, if the international community is perceived to have granted a de facto amnesty to the major perpetrators, it will send a signal to other rogue regimes throughout the world that they have nothing to lose by engaging in such criminal acts.

C. Peace and Stability

1. Within Bosnia

The apprehension and prosecution of war criminals will remove a key source of violence and institutional corruption in Bosnia and, in so doing, will foster peace and the establishment of democracy.

According to International Tribunal president Antonio Cassese, the apprehension and prosecution of war criminals "is essential to the restoration of peaceful and normal relations especially for people who have had to live under a reign of terror [because] [i]t breaks the cycle of violence, hatred, and extrajudicial retribution."[6] As such, the identification, apprehension, prosecution, and punishment of war criminals is a precondition for the successful implementation of Western policies to end the cycle of violence in Bosnia. The application of war crimes procedures to the Dayton signatories would acknowledge the parties' willingness to accept Western legal norms as a legal foundation for the genuine ending of conflict and would lay to rest the territorial ambitions that caused the fighting.

Apprehension and prosecution of war criminals further promotes stability in the former Yugoslavia by dismantling institutions and discrediting the leaders who have enabled crimes against humanity to occur. When a government enacts policies of ethnic cleansing or systematically denies human rights, it is often done through legal structures. South Africa's apartheid government, for instance, used its constitution to oppress, and special government forces to torture and murder, members of black opposition groups. In order to remove the stigma of past wrongs from new governmental institutions, the South African Truth and Reconciliation Commission was given the task of documenting the full extent of government involvement in racial killings. In Yugoslavia, government leaders and government forces were also a driving force behind much of the ethnic killing. It is thus imperative that the war's leaders be removed from power so that people may have faith in the common institutions created by the Dayton Accords.

Local stability will be further enhanced where free and fair elections are held. In the long term, a renewed effort to apprehend and prosecute war criminals will help to create the proper atmosphere for the municipal elections and any subsequent elections, as it will bring justice to citizens who were the victims of the most significant atrocities committed in Europe since World War II. Moreover, a renewed effort will assist with the reconciliation of the various divergent ethnic groups in the country by removing those with a vested interest in seeing the Dayton Accords fail.

2. Within the Balkan Region

The apprehension and prosecution of war criminals will foster stability within the Balkan region by advancing the assimilation of the Bosniac-Croat Federation and the Bosnia Serb entity into a unitary state and the integration of Bosnia within a stable and democratic post–cold war Europe.

Unfortunately, the current status of the war crimes effort provides cause for some of the three parties to seek recourse to the battlefield to redress their grievances. The possible resumption of the fighting raises the specter of the spread of conflict to other states in the region that were not directly involved in the war, particularly Albania and Macedonia.

II. International Involvement in the War Crimes Aspects of the Yugoslav Conflict

A. The UN Creation of the International Criminal Tribunal for the Former Yugoslavia

Determining that the situation in the former Yugoslavia constituted a threat to international peace and security, on May 25, 1993, the UN Security Council created the International Criminal Tribunal for the former Yugoslavia. The purpose of the International Tribunal was to contribute to the restoration and maintenance of peace in the territory of the former Yugoslavia. Its specific mission was to assist the Security Council in bringing to an end the commission of war crimes in that country by ensuring that those responsible for the atrocities were brought to justice.[7] The International Tribunal was charged with the jurisdiction and competence to prosecute any individuals responsible for serious violations of international humanitarian law in the former Yugoslavia from January 1991.[8]

1. Obligation of States to Comply with the Orders of the International Tribunal

Whereas judicial cooperation and mutual assistance between states with respect to national criminal investigations or prosecutions is usually governed by bilateral or multilateral agreements, the obligation of states to provide the necessary cooperation and assistance to the International Tribunal stems directly from its establishment by a Security Council decision under Chapter VII that creates binding obligations for all states by virtue of Articles 2 (6) and 25 of the United Nations Charter.[9] The secretary-general's report describes the nature of state obligations with respect to the International Tribunal as follows: "The establishment of the International Tribunal on the basis of a Chapter VII decision creates a binding obligation on all states to take whatever steps are required to implement the decision."[10] Specifically, Security Council Resolution 827 requires all states to "cooperate fully with the International Tribunal and its organs in accordance with the present resolution and the Statute of the International Tribunal."

Although some states and substate entities, such as Serbia/Montenegro and the Bosnian Serb entity, assert they lack the necessary domestic legislation to comply with the indictments and orders issued by the International Tribunal, Resolution 827 explicitly requires all states to take any measures necessary under their domestic law to implement the provisions of the Resolution. Under international law a state has a duty to comply with its international legal obligations, including binding Chapter VII Security Council Resolutions, which take precedence over all domestic legal obligations.[11] Therefore, a state may not assert that it is unable to fulfill its international legal obligations on the basis that it is prohibited from doing so by domestic legislation, or that it lacks the necessary domestic authority.[12]

The obligation of all states to cooperate with the International Tribunal is further set forth in Article 29 of the tribunal's statute, which provides for (1) the general obligation to provide any cooperation that may be required to facilitate the investigation or prosecution of alleged perpetrators by the International Tribunal, and (2) the obligation to comply without undue delay with a specific request or order issued by a trial chamber, including arrest warrants. The tribunal may notify the Security Council of the failure of a state to provide the necessary cooperation or assistance in response to a specific request or order.

B. The Dayton Accords

In November 1995, the parties to the Yugoslav conflict and representatives of the Contact Group gathered in Dayton, Ohio, to negotiate a series of accords designed to bring about the peaceful reintegration of Bosnia. Although the various parties to the negotiations held differing views as to the role of justice in promoting peace and the extent to which the Dayton Accords should create obligations to bring war criminals to justice, the parties agreed that the accords must to some degree incorporate the obligations set forth in Resolution 827.

As such, the Dayton Accords provided that the parties were obligated "to cooperate in the investigation and prosecution of war crimes and other violations of international humanitarian law,"[13] and that "no person who is serving a sentence imposed by the [International Tribunal], and no person who is under indictment by the [International Tribunal] . . . may stand as a candidate or hold any appointive, elective, or other public office in the territory of Bosnia and Herzegovina."[14] In addition, the Bosnian delegation extracted an implicit promise from the NATO representatives that IFOR, the international force keeping the peace in Bosnia, would neither interact with indicted war criminals nor tolerate their presence in the area of operation. The parties took this to mean that NATO forces would actively participate in the apprehension of indicted war criminals.

III. The Current State of Implementation of Obligations to Apprehend Indicted War Criminals

Although the two provisions included in the Dayton Accords represent what might be considered minimum commitments necessary to fulfill the role of justice in promoting peace, even they have not yet been fully implemented. Serbia, Croatia, and the Bosnian-Serb entity have played a part, to different degrees, in obstructing the judicial process, thereby jeopardizing the peace.

The Bosniac leaders of Bosnia and Herzegovina have, however, cooperated fully with the International Tribunal on a variety of issues. In contrast, the United States and its allies have failed to exert sufficient pressure to compel the cooperation of Croatia, Serbia, the Bosnian Serb entity, and the de facto authorities in Bosnian Croat regions of Bosnia. In recent months, Western governments have attempted to deflect criticism of their policies by claiming that the Balkan parties have failed to act. The Dayton Accords oblige the signatory parties to cooperate with the International Tribunal, making such claims disingenuous. In the four above-mentioned entities and states, the failure of Western governments to implement key reintegrative provisions of the accords has further entrenched and empowered leaders who orchestrated the war and who are widely believed to have committed indictable offenses.

A. Serbia/Montenegro

In Serbia/Montenegro there has not been any significant cooperation with the International Tribunal. Specifically, none of the indicted individuals residing within Serbian/Montenegrin territory have been extradited to the International Tribunal. Serbia/Montenegro explicitly refuses to extradite these indicted war criminals on the grounds that it claims not to possess the necessary domestic legislation for extradition to the International Tribunal. As noted, however, the lack of domestic authority is not a valid excuse for the breach of international legal obligations to arrest indicted war criminals and extradite them to the International Tribunal.

Belgrade has not only provided less support to the International Tribunal than other nations but has also actively obstructed its work. It has declined most of the International Tribunal's requests for cooperation; with others it has agreed to cooperate, but only in a minimal form and only after considerable delays. Although Belgrade is a party to the Dayton Accords and Serbian president Slobodan Milosevic committed verbally at Dayton to remove Ratko Mladic and Radovan Karadzic from political life, Belgrade has not surrendered war criminals under its de facto control to the International Tribunal's custody. Belgrade has also failed to prevent indicted war criminals from traveling to and from Serbia. In 1996, it allowed Serb army officials to attend and participate in a public funeral for Djordje Djukjic, a Serbian military officer who was in charge of the Bosnian Serb forces' logistics and who had been released from the International Tribunal's custody on medical grounds. The Bosnian Serb war effort and other individual Serbian indictees were venerated at the ceremony.

B. The Republic of Croatia

Croatia also refuses to cooperate with the International Tribunal and, aside from General Tihomir Blaskic's voluntary appearance at The Hague and the recent extradition of Saso Aleksouski, none of the indictees residing in Croatia have been extradited.[15] Although Croatia possesses the necessary domestic legislation for extradition, it claims to be unable to find any indictees residing on its territory, notwithstanding the fact that they are all represented by the same Zagreb lawyer, Zvonimir Hodak, and at least two of them have been located by local independent newspapers.

While the United States has begun to place increasing pressure on the Croatian government to comply with the International Tribunal, most recently by postponing loans to Zagreb from international lending institutions, the recent reelection of President Franjo Tudjman by a comfortable margin has emboldened the Croatian government to stonewall on the war crimes issue.

C. Bosnia and Herzegovina

The central government has complied with all the requests made by the International Tribunal. However, its effectiveness is undermined by power sharing between the country's two constituent entities and by Dayton-mandated constitutional provisions for an entity's veto of central policies. These endemic weaknesses, together with the West's unwillingness to challenge the ongoing territorial control of parts of Bosnia by ethnic Serb and Croat separatists, have led the International Tribunal to attempt to cooperate instead with the country's two constituent parts (see below) and the de facto leadership of Croatian regions and thus to treat Bosnia as three separate countries.

1. The Bosnian Serb Entity

Since signing the Dayton Accords, not one of the forty-eight publicly indicted war criminals residing on the territory of the Bosnian Serb entity has been turned over to the International Tribunal. In fact, Pale has openly declared that it has no intention of cooperating with the International Tribunal, yet it is not subject to international sanction. Bosnian Serb president Biljana Plavsic has frequently pointed out that the Bosnian Serb constitution bans extradition and that her government will not turn over Karadzic, Mladic, or any other indictees to the International Tribunal.[16]

Specifically, Plavsic informed UN secretary-general Kofi Annan, via a "diplomatic letter," that the International Tribunal's indictments are no longer considered valid since the fighting has ceased and there have been no recent reports of war crimes being committed in the Bosnian Serb entity. In the letter, she declared, "any such trials now fall outside the scope of the International Tribunal's constitutional framework" because the International Tribunal was established when war crimes were a threat to peace. Plavsic argued that without further reports of war crimes committed in the Bosnian Serb entity, the International Tribunal's mandate has "disappeared." This position, moreover, has hardened since the recent stabilization force (SFOR) operation in Prijedor.

As to removing war criminals from power, it took significant pressure from the international community to persuade the Bosnian Serb authorities to remove Karadzic from official public office. However, a number of wanted war criminals continue to serve in local police forces and hold other influential public positions in Prijedor, Omarska, and Bosanski Samac.[17] Similarly, although both Karadzic and Mladic have been formally removed from office, they remain within the territory of the Bosnian Serb entity and continue to wield significant political and military authority.[18] Indeed, Karadzic is generally acknowledged to be the dominant political figure in the Bosnian Serb entity.[19]

2. Federation of Bosnia and Herzegovina

With respect to the Bosnian Federation, other than the recent reluctance of the minister of defense to cooperate with the International Tribunal on the Blaskic case, the Federation has complied with the indictments issued by the International Tribunal and has extradited to The Hague Zejnil Delalic, Hazim Delic, Zdravko Mucic, and Esad Landzo.

In contrast to Federation areas under the control of Bosniac officials, conditions in Bosnian Croat-controlled parts of Bosnia are virtually identical to those in the Bosnian Serb entity: indicted war criminals live and work in public positions with impunity and with the full knowledge and complicity of Bosnian Croat leaders. Bosnian Croat leaders of the Croatian Democratic Union (HVO), Tudjman's party, claim they support the work of the International Tribunal but assert disingenuously that they lack the laws and institutions to cooperate because there is no parliament for their de facto entity in Bosnia.

D. International Community

1. Financial and Other Support for the International Tribunal

Since its inception, the UN International Tribunal has suffered from a chronic lack of political, financial, and evidentiary support. Although the United States has provided more support than other nations, the paucity of its voluntary and other in-kind contributions—totaling only $18 million in the first three years of operations—has prevented the International Tribunal from carrying out more than a fraction of its functions and responsibilities. This is reflected, generally, in the dearth of indictments issued to date and, more specifically, in the small scale of the court's investigatory operations.

Other major powers have not even approached the United States' low level of support for the International Tribunal. In fact, Micronesia has provided more voluntary assistance than either Britain or France. For four years, Western governments have paid rhetorical tribute to the International Tribunal's importance. At the same time, they have not only failed to provide genuine support but have also enacted broader, contradictory policies that are undermining the International Tribunal's work and condemning it to irrelevance.

2. NATO Military Forces

In the face of breaches of the Dayton Accords provision requiring cooperation with the International Tribunal by most of the parties, NATO forces have, until the SFOR operation in Prijedor, steadfastly refused to exercise their authority to apprehend those indicted for war crimes. Until recently, NATO's official policy has permitted its forces to attempt to apprehend only indicted criminals they should happen to encounter, when doing so posed no risks to those forces.

In reality NATO's policy has been for its forces to avoid any interaction with indictees at all costs and to circumvent areas where indictees are believed to operate. In the event that contact was made, NATO forces were to remove themselves quickly from the area and deny their recognition of the indictees.[20] The Prijedor operation appears to represent a change in NATO policy. However, the procedure of avoiding contact with war criminals is still evidently in place.

IV. The Specific Effects of the Lack of Implementation

The decision by NATO forces not to implement Dayton's provisions on apprehending war criminals has impeded the enforcement of other requirements of the agreement and thus reduced the chances for a peaceful reunification of Bosnia.

A. Barrier to the Return of Refugees and Freedom of Movement

Only one in ten of the country's 2.2 million displaced persons has returned, and an even smaller fraction of this 10 percent has actually returned home. Instead, the displaced are resettling—or being resettled—in areas in which, by ethnicity or religion, they are part of the majority. The failure to apprehend indicted war criminals has exacerbated the refugee situation, as many refugees seeking to return to their place of residence are inhibited from doing so by fear of attack or intimidation in communities where war criminals hold power or by police forces that include former war criminals.

B. Unfree and Unfair Elections

Regrettably, the lack of action on the war criminals issue allowed and even encouraged indicted war criminals to participate openly in last year's municipal elections in Bosnia. Free and fair elections, which are necessary for Bosnia's recovery and progress as a nation, are not possible as long as war criminals continue to flout justice and execute their policies of ethnic supremacy and separatism.

C. Impediment to Reconstruction

The failure to apprehend war criminals has seriously impeded the efforts to rebuild the Bosnian economy. Only 2 percent of international aid for reconstruction in 1996 went to the Bosnian Serb entity in part because of its noncompliance with the International Tribunal. Moreover, some of this aid has been awarded to firms owned by war crimes suspects. Suspected war criminals have also restricted the ability of legitimate businesses to win contracts for reconstruction projects. As long as war criminals remain at large, the reconstruction of Bosnia will be adversely affected.

Croatia has also recently begun to feel the effects of its failure to turn over indicted war criminals on its territory. The World Bank, under pressure from the United States, Canada, Japan, and major allies in Europe, has delayed two loans. And Serbia, although no longer under UN sanction, is still shunned by the international economic community for its failure to cooperate in efforts to bring indicted war criminals to The Hague.

D. Regional Instability

Over the long term, the sense of injustice stemming from the failure to arrest war criminals has the potential to act as a destabilizing factor not only within Bosnia, as recent political unrest in the Bosnian Serb entity has shown, but also in Croatia, Serbia, and other parts of the Balkans. Until the war crimes issue is resolved, the potential for regional instability remains significant.

E. Sanctioning of Agenda of Ethnic Purity

Even if the partition holds and fighting does not resume in Bosnia, the precedent of seizure of territory by force has been reconfirmed as a functional model for post–cold war state behavior. The West, under the active leadership of the United States, has rhetorically sanctioned Milosevic's ends toward a "Greater Serbia" while condemning—but not redressing—his means: aggression, destruction of pluralism and democracy, genocide, and the forcible transfer of populations.

By shirking their responsibilities to defend their values in Central Europe—and arresting war criminals is one such—the Western allies devalue democracy and raise questions about their fundamental commitment to collective defense and religious, ethnic, and cultural pluralism beyond their own borders.

F. Negative Precedent for the Future Implementation of the Rules Governing Armed Conflict

The establishment of the International Criminal Tribunal for the former Yugoslavia in 1993 was intended to bring a halt to what the international community rightly believed were "grave breaches" of the Geneva Conventions of 1949 and Protocol I added in 1977. If the mandate of the International Tribunal is not executed, it will set a disturbing precedent; namely, that the rules governing armed conflict between states can be disregarded with impunity. As Secretary of State Madeleine Albright recently stated, "t[he] tribunal represents a chance not only for Bosnia . . . but for the world. . . . We can presume to forget what only God and the victims have standing to forgive, or we can heed the most searing lesson of this century, which is that evil—when unopposed—will spawn more evil."[21]

V. Options and Recommendations for Improving the Likelihood for the Apprehension and Successful Prosecution of Indicted War Criminals

As the second anniversary of the signing of the Dayton Peace Accords approaches, it is clear that the recent American and European policy on the apprehension of indicted war criminals has been a political and moral failure. Some recent, laudable steps have been taken by the United States to increase pressure on Croatia, Serbia, and the Bosnian Serb entity to hand over those indicted for war crimes and to support the recent apprehension of two indicted war criminals.

A. Impose Political and Diplomatic Sanctions

As Secretary of State Albright stated: "We cannot achieve our objectives in Bosnia by doing just enough to avoid immediate war; we must do all we can to help the people of Bosnia to achieve permanent peace." These words should be backed up by a stronger U.S. policy of intensive diplomatic pressure on Serbia and Croatia through the UN, the EU, the Council of Europe, NATO, and the OSCE.

Recommendations:

(1) *The United States and its allies should consider recalling their ambassadors to Belgrade and Zagreb and formally downgrading their diplomatic relations with Serbia and Croatia until those states cooperate fully with the International Tribunal. This cooperation should include:*

(a) *surrender of all suspects on territory under Belgrade's and Zagreb's control;*

(b) *suspension of all political, military, and economic cooperation with their Bosnian client-entities and proxies for as long as those entities and proxies harbor war criminals;*

(c) *full political, financial, and evidentiary support for the International Tribunal and its work.*

(2) *The United States and its allies should suspend diplomatic contact with—and political, military, economic, and any other support for—the Bosnian Serb entity and entities and institutions under Bosnian Croat control until the Republic and those entities and institutions surrender all suspects on territory under their control and provide full political, financial, and evidentiary support for the International Tribunal and its work.*

(3) *The United States and its allies should terminate or prevent the acquisition of Partnership for Peace status for countries that harbor war criminals and/or provide less than full support for the International Tribunal and its work.*

(4) *Members of the European Union should terminate or prevent EU association with countries that harbor war criminals and/or provide less than full support for the International Tribunal and its work. Specifically, the EU should investigate and demand a full accounting by Cyprus of its support for the financial and business activities of indicted war criminal Radovan Karadzic.*

B. Impose Economic Options

1. Enact UN Sanctions against States

Through the adoption of Resolutions 757, 787, and 820, the Security Council imposed sweeping trade sanctions on Serbia and the Bosnian Serb entity. The sanctions included an embargo on exports to Serbia and the Bosnian Serb entity, a prohibition on imports from Serbia and the Bosnian Serb entity, the freezing of all Serb government assets, the impounding of all Serb-owned vessels, and the prohibition of Serb participation in international sporting events.

In November 1995, the Security Council adopted Resolution 1022, conditionally lifting the trade sanctions on Serbia and the Bosnian Serb entity. In that resolution, the Security Council reiterated that compliance with the orders of the International Tribunal was integral to the obligations of Serbia and the Bosnian Serb entity under the Dayton agreement. The resolution provided that if either the commander of IFOR or the United Nations high representative reported that those governments had significantly failed to carry out their obligations, then the sanctions were to be automatically reimposed. Yet no such action was taken when International Tribunal president Antonio Cassese called for the reimposition of sanctions against Serbia for failing to execute arrest warrants.[22] The Security Council responded with a statement that it "deplores the failure to date of the Federal Republic of Yugoslavia (Serbia and Montenegro) to execute the arrest warrants," but it neither threatened nor took any further action.[23] It later permanently lifted the trade sanctions by adopting Resolution 1074, thereby eliminating any inducement to cooperate with the International Tribunal.

Recommendations:

(5) *The United Nations Security Council should reimpose select sanctions against Serbia and the Bosnian Serb entity that would include (on a phased-in basis):*

(a) *the suspension of all rail, sea, air, and postal links with Serbia/Montenegro;*

(b) *the suspension of high-level diplomatic contacts with Serbia/Montenegro and the recall of ambassadors;*

(c) *an embargo on exports to Serbia/Montenegro and the Bosnian Serb entity;*

(d) *a prohibition on imports from Serbia/Montenegro and the Bosnian Serb entity;*

(e) *the freezing of all Serb government assets;*

(f) *the impounding of all Serb-owned vessels;*

(g) *the prohibition of Serb participation in international sporting events.*

2. Enact UN Sanctions against Individuals

In the context of the United Nations' efforts to dislodge the military regime from Haiti in 1993, the Security Council adopted Resolution 841, which required UN member states to freeze the assets located within their jurisdiction of known supporters of the military regime. This was the first time the Security Council acted under Article 41 of the UN Charter to freeze the assets of private individuals rather than a government. Drawing upon this precedent, the Security Council could pass a resolution requiring states to seize and freeze the assets of any person indicted by the International Tribunal. Such action would (1) further isolate persons indicted by the International Tribunal, (2) serve as an effective penalty even if such persons evade justice, and (3) induce such persons to surrender themselves to the International Tribunal since their assets would be unfrozen upon their acquittal. Because these sanctions would be targeted at specific indicted individuals, not governments, it would be much easier to gain support of the members of the Security Council for such a measure.

RECOMMENDATION:

(6) *The Security Council should act under the authority of Article 41 of the UN Charter to require states to freeze the assets of individuals indicted by the International Tribunal.*

3. IMPLEMENT UNILATERAL U.S. SANCTIONS AND INDUCEMENTS

a. Impose Unilateral Sanctions. When the UN Security Council adopts a binding sanctions resolution under Chapter VII of the UN Charter, the United States implements the sanctions by virtue of an executive order promulgated under the authority of the UN Participation Act, 22 U.S.C. Section 287(c). In the absence of a Security Council resolution, the president can promulgate unilateral economic sanctions, exercising his authority under the International Emergency Economic Powers Act (IEEPA), 50 U.S.C. Section 1702. As a prerequisite for such action, IEEPA requires the president to make a determination that the situation constitutes an "unusual and extraordinary threat to national security." Because of the linkage between the successful operation of the International Tribunal and peace and reconciliation in the Balkans, and because of the presence of a large number of U.S. troops in SFOR, this situation would qualify as a case of an "unusual and extraordinary threat to national security" as required for action under IEEPA. In addition to authorizing an embargo of imports and exports, the president can use his authority under IEEPA to seize and freeze foreign assets, as discussed below. These actions would almost certainly be supported by Congress, where sentiment is growing that the administration should condition assistance for Balkan states on cooperation with the Dayton Accords, especially on the issue of war criminals.

RECOMMENDATION:

(7) *Acting under the International Emergency Economic Powers Act, President Clinton should impose an economic embargo on all*

U.S. imports to or exports from Serbia and the Bosnian Serb entity.

b. Unilateral Seizure of Domestic Assets. In 1996, the president of the United States, exercising his authority under the International Emergency Economic Powers Act, promulgated executive orders to freeze the assets of persons designated (1) as having assisted terrorists or committed acts of terrorism (Executive Order No. 12947, January 23, 1995) or (2) as having assisted or played a significant role in international drug trafficking centered in Colombia (Executive Order No. 12978, October 21, 1995). IEEPA authorizes the president to freeze assets in the United States and held in U.S. banks abroad in the case of an "unusual and extraordinary threat to national security."

IEEPA has been used in the past to freeze the assets of foreign governments and their ruling elites, including the assets of the government of Iran when Americans were taken hostage, the assets of Iraq during the Persian Gulf crisis, and the assets of Haitian leaders during the reign of the military regime. With the 1996 executive orders, IEEPA has now been used against individual international terrorists and drug traffickers. Based on this precedent, the president of the United States, through promulgation of an executive order, could freeze assets in the United States of individuals under indictment by the International Tribunal and assets held in U.S. banks abroad.

Recommendations:

(8) *Acting under the International Emergency Economic Powers Act, President Clinton should order that the personal assets located in the United States of all indicted war criminals be seized.*

(9) *The president should immediately suspend all financing by the Export-Import Bank (Eximbank) and the Overseas Private Investment Corporation (OPIC) of U.S. businesses working in Croatia, Serbia, and the Bosnian Serb entity.*

(10) *The president should suspend all existing or planned U.S. Agency for International Development (AID) assistance in the Bosnian Serb entity.*

C. Apprehend Indicted Criminals

1. Legal Authority for Military Options

U.S. military forces operating in the theater of the former Yugoslavia have the technical capability to apprehend indicted war criminals. Prior to the successful Prijedor operation of July 10, 1997, NATO forces in Bosnia and Herzegovina declined to arrest suspects indicted by the International Tribunal. Official NATO policy had been to avoid searching for suspects, but to allow soldiers to arrest indicted suspects if the soldiers encountered them in the normal course of their operations and it was deemed prudent to arrest them.

Yet NATO forces never found it prudent to arrest indicted suspects, however frequently encountered. When criticized for this policy, NATO claimed that it was not SFOR's mandate to search for suspects. By basing its position on the mandate (which, in this case, was established by the North Atlantic Council), NATO sidestepped the crucial question of whether Western national forces in Bosnia were legally authorized and possibly obligated to arrest suspected war criminals.

Unequivocal legal authority exists for UN military personnel to engage in operations in Bosnia to apprehend indicted war criminals. This authority may be derived from conventional international law, at least two United Nations Security Council resolutions, and the consent of the Bosnian government. A strong legal case can be made that U.S. military personnel have a legal obligation to arrest indicted war criminals. This obligation is derived from the Geneva Conventions, UN Security Council resolutions, and the Genocide Convention.

2. Political Risks of Successful Apprehension

A major stumbling block to the forceful apprehension of war criminals has been the supposed political risks associated with it. The most oft-cited concern is that Serbia, Croatia, and/or their proxies in Bosnia will withdraw their support for the peace implementation process. Each of these entities' support, however, has been minimal to date. Furthermore, that support has actually decreased as the United States, first, has failed to honor its own commitments to implement key parts of the Dayton Accords and, second, has failed to exert meaningful pressure on the parties to the accords.

The forceful apprehension of war criminals should be seen as part of a comprehensive policy to reverse this process. If combined with significant political and economic pressure on Serbia, Croatia, and their Bosnian proxies, arresting war criminals poses little risk of derailing or even stalling the peace implementation process. Indeed, it should demonstrate that the United States and its allies are, at long last, taking their commitments seriously.

3. Operational Risks

As the recent SFOR operation in Prijedor has shown, there are risks inherent in any military action, and they are especially high when a quick and precise action is needed to achieve success. These risks are reduced, however, in the context of Bosnia by the fact that SFOR has unlimited freedom of movement throughout the country, including the Bosnian Serb entity. As the recent British SAS preparations for the Prijedor operations reveal, this is an ideal situation, from the intelligence standpoint, in which to use special forces against selected targets in hostile territory.

Although the recent Bosnian Serb attacks against the UN and OSCE and threats by Pale of widespread retaliation against NATO give cause for concern, this should not distract the United States and its allies from undertaking further operations to arrest war criminals. It should be recalled that the Bosnian Serbs regularly used such intimidation tactics during the war but desisted from employing them when overwhelming force was brought against them. The risk of eventual Serbian action against U.S. or IFOR troops is equally small. However, no chances should be taken. Any action to apprehend war criminals must be accompanied by U.S. readiness to use force in the most decisive manner.

Recommendations:

(11) *NATO military operations should continue and should be directed toward the seizure of high-level indictees.*

(12) *President Clinton should instruct the U.S. forces operating in Bosnia to seek out and apprehend Radovan Karadzic and Ratko*

Mladic, as well as those responsible for operating concentration camps.

(13) *NATO forces should assist the civilian mechanism in vetting the local police forces of suspected war criminals.*

(14) *The member states of NATO should deliver an unequivocal diplomatic message to Pale that it will be held directly responsible and accountable for any and all violent actions against SFOR, the OSCE, the UN, etc. in response to legal military actions to arrest war criminals and that failure to prohibit such actions will lead to a firm response by NATO against Bosnian Serb military assets.*

D. Improve the Effectiveness of the International Tribunal

To improve the effectiveness and relevance of the International Tribunal it is necessary to develop an alternative prosecution strategy that focuses on:

- pursuing the principal figures responsible for orchestrating ethnic cleansing and genocide in Bosnia and Croatia;
- establishing a meaningful witness protection program;
- utilizing the authority of the International Tribunal to mandate the apprehension of indicted war criminals;
- conducting an independent review of the effectiveness of the International Tribunal.

1. Prosecute Principal Figures

When the International Tribunal was established, the goal was to indict publicly both low-level and high-ranking war criminals. Former prosecutor Richard Goldstone explained the Tribunal's strategy of investigating "lower-level persons directly involved in carrying out the crimes in order to build effective cases against the military and civilian leaders who were party to the overall planning and organization of those crimes."[24] Unfortunately, given its limited resources and the fact that the International Tribunal has only two courtrooms to try cases, the tribunal has not been able to carry out this plan of action. To date, the majority of those indicted are low-level figures, including prison guards and foot soldiers. Many of the most culpable higher-level figures have still not been publicly indicted.[25]

Recommendations:

(15) *The International Tribunal should refocus its scarce resources on investigations of those primarily responsible for orchestrating ethnic cleansing and genocide in Bosnia and Croatia, including heads of state and notorious paramilitary leaders.*

(16) *The International Tribunal should abandon its perplexing policy of issuing formal letters or certificates to potential indictees stating that the International Tribunal has not indicted them.*

2. Establish a Meaningful Witness Protection Program

One of the International Tribunal's challenges is setting up a functioning witness protection program. Owing to the reluctance of witnesses to participate, over the strenuous objections of the defense, the International Tribunal has ruled that various witnesses could testify anonymously in order to protect themselves and their families from retribution.[26] However, this decision has been criticized on the grounds that the right to examine or cross-examine witnesses guaranteed by the International Tribunal's statute cannot be effective without the right to know the identity of adverse witnesses.[27]

Recommendations:

(17) *The International Tribunal should develop a plan for an adequate and effective witness protection program.*

(18) *The International Tribunal's witness protection program should receive additional funding to support its work.*[28]

(19) *Given the difficulties involved in securing cooperation from potential witnesses in the Bosnian Serb entity, and because the International Tribunal does not have a police force to compel witnesses to testify, available defense witnesses should be provided safe conduct. Orders for safe conduct should grant witnesses limited immunity from prosecution when appearing in The Hague to give testimony. Although orders for safe conduct are not specifically provided for in the International Tribunal's statute or the rules, the trial chamber could find authority in Rule 54.*[29]

(20) *If safe conduct is not feasible, the trial chamber should liberally permit defense witnesses to give testimony by means of video-link. The trial chamber has recently ruled that defense witnesses can offer testimony via video conferencing if they cannot or will not travel to The Hague. The video-link could be a live television link between the trial chamber and a safe harbor such as an embassy in Bosnia-Herzegovina.*

(21) *To mitigate the very real threat of reprisals against witnesses who testify, the trial chamber should refrain from disclosing witnesses' identities to the public. This elementary form of witness protection is supported by the statute and the rules,*[30] *each of which contains a provision to guarantee confidentiality.*

3. Utilize the Authority of the International Tribunal to Mandate the Apprehension of Indicted War Criminals

Article 29 of the substantive law of the International Tribunal mandates the arrest or detention,[31] as well as the surrender or transfer,[32] to the tribunal of any accused individual. The International Tribunal's enforcement powers are more fully spelled out in its rules.[33] Under Rule 40, the prosecutor is also permitted in urgent situations to request the provisional arrest of a suspect even before he or she has been formally accused by the International Tribunal.[34] To further the success of the International Tribunal's mandate, the prosecutor, in such situations, is also given the power to request "all necessary measures to prevent the escape of a suspect or an accused, injury to or intimidation of a victim or witness, or the destruction of evidence."[35]

Should a lack of cooperation with the International Tribunal result in a failure to execute a warrant of arrest, the president of the tribunal is empowered to notify its parent body, the UN Security Council, for further action.[36] In this event, when a warrant has not been properly executed,[37] a judge of the International Tribunal chamber *must* issue an international arrest warrant for the accused.[38] Under generally accepted public international law, the individual then becomes an accused enemy of all mankind and thus subject to arrest anywhere in the world under universal jurisdiction.

Moreover, since "all states can be held to have a legal interest" in the arrest, detention, and surrender of the individual, they are all under an obligation *erga omnes*[39] to conform to the authority of the UN Security Council and the International Tribunal, as the alleged crimes of the accused concern "the basic rights of the human person."[40] The International Court of Justice has held that such obligations "have entered into the body of general international law."[41] This is no less than a "recognition of supremacy of the law of humanity" for protection against any and all violations "of elementary human rights in a manner which may justly be held to shock the conscience of mankind."[42]

Recommendations:

(22) *The International Tribunal should more regularly report to the UN Security Council those states failing to comply with its orders.*

(23) *The International Tribunal should more regularly and openly request the extradition of indicted war criminals from specific states.*

(24) *The International Tribunal should more regularly and openly request that certain states provide it with information regarding indicted or suspected war criminals.*

(25) *The International Tribunal should request that the contributing states to SFOR actively seek to arrest and transfer to The Hague indicted war criminals living in their theater of operation.*

(26) *The International Tribunal should request apprehension by specific states whose forces patrol zones where indicted war criminals are suspected to reside and/or visit frequently.*

4. Provide Adequate Funding for the Work of the International Tribunal

One of the highest priorities for the International Tribunal is to increase its budget for 1998. The UN Secretariat has frozen the International Tribunal's budget for the first quarter of 1997 at 1996 levels. Although established in 1993, the International Tribunal did not receive any significant allocation of funding from the United Nations until 1994, and even this amount was minimal. The International Tribunal's total budget for 1994-95 was $32.6 million. More than $22 million, however, was directed toward salaries and administrative costs. The two-year budget for investigative expenses was approximately $560,000. The relatively small amount of funding has slowed down the investigative process for the International Tribunal. Without further financial support, the International Tribunal will be at a crossroads, where active investigations may have to stop and programs for defense preparation, witness protection, and resettlement will be compromised.

Complicating the dire financial situation of the International Tribunal has been the insistence that all member states that seconded personnel to the International Tribunal pay a 13 percent surcharge to defray costs associated with accepting gratis personnel. Although applied throughout the United Nations system, this surcharge, and the unwillingness of certain states to pay it, particularly affects the International Tribunal, as its 55 gratis personnel represent 23 percent of its professional staff.

Recommendations:

(27) *Governments and nongovernmental organizations must actively lobby the UN's Advisory Committee on Administrative and Budgetary Questions and the Fifth Committee (particularly countries represented*

in both committees)[43] *to support the necessary increase in financial support for the International Tribunal.*

(28) *The United Nations' November 21, 1996,* Report on Gratis Personnel *should be amended to eliminate the 13 percent surcharge for program support costs related to gratis personnel provided by governments and other entities to the International Tribunals. The current requirements that all secondees be preapproved by the relevant International Tribunals and adhere to all International Tribunal regulations are appropriate and will ensure that gratis personnel possess the required expertise and comply with all International Tribunal instructions.*

(29) *The UN secretary-general should adhere to Security Council Resolution 827, which unambiguously supports the use of gratis personnel for the International Tribunal.*

(30) *The United States should urge a non-UN-affiliated review of the effectiveness of the International Tribunal and means for improving its operation.*

E. Establish Nonprosecutorial Mechanisms

To augment the work of the International Tribunal, a truth commission/vetting mechanism must be established to enhance the application of noncriminal sanctions and to develop a victim compensation program.

1. Establish a Truth Commission/Vetting Mechanism

Given the vast number of atrocities in Yugoslavia, the truth needs to be told before successful reconciliation can occur. Criminal prosecutions, which by their nature focus on individual liability, are unable to tell the whole story of abuses. Cherif Bassiouni, former chairman of the Yugoslavia War Crimes Commission, had proposed that his commission be "folded into the Yugoslavia Tribunal."[44] While the Yugoslavia War Crimes Commission was instead terminated when the International Tribunal's Office of Prosecutor was established, precedent exists for imbuing a prosecutor's office with the additional functions of a high-level truth commission in the mandate given to Lawrence Walsh, independent prosecutor for the Iran-contra investigation, pursuant to Section 595(b)(2) of Title 28 of the United States Code.[45] His three-volume report provides a comprehensive "account of the Independent Counsel's investigation, the prosecutions, the basis for decisions not to prosecute, and overall observations and conclusions on the Iran/Contra matters."[46] The Office of the Prosecutor of the International Tribunal should be given a similar mandate by the Security Council to prepare a comprehensive report based on its investigations.

Moreover, there is an ongoing need to remove from positions of influence those responsible for or reasonably suspected of committing war crimes. In particular, these individuals should be excluded from the military and police forces and should be denied the opportunity to hold public office. Currently the International Police Task Force is assisting with the restructuring of the police forces in Sarajevo and Tuzla to exclude individuals suspected of committing atrocities. A broader precedent for such action would include the American vetting and retraining of the Haitian police force and efforts by Germany to exclude from its judiciary former Communist party members. Because the situation in Bosnia might as of yet not be sufficiently stable to permit the parties to vet indicted and suspected war criminals unilaterally, a joint process should be set up with the participation of the international community.

Recommendations:

(31) *The Office of the Prosecutor should be provided with an additional mandate and staff to serve as a high-level truth commission responsible for creating an accurate and unbiased historical record of the ethnic cleansing and genocide that occurred in Bosnia.*

(32) *The United Nations, in conjunction with the above recommendation, should authorize the creation of a number of local truth commissions to assemble a historical record of specific atrocities. These commissions should include members of the local community and a staff of psychologists and victims' advocates to address the trauma associated with the presentation of testimony by witnesses.*[47]

(33) *The existing local truth commissions should come under supervision of the United Nations to ensure the creation of an unbiased historical record.*

(34) *The IPTF should continue and expand its efforts to reconstitute the police forces in Bosnia and begin to include forces from the Bosnian Serb entity.*

(35) *An entity separate from the United Nations should establish a mechanism for the purpose of investigating nonparty complicity in ethnic cleansing and genocide, including the Sarajevo siege and the Srebrenica massacre.*

(36) *The United States should create a WatchList to deny U.S. entry visas to suspected war criminals. The United States should further instruct government officials to avoid any and all contact with individuals on the list.*

2. Create a Victim Compensation Program

The Universal Declaration of Human Rights, the Covenant on Civil and Political Rights, and the Torture Convention all recognize the right of victims of human rights abuses to receive compensation for their injury.[48] Compensable damages include loss of life, physical or psychological injury, loss of liberty, loss or damage to property, loss of opportunity, and other injuries proximately caused by the abuses.[49] Compensation for these damages can either be monetary or in the form of nonmonetary reparation such as provision of new employment, pension rights, medical and educational services, social security, and housing.[50] Although the Dayton Accords provide for the creation of a compensation commission, its jurisdiction is limited to property claims.

Without international action, there is little likelihood that victims of atrocities in the former Yugoslavia will obtain compensation from the individual perpetrators or the governments responsible for their suffering. The international community should help in two ways: first, the United Nations could set up a victim compensation fund and urge foreign governments to allocate a certain percentage of their aid to the countries of the former Yugoslavia to that fund; second, the Security Council should establish a compensation commission modeled after the one put together in 1991, which created a fund and oversaw the payment of compensation for claims against Iraq "for any direct loss, damage, including environmental damage and the depletion of natural resources, or any injury to foreign Governments' nationals and corporations, as a result of Iraq's unlawful invasion and occupation of Kuwait."[51] Such a mechanism was originally contemplated for the International Tribunal. Although the statute of the International Tribunal does not give it the power to award victim compensation, a clause was included in Security Council Resolution 827 declaring that the creation of the International Tribunal would not prejudice the future establishment of a victim compensation program.[52]

Recommendations:

(37) *The UN Security Council should create a voluntary fund for the provision of financial compensation to the victims of atrocities.*

(38) *The Security Council should order that certain assets of the Republic of Serbia, the Bosnian Serb entity, and the Republic of Croatia be frozen and then contributed to this fund.*

(39) *The Security Council should order that the individual assets of indicted war criminals be seized and transferred to this fund.*

(40) *The United States and its allies, maintaining their freeze on assets, should divide those assets according to the Brussels negotiations and transfer a certain share of the assets identified as belonging to the Republic of Serbia and the Republic of Croatia to an internationally administered compensation fund.*

F. Improve the Quality and Effectiveness of Domestic Prosecutions

1. Revamp the Rules of the Road Agreement

On February 18, 1996, the parties to the Dayton Accords sought to strengthen the peace process by agreeing that persons other than those indicted by the International Tribunal could be arrested and detained for war crimes only pursuant to a previously issued order, warrant, or indictment that had been reviewed by the Office of the Prosecutor for the International Tribunal and deemed consistent with international legal standards. This agreement was known as the "Rules of the Road" agreement and became effective immediately.

To date, the Bosnian government has submitted approximately 350 cases to the International Tribunal for review; however, it continues to detain a number of suspects whose files it has not transferred to the International Tribunal. Furthermore, the Croatian government, which has declared its intentions to prosecute more than 150 persons for war crimes, has not submitted its files to the International Tribunal. Similarly, the Bosnian Serb entity has submitted only a few files to the tribunal.

For its part, the prosecutor's office has failed to marshal or commit the resources necessary to review promptly the files that have been presented by the states. Thus, only a small fraction of the files have been reviewed, effectively blocking national efforts to prosecute war crimes by those states that have complied with the Rules of the Road agreement.

Recommendations:

(41) *The International Tribunal should be provided with additional financial and personnel resources to enable the prosecutor to review the large number of case files expected to fall under the Rules of the Road agreement.*

(42) *The prosecutor should establish guidelines and assemble lawyers, prosecutors, and translators to begin reviewing files.*[53]

(43) *The international community should increase pressure on all parties to adhere to the procedures established in the Rules of the Road agreement, specifically, the requirement to seek International Tribunal authorization before arresting or detaining any individual suspected of committing a war crime.*

(44) *The international community should increase pressure on all parties to release any individual in custody whose case has been reviewed by the International Tribunal and has been found to lack adequate evidence necessary for prosecution of war crimes.*

(45) *The international community should increase pressure on all parties to ensure that all suspects are afforded their due process rights by local authorities. These rights include access to counsel, limited detention at police headquarters, informing the suspect's family of his/her whereabouts, speedy trial, periodic judicial review, and adequate medical care.*

2. Increase the Domestic Capacity for the Prosecution of War Criminals

There are two competing views regarding the role of national courts in prosecuting war crimes. The first advocates a strong role for the International Tribunal in prosecuting all alleged war criminals. This view is premised on the argument that national courts cannot handle these types of cases because of the complexities involved and because the courts are struggling to restructure their own legal systems. The second view is that the International Tribunal simply does not have the capacity to prosecute a large number of alleged war criminals; rather, it should focus on the "key players." Thus, there is little choice but to rely on the national courts to prosecute the remaining alleged war criminals.

Although the International Tribunal has primacy over national courts, which defer to its competence, it still has recognized the right of national courts to conduct war crimes trials. In creating the International Tribunal, the UN Security Council made clear its intention to encourage states to prosecute war criminals.

However, the reality of the situation on the ground in Bosnia and Herzegovina is that the legal system has not yet sufficiently matured to undertake a prominent role in prosecuting persons accused of violating international humanitarian law. Problems in the current legal system include the lack of cooperation between the Federation and the Bosnian Serb entity on judicial matters, the lack of procedural laws to effectively prosecute and defend effectively alleged war criminals, the inability to monitor trials, the lack of qualified defense attorneys, and the inability to subpoena witnesses. In short, the legal system in Bosnia and Herzegovina (in both the Federation and the Bosnian Serb entity) cannot yet guarantee a fair and politically unbiased judicial process.

The international effort in Ethiopia provides Bosnia with a model for international community involvement in the reconstruction of domestic capacity to prosecute war crimes. In Ethiopia, the international community recently provided funding, attorneys, and judges to facilitate the prosecution of some three thousand officials of the fallen Mengistu regime.[54]

RECOMMENDATIONS:

(46) *In cooperation with the International Tribunal, a regular trial observance system should be implemented immediately by an international legal nongovernmental organization.*

(a) *The trial observers should be experienced lawyers familiar with the civil law system and the jurisdiction of the legal system in Bosnia and Herzegovina. They should also have knowledge of international human rights standards as pertinent to criminal trials.*

(b) *If it is not possible to obtain support from an international legal NGO, the two entities in Bosnia and Herzegovina should conduct joint observation teams, with representatives from both entities.*

(47) *In the short term, the international community must pressure the Bosnian Serb entity to permit suspects to be represented by the lawyers of their choice. In the medium term, a joint commission composed of members of the Federation's Lawyers Association and the Bosnian Serb entity's Lawyers Association must be formed to create a reciprocity agreement that would permit inter-entity representation.*

(48) *The international community should pressure local government authorities to:*

(a) *ensure an immediate end to torture and mistreatment of suspects by local police (this is particularly the case in the Una Sana Canton);*

(b) *void any prosecution where there is evidence of due process violations;*

(c) *prosecute any law enforcement personnel who violate the due process rights of suspects.*

(49) *The international community should provide assistance to local government authorities for the purposes of:*

(a) *increasing the training of local police with respect to the rights of suspected war criminals;*

(b) *conducting a series of training programs for judges regarding the prosecution of alleged war criminals;*

(c) *creating an international team of legal experts to assist the national and local courts in preparing for and conducting war crimes trials;*

(d) *assisting the national governments in drafting domestic legislation and in creating mechanisms that would provide an opportunity for victims to seek civil redress for war crimes.*

VI. Conclusion

There can be no lasting peace nor an end to the long national nightmare of Bosnia until all war criminals are arrested and brought to justice. Neither Croatia nor Serbia will be able to join the community of nations with all the rights and privileges that entails until they honor their obligations to the International Tribunal. The North Atlantic Treaty Organization will have undermined its raison d'être—the freedom and security of Europe—if it does not execute fully its authority to arrest indicted war criminals. The International Criminal Tribunal for the former Yugoslavia will not have accomplished its mission if it does not move more efficiently and effectively in its pursuit and prosecution of those who have committed war crimes in Bosnia and Croatia. And the United States and its allies will have failed a profound test of their moral, ethical, political, and military leadership in the world if they do not act decisively to end the illegitimate freedom of men who have committed and condoned grave and heinous crimes against humanity.

Appendix

Composite List of Recommendations

Political and Diplomatic Recommendations

(1) The United States and its allies should consider recalling their ambassadors to Belgrade and Zagreb and formally downgrading their diplomatic relations with Serbia and Croatia until those states cooperate fully with the International Tribunal. This cooperation should include:

(a) surrender of all suspects on territory under Belgrade's and Zagreb's control;

(b) suspension of all political, military, and economic cooperation with their Bosnian client-entities and proxies for as long as those entities and proxies harbor war criminals;

(c) full political, financial, and evidentiary support for the International Tribunal.

(2) The United States and its allies should consider suspending diplomatic contact with—and political, military, economic, and any other support for—the Bosnian Serb entity and entities and institutions under Bosnian Croat control until those

entities and institutions surrender all suspects on territory under their control and provide full political, financial, and evidentiary support for the International Tribunal and its work.

(3) The United States and its allies should terminate or prevent the acquisition of Partnership for Peace status for countries that harbor war criminals and/or provide less than full support for the International Tribunal and its work.

(4) Members of the European Union should terminate or prevent EU association with countries that harbor or support war criminals and/or provide less than full support for the International Tribunal and its work. Specifically, the EU should investigate and demand a full accounting by Cyprus of its support for the financial and business activities of indicted war criminal Radovan Karadzic.

Economic Recommendations

(5) The United Nations Security Council should reimpose select sanctions against Serbia and the Bosnian Serb entity that would include:

(a) the suspension of all rail, sea, air, and postal links with Serbia/Montenegro;

(b) the suspension of high-level diplomatic contacts with Serbia/Montenegro and the recall of ambassadors;

(c) an embargo on exports to Serbia/Montenegro and the Bosnian Serb entity;

(d) a prohibition on imports from Serbia/Montenegro and the Bosnian Serb entity;

(e) the freezing of all Serb government assets;

(f) the impounding of all Serb-owned vessels;

(g) the prohibition of Serb participation in international sporting events.

(6) The Security Council should act under the authority of Article 41 of the UN Charter to require that states freeze the assets of individuals indicted by the International Tribunal.

(7) Acting under the International Emergency Economic Powers Act, President Clinton should impose an economic embargo on all U.S. imports to or exports from Serbia and the Bosnian Serb entity.

(8) Acting under the International Emergency Economic Powers Act, President Clinton should order that the personal assets located in the United States of all indicted war criminals be seized.

(9) The president should immediately suspend all financing by the Export-Import Bank (Eximbank) and the Overseas Private Investment Corporation (OPIC) of U.S. businesses working in Croatia, Serbia, and the Bosnian Serb entity.

(10) The president should suspend all existing or planned U.S. Agency for International Development (AID) assistance in the Bosnian Serb entity.

Recommendations for Apprehension of Indicted Criminals

(11) NATO military operations should continue and be directed toward the seizure of high-level indictees.

(12) President Clinton should instruct the U.S. forces operating in Bosnia to seek out and apprehend Radovan Karadzic and Ratko Mladic, as well as those responsible for operating concentration camps.

(13) NATO forces should assist the civilian mechanism in vetting local police forces of suspected war criminals.

(14) The member states of NATO should deliver an unequivocal diplomatic message to Pale that it will be held directly responsible and accountable for any and all violent actions against SFOR, the OSCE, the UN, etc. in response to legal military actions to arrest war criminals and that failure to prohibit such actions will lead to a firm response by NATO against Bosnian Serb military assets.

Recommendations for Improving the Effectiveness of the International Tribunal

(15) The International Tribunal should refocus its scarce resources on investigations of those primarily responsible for orchestrating ethnic cleansing and genocide in Bosnia and Croatia, including heads of state and notorious paramilitary leaders.

(16) The International Tribunal should abandon its perplexing policy of issuing formal letters or certificates to potential indictees stating that the International Tribunal has not indicted them.

(17) The International Tribunal should develop a plan for an adequate and effective witness protection program.

(18) The International Tribunal's witness protection program should receive additional funding to support its work.

(19) Given the difficulties involved in securing cooperation from potential witnesses in the Bosnian Serb entity, and because the International Tribunal does not have a police force to compel witnesses to testify, available defense witnesses should be provided safe conduct. Orders for safe conduct should grant witnesses limited immunity from prosecution when appearing in The Hague to give testimony. Although

orders for safe conduct are not specifically provided for in the International Tribunal's statute or the rules, the trial chamber could find authority in Rule 54.

(20) If safe conduct is not feasible, the trial chamber should liberally permit defense witnesses to give testimony by means of video-link. The trial chamber has recently ruled that defense witnesses can offer testimony via video conferencing if they cannot or will not travel to The Hague. The video-link could be a live television link between the trial chamber and a safe harbor such as an embassy in Bosnia-Herzegovina.

(21) To mitigate the very real threat of reprisals against witnesses who testify, the trial chamber should refrain from disclosing witnesses' identity to the public. This elementary form of witness protection is supported by the statute and the rules, each of which contains a provision to guarantee confidentiality.

(22) The International Tribunal should more regularly report to the UN Security Council those states failing to comply with its orders.

(23) The International Tribunal should more regularly and openly request the extradition of indicted war criminals from specific states.

(24) The International Tribunal should more regularly and openly request that certain states provide it with information regarding indicted or suspected war criminals.

(25) The International Tribunal should request that the contributing states to SFOR actively seek to arrest and transfer to The Hague indicted war criminals living in their theater of operation.

(26) The International Tribunal should request apprehension by specific states whose forces patrol zones where indicted war criminals are suspected to reside and/or visit frequently.

(27) Governments and nongovernmental organizations must actively lobby the UN's Advisory Committee on Administrative and Budgetary Questions and the Fifth Committee (particularly countries represented in both committees) to support the necessary increase in financial support for the International Tribunal.

(28) The United Nations' November 21, 1996, *Report on Gratis Personnel* should be amended to eliminate the 13 percent surcharge for program support costs related to gratis personnel provided by governments and other entities to the International Tribunals. The current requirements that all secondees be preapproved by the relevant International Tribunals and adhere to all International Tribunal regulations are appropriate and will ensure that gratis personnel possess the required expertise and comply with all International Tribunal instructions.

(29) The UN secretary-general should adhere to Security Council Resolution 827, which unambiguously supports the use of gratis personnel for the International Tribunal.

(30) The United States should urge a non-UN-affiliated review of the effectiveness of the International Tribunal and means for improving its operation.

Recommendations for Establishing Nonprosecutorial Mechanisms

(31) The Office of the Prosecutor should be provided with an additional mandate and staff to serve as a high-level truth commission responsible for creating an accurate and unbiased historical record of the ethnic cleansing and genocide that occurred in Bosnia.

(32) The United Nations, in conjunction with the above recommendation, should authorize the creation of a number of local truth commissions to assemble a historical record of specific atrocities. These commissions should include members of

the local community and a staff of psychologists and victims' advocates to address the trauma associated with the presentation of testimony by witnesses.

(33) The existing local truth commissions should come under supervision of the United Nations to ensure the creation of an unbiased historical record.

(34) The IPTF should continue to expand its efforts to reconstitute the police forces in Bosnia and begin to include forces from the Bosnian Serb entity.

(35) An entity separate from the United Nations should establish a mechanism for the purpose of investigating nonparty complicity in ethnic cleansing and genocide, including the Sarajevo siege and the Srebrenica massacre.

(36) The United States should create a WatchList to deny U.S. entry visas to suspected war criminals. The United States should further instruct government officials to avoid any and all contact with individuals on the list.

(37) The UN Security Council should create a voluntary fund for the provision of financial compensation to the victims of atrocities.

(38) The Security Council should order that certain assets of the Republic of Serbia, the Bosnian Serb entity, and the Republic of Croatia be frozen and then contributed to this fund.

(39) The Security Council should order that the individual assets of indicted war criminals be seized and transferred to this fund.

(40) The United States and its allies, maintaining their freeze on assets, should divide those assets according to the Brussels negotiations and transfer a certain share of the assets identified as belonging to the Republic of Serbia and the Republic of Croatia to an internationally administered compensation fund.

Recommendations for Improving the Quality and Effectiveness of Domestic Prosecutions

(41) The International Tribunal should be provided with additional financial and personnel resources to enable the prosecutor to review the large number of case files expected to fall under the Rules of the Road agreement.

(42) The prosecutor should establish guidelines and assemble lawyers, prosecutors, and translators to begin reviewing files.

(43) The international community should increase pressure on all parties to adhere to the procedures established in the Rules of the Road agreement, specifically, the requirement to seek International Tribunal authorization before arresting or detaining any individual suspected of committing a war crime.

(44) The international community should increase pressure on all parties to release any individual in custody whose case has been reviewed by the International Tribunal and has been found to lack adequate evidence necessary for prosecution of war crimes.

(45) The international community should increase pressure on all parties to ensure that all suspects are afforded their due process rights by local authorities. These rights include access to counsel, limited detention at police headquarters, informing the suspect's family of his/her whereabouts, speedy trial, periodic judicial review, and adequate medical care.

(46) In cooperation with the International Tribunal, a regular trial observance system should be implemented immediately by an international legal nongovernmental organization.

(a) The trial observers should be experienced lawyers familiar with the civil law system and the jurisdiction of the legal system in Bosnia and Herzegovina. They should also have knowledge of international human rights standards as pertinent to criminal trials;

(b) If it is not possible to obtain support from an international legal NGO, the two entities in Bosnia and Herzegovina should conduct joint observation teams, with representatives from both entities.

(47) In the short term, the international community must pressure the Bosnian Serb entity to permit suspects to be represented by the lawyers of their choice. In the medium term, a joint commission composed of members of the Federation's Lawyers Association and the Bosnian Serb entity's Lawyers Association must be formed to create a reciprocity agreement that would permit inter-entity representation.

(48) The international community should pressure local government authorities to:

(a) ensure an immediate end to torture and mistreatment of suspects by local police (this is particularly the case in the Una Sana Canton);

(b) void any prosecution where there is evidence of due process violations;

(c) prosecute any law enforcement personnel who violate the due process rights of suspects.

(49) The international community should provide assistance to local government authorities for the purpose of:

(a) increasing the training of local police with respect to the rights of suspected war criminals;

(b) conducting a series of training programs for judges regarding the prosecution of alleged war criminals;

(c) creating an international team of legal experts to assist the national and local courts in preparing for and conducting war crimes trials;

(d) assisting the national governments in drafting domestic legislation and in creating mechanisms that would provide an opportunity for victims to seek civil redress for war crimes.

Notes

1. Report to the United Nations Security Council, UN Doc. A/49/342, S/1994/1007 (1994).

2. Priscilla B. Hayner, "Fifteen Truth Commissions—1974 to 1994: A Comparative Study," 1 *Transitional Justice* 225-62 (1994). "The great virtue of legal proceedings," writes one scholar of nationalism, "is that their evidentiary rules confer legitimacy on otherwise contestable facts." Michael Ignatieff, "Articles of Faith," *Index on Censorship* (September/October 1996).

3. See *Report to the President from Justice Robert H. Jackson, Chief of Counsel for the United States in the Prosecution of Axis War Criminals,* June 7, 1945, reprinted in *AJIL* 178, 184 (Supp. 1945).

4. "Healing Wounded People," speech by Justice Richard Goldstone at the United States Holocaust Memorial Museum, Washington, D.C., January 27, 1997.

5. Hitler's speech to chief commanders and commanding generals, August 22, 1939, quoted in M. Cherif Bassiouni, *Crimes Against Humanity in International Criminal Law* 176, no. 96 (1992).

6. International Criminal Tribunal for the Former Yugoslavia, press release, CC/PIO/027-E, The Hague, November 24, 1995.

7. Preamble to United Nations Security Council Resolution 827, May 25, 1993.

8. United Nations Security Council Resolution 827. The International Tribunal consists of a prosecutor and his staff, chambers, including two trial chambers and an appeals chamber, and a registry. See Article 11 of the *Statute of the International Criminal Tribunal for the Former Yugoslavia,* at 13 (May 25, 1993).

9. Articles 2 (6) and 25 of the United Nations Charter establish the respective obligations of nonmember and member states to comply with Security Council decisions when necessary for the maintenance of international peace and security.

10. Report to the United Nations Security Council, UN Doc. A/49/342, S/1994/1007, p. 31.

11. Chapter VII, *Charter of the United Nations.*

12. See Articles 25 and 103 of the United Nations Charter and Article 46 of the Vienna Convention on the Law of Treaties (Article 46 is considered to reflect accurately customary international law).

13. Dayton Peace Accords (November 21, 1995), *General Framework Agreement,* Article IX.

14. Article IX of Annex 4 to the *General Framework Agreement.*

15. Despite the indictment of General Blaskic for war crimes and crimes against humanity, Croatian president Franjo Tudjman awarded General Blaskic a military medal for his role in retaking the Knin region in 1995. "Medal for Indicted Croat," *New York Times,* December 10, 1996. Moreover, as recently as July 21, 1997, the Croatian government indicated that "it would use all legal means available" to avoid turning over documents in the Blaskic case requested by the International Tribunal; see "Bosnian Serb Leader Urges Democracy," *International Herald Tribune,* July 22, 1997.

16. "Bosnian Serbs Resist UN Order," *Washington Post,* January 11, 1997.

17. Zeljko Mejakic, Mladen Radic, Miroslav Kvocka, and Nedeljko Timarac hold positions as police officers, while Blagoje Simic and Stevan Todorovic hold influential public positions in Bosanski Samac. Elizabeth Neuffer, "Indicted Serb Town Official 'Not Uncatchable,'" *Boston Globe,* November 1, 1996.

18. Chris Hedges, "Bosnian Serb Area Destitute and Vulnerable," *New York Times,* March 11, 1997.

19. Chris Hedges, "Bosnian Serb Chief Fears for Life," *International Herald Tribune,* July 7, 1997. The current power struggle between Plavsic and Karadzic has caused a split within the ranks of the Bosnian Serbs, with Karadzic accusing Plavsic of complicity with NATO in the recent Prijedor operation and Plavsic threatening to arrest Karadzic for corruption.

20. At the heart of this policy was the belief that it was better to avoid apprehending war criminals on account of the risk it posed to NATO forces in Bosnia. However, this concern focused on the short-term risks of apprehension rather than the long-term moral, legal, and political necessity of arresting individuals charged with grave crimes against humanity. Note in this regard the statement by Klaus Naumann, chairman of NATO's military command: "Soldiers never make good policemen. If politicians ask us to take action against war criminals, they should realize the operative risks may last a long time. We do not know what the aftermath would be because many people regard these criminals as heroes

worth defending." Quoted in William Droszdiak, "NATO Rejects Hunting Bosnia Crimes Suspects," *International Herald Tribune,* June 14, 1997. A criminal's so-called status as a hero cannot be used to excuse a failure to bring him to justice. It should only be employed to justify a planned operation for his arrest that takes into account these complexities.

21. *New York Times,* June 6, 1997.

22. Press statement by the prosecutor, Justice Richard Goldstone, in conjunction with the announcement of indictments, International Criminal Tribunal for the former Yugoslavia, The Hague, July 25, 1995.

23. Statement of the president of the UN Security Council, S/PRST/1996/13, May 8, 1996. In October 1996, the Security Council adopted Resolution 1074, permanently lifting the sanctions imposed on Serbia and the Bosnian Serb Republic.

24. Press statement of Justice Goldstone.

25. This prosecution strategy has come under implicit criticism by the inspector general of the United Nations. In a February 1997 report focusing on the Rwanda Tribunal, which may also be applicable to the International Tribunal, the inspector general concluded that the failure of the prosecutor to ensure that the limited resources of his office were redirected to pursue key figures in the genocide "is the single most significant failing. Unless that is corrected, the Tribunal will have been created to little effect; the Rwandans will be right to suspect that justice delayed is justice denied; and the United Nations will have failed in its promise to put an end to such crimes and to take effective measures to bring to justice the persons who are responsible for them. " *Report of the Secretary-General on the Activities of the Office of Internal Oversight Services,* UN Doc. A/51/789, February 6, 1997 (Annex), at para. 59.

26. Decision on the prosecutor's motion for protective measures for victims and witnesses, International Criminal Tribunal for the former Yugoslavia, The Hague, August 10, 1995, IT Doc. IT-94-I-T.

27. Monroe Leigh, *Yugoslav Tribunal: Use of Unnamed Witnesses against Accused,* 90 AJIL 235 (1996).

28. For a full discussion of recommendations 19-22, see Mark Ellis, "Justice before the International War Crimes Tribunal—Needed Changes for Defense Council," *Duke Journal of Comparative and International Law,* 3.2 (1997).

29. Rule 54 of the International Tribunal's Rules and Procedures reads, "At the request of either part or *proprio motu* a judge or a Trial Chamber may issue such orders, summonses, subpoenas, warrants and transfer orders as may be necessary for the purposes of an investigation or the preparation or conduct of the trial."

30. Statute of the International Criminal Tribunal for the former Yugoslavia, The Hague, Article 204, Rule 69.

31. Ibid., Article 29(2)(d)

32. Ibid., Article 29(2)(e).

33. M. Cherif Bassiouni, *The Law of the International Criminal Tribunal for the Former Yugoslavia* 789 (1996).

34. "Rules of Procedures of the International Criminal Tribunal," Rule 40(I).

35. Rule 40(iii).

36. Rule 59.

37. Rule 61(A).

38. Rule 61(D).

39. *Case Concerning Barcelona Tradition (Belgium v. Spain)* 1970, ICJ 3, para. 33.

40. Ibid, para. 34.

41. Ibid.

42. Robert Jennings and Arthur Watts, *Oppenheim's International Law* 998 (1992).

43. Members of the Advisory Committee on Administrative and Budgetary Questions come from Barbados, Brazil, China, Cuba, France, Germany, India, Italy, Japan, Mali, New Zealand, Romania, Russia, Syria, Tanzania, and Tunisia.

44. Iain Guest, *On Trial: The United Nations, War Crimes, and the Former Yugoslavia,* an unpublished report of the Refugee Policy Group, September 1995, at 90.

45. 28 U.S.C. Section 595(b)(2) "establishes a stand-by mechanism for the appointment of a temporary special prosecutor when needed." Its purpose is "to preserve and promote the accountability and integrity of public officials and of the institutions of the Federal Government and to invigorate the Constitutional separation of powers between the three branches of Government." See legislative history of P.L. 95-521, reproduced in Lawrence E. Walsh, 3 *Final Report of the Independent Counsel for Iran/Contra Matters* 4217, United States Court of Appeals for the District of Columbia Circuit (August 4, 1993).

46. Lawrence E. Walsh, 1 *Final Report of the Independent Counsel for Iran/Contra Matters* xvi, United States Court of Appeals for the District of Columbia Circuit (August 4, 1993).

47. See Suzanne Daley, "In Apartheid Inquiry, Many Only Relived the Pain," *International Herald Tribune,* July 18, 1997.

48. Diane F. Orentlicher, "Addressing Gross Human Rights Abuses: Punishment and Victim Compensation," in *Human Rights: An Agenda for the Next Century,* ed. Louis Henkin and John Lawrence Hargrove (1994),

at 448–49; *Study Concerning the Right to Restitution, Compensation and Rehabilitation for Victims of Gross Violations of Human Rights and Fundamental Freedoms, United Nations Commission on Human Rights, Sub Commission on Prevention of Discrimination and Protection of Minorities, Theo van Boven, Special Rapporteur,* UN Doc. E/CN.4/Sub.2/1990/10, July 26, 1990, reproduced in 1 *Transitional Justice* 505, 515 (1995).

49. Ellen L. Lutz, "After the Elections: Compensating Victims of Human Rights Abuses," 1 *Transitional Justice* 551, 559 (1995).

50. Theo van Boven, "Seminar on the Right to Restitution, Compensation and Rehabilitation for Victims of Gross Violations of Human Rights and Fundamental Freedoms: Summary and Conclusions," 1 *Transitional Justice* 500 (1995).

51. United Nations Security Council Resolution 687 (1991), para. 18. The Iraqi Compensation Commission has received more than 2,335,000 claims submitted by seventy-eight governments on behalf of their citizens. *Letter Dated 17 January 1994 From the President of the Governing Council of the United Nations Compensation Commission Addressed to the President of the Security Council,* UN Doc. S/1994/107, February 2, 1994.

52. However, the Security Council later unfroze the assets of Serbia and the Bosnian Serbs (via Resolution 1074), thereby for the time being removing any possibility for such a program for the victims of ethnic cleansing in the Balkans. If the Security Council were to freeze the assets of indicted Yugoslav war criminals again, those assets could be used for this purpose.

53. The International Tribunal needs immediate assistance in reviewing the case files now in their possession. The American Bar Association's Central and East European Law Initiative (CEELI), through its Coalition for International Justice (CIJ), will provide the tribunal with three U.S. criminal lawyers and three translators. The prosecutor will ultimately decide the fate of each file. The Rome Agreement requires that the prosecutor, and not a third party, make a determination as to the strength of the evidence against persons suspect to investigation, arrest, or detention by local authorities. The CEELI attorneys will conduct the analytical review. They will prepare memorandums in which they assess the strength of the evidence in the dossiers against the accused.

54. See Luc Huyse, "Justice after Transition: On the Choices Successor Elites Make in Dealing with the Past," 1 *Transitional Justice* 335 (1995). See also "Ethiopia: Report of the Office of the Special Prosecutor" (February 1994), reprinted in 3 *Transitional Justice* 107 (1995).

Responsibilities of States Participating in Multilateral Operations with Respect to Persons Indicted for War Crimes

Diane F. Orentlicher

Acknowledgments

I am grateful to Graham T. Blewitt, Robert K. Goldman, Christopher Keith Hall, W. Hays Parks, Yves Sandoz, and Bruno Zimmermann for comments on earlier drafts of this paper, and to Amjad Atallah and Ewen Allison for research assistance. This paper was presented at the International Conference on Reining in Impunity for International Crimes and Serious Violations of Fundamental Human Rights, International Institute of Higher Studies in Criminal Sciences, Siracusa, Italy, September 16–20, 1997.

INTRODUCTION

The creation of two international criminal tribunals in recent years has presented a raft of novel issues relating to the interaction of national and international legal authority. Among these, surely none has greater practical importance than questions bearing on responsibility for apprehending indicted suspects.

When the United Nations Security Council established the Yugoslavia and Rwanda tribunals, it was contemplated that responsibility for apprehending indicted suspects would fall to state authorities.[1] In the case of the Yugoslavia tribunal, it soon became clear that reliance solely on national authorities would hobble the tribunal's operation, as those in a position to arrest most of the indicted suspects were determined to shield them from prosecution.

Thus, attention naturally turned to the possibility of arrest authority being conferred upon an international entity. This possibility was realized through the Dayton Peace Agreement, concluded in late 1995, which authorizes but does not require the NATO force deployed in Bosnia—originally the Implementation Force (IFOR) and now the Stabilization Force (SFOR)—to arrest suspects indicted by the International Criminal Tribunal for the former Yugoslavia (ICTY).[2] While the North Atlantic Council could act on that authorization by encouraging SFOR to search for and arrest suspects indicted by the ICTY, it has instead made clear that arrests are to be made only if SFOR troops encounter indicted suspects without searching for them and the circumstances make it prudent to effect an arrest. It took nineteen months before NATO commanders deemed it appropriate to make such an arrest, and SFOR has to date attempted to arrest only two suspects.*

Public debate concerning NATO's controversial stance has focused principally on policy concerns. While this is scarcely surprising, it is incorrect to assume that NATO's position on apprehension is solely a matter of policy: this question is also governed by law. Several sources of international law require SFOR to search for and, where reasonably possible, to arrest suspects indicted by the ICTY.

Obligations Relating to Grave Breaches of the Geneva Conventions and Protocol I

One source of a duty to search for and arrest indicted suspects is the Geneva Conventions of 1949 and Additional Protocol I of 1977.[3] Each of these conventions, which establish rules governing armed conflicts between states,[4] identifies certain violations as "grave breaches." For example, the Fourth Geneva Convention of 1949 identifies the following as "grave breaches" when committed against protected persons: "wilful killing, torture or inhuman treatment . . . wilfully causing great suffering or serious injury to body or health, unlawful deportation or transfer or unlawful confinement of a protected person . . . , taking of hostages and extensive destruction and appropriation of property, not justified by military necessity and carried out unlawfully and wantonly."[5]

Although parties to these conventions are required to suppress all violations,[6] they have special enforcement duties with respect to grave breaches. The conventions provide in clarion terms that "each High Contracting Party shall be under the obligation to search for persons alleged to have committed, or to have ordered to be committed, such grave breaches, and shall bring such persons, regardless of their nationality, before its own courts" or hand such persons over for trial to another high contracting party.[7]

---

* Since this paper was first presented, the NATO force in Bosnia had arrested (as of April 8, 1998) five additional indicted suspects.

There can be no doubt that "persons alleged to have committed, or to have ordered to be committed," grave breaches are at large in Bosnia. Virtually all of the suspects who have been publicly indicted by the tribunal have been charged with committing or ordering grave breaches.[8] The issue is whether the duty to search for and arrest these men applies to SFOR.

Extraterritorial Application of Geneva Conventions

Military lawyers in the U.S. government, which commands SFOR, as well as NATO legal advisers have argued that SFOR is not bound by this obligation. These lawyers have put forth two principal arguments in support of their position. First, the Pentagon's general counsel asserts that the duty of high contracting parties to search for and arrest persons alleged to have ordered or committed grave breaches does not apply extraterritorially. In her view, the United States is obligated to search for and arrest suspects in its own territory, even when the alleged grave breaches were committed in Bosnia—but this duty stops at the borders of the United States.[9]

While U.S. officials have not elaborated the grounds for this position, one possible basis may be that treaties typically have territorial application.[10] But this is a general, and not exclusive, rule. That the Geneva Conventions and Protocol I are exceptions to the general rule is plain. These conventions, which establish rules principally governing the conduct of interstate armed conflict,[11] would be meaningless if their provisions applied only within the territory of contracting parties.

A second possible and interrelated claim in support of the U.S. position is that, even if other provisions of the Geneva Conventions apply extraterritorially, the provisions establishing a duty to search for and arrest suspected war criminals should be interpreted as applying on a territorial basis in view of the fact that, under international law, states generally can exercise police powers only within their own territory.[12]

But there are well-established exceptions to this general rule. For example, combatants have long been liable to arrest on war crimes charges in the theater of war,[13] and occupying forces have broad police and judicial authority in occupied territories.[14] Most important for present purposes, states may exercise police powers outside their own territory with the consent of the host state.[15] The Bosnian government has consented to NATO's exercise of police powers (and, indeed, has repeatedly urged it to arrest war crimes suspects). By letter dated December 21, 1995, the Bosnian minister of foreign affairs, Muhamed Sacirbey, agreed as follows:

> With regard to the arrest warrant of the International war crimes Tribunal in the Hague concerning the citizens of the Republic of Bosnia and Herzegovina we agree that these tasks be performed, along with our police force, also by members of the IFOR.
>
> We also agree that those persons arrested in connection with the warrants of the tribunal be handed over by the IFOR to the International Tribunal for war crimes.[16]

The legal adviser to NATO's Supreme Headquarters Allied Powers Europe (SHAPE) has conceded that, "with that authorization," his office's "concerns about a possible affront to [the Bosnian government's] sovereignty and, more importantly, actual authority for IFOR personnel to do what the NAC [North Atlantic Council] allowed, evaporated."[17]

Further, the Dayton Peace Agreement and various UN Security Council resolutions make clear that NATO forces may lawfully exercise police powers in Bosnia.[18] Pursuant to this authority and based on consultations between NATO and ICTY officials, tribunal judges amended the ICTY's rules of procedure and evidence to make clear that NATO forces are authorized to arrest indicted suspects.[19]

The drafting history of the Geneva Conventions and Protocol I provides scant insight into the scope of the duty to search for and arrest persons allegedly responsible for grave breaches, but an authoritative commentary published by the International Committee of the Red Cross (ICRC) suggests that the drafters anticipated at least some extraterritorial applications of the duty. It was, to be sure, contemplated that a principal venue for fulfilling this obligation would be the territory of high contracting parties.[20] But the Commentary on Protocol I published by the ICRC implicitly recognizes that this duty was also intended to apply extraterritorially when possible and appropriate. Writing of the duty established by the four conventions of 1949 and Protocol I to search for, arrest, and ensure prosecution of someone alleged to have ordered or committed a grave breach, the commentary explains:

> The possibility of handing over the accused to be tried by another Contracting Party willing to prosecute him is an option open to the Contracting Party *in whose territory the accused is or in whose hands he has fallen.*[21]

In larger perspective, the object and purpose of the "grave breaches" provisions is best served if the duty to search for and arrest persons alleged to have ordered or committed grave breaches applies wherever high contracting parties lawfully exercise arrest authority with respect to such persons. The core aim of the "grave breaches" provisions, which establish mandatory universal jurisdiction, is to foreclose impunity for such breaches.[22] This aim would be ill served if contracting parties' obligations were inapplicable in territories where those states exercise lawful power to arrest twenty-one persons allegedly responsible for grave breaches.[23]

A variation on the claim that the duty to search for and arrest persons alleged to have ordered or committed grave breaches does not apply to the NATO force in Bosnia is the observation, which has been put forth by NATO and U.S. military lawyers, that IFOR/SFOR "is not an army of occupation."[24] But that fact does not negate its authority pursuant to the Dayton Peace Agreement, various Security Council resolutions, and the Bosnian government's consent to arrest suspects indicted by the ICTY.

Application of Geneva Conventions to Multilateral Operations

The second principal argument offered in support of the U.S./NATO position is that neither NATO nor SFOR is a party to the Geneva Conventions and Protocols; only states are parties. This position has been urged by, among others, NATO legal adviser Max S. Johnson, Jr.[25]

But this misses the point: the issue is not whether NATO or SFOR themselves are bound by the conventions (although some legal experts believe they are).[26] The core question is whether parties to the conventions, such as the United States, may evade their commitments by joining a multinational force. This question fairly answers itself. By Mr. Johnson's logic, any state could violate the Geneva Conventions with impunity merely by joining other countries in a military alliance.

The ICRC has consistently taken the position that each state remains individually responsible for applying these treaties when it contributes contingents to multilateral peacekeeping forces.[27] It has also taken the position that breaches of the conventions must be "repressed" by the national authorities of the contingent concerned,[28] making clear its view that states' obligations as high contracting parties do not vaporize when they participate in multilateral operations.

The United States and other states that have contributed forces to multilateral operations have repeatedly acted in accordance with the ICRC's position. In fact, various states have insisted that their contingents remain subject to national authority, notwithstanding a unified command structure governing multinational operations, for such purposes as disciplining troops who commit war crimes.[29]

In the wake of recent revelations about abuses committed by Italian contingents participating in a U.S.-led operation in Somalia, for example, American officers stated that, although they were aware of the abuses, they believed they "had no power of jurisdiction to investigate or punish."[30] A U.S. officer who commanded the Somalia operation told a reporter,

> When the first incidents took place we sat down with our judge advocate and asked ourselves, "what is the U.S. responsibility as the lead element with operational control?" We decided that although we have tactical control and combatant command, we don't have discretionary authority [over discipline]. That rests with the national forces.[31]

Accordingly, when U.S. officials received word of possible abuses by non-American troops participating in the operation, they turned over the information for investigation by the relevant national authority.[32]

Alleged abuses by troops participating in this and other multinational operations in Somalia[33] have in fact been investigated by their own national authorities. Reports of possible abuses by U.S. soldiers participating in the U.S.-led Somalia operation were investigated and in one case prosecuted by U.S. military authorities.[34] Alleged abuses by Italian, Canadian, and Belgian soldiers who participated in multilateral operations in Somalia have also been investigated and in some cases prosecuted by their respective national authorities.[35]

The United Nations likewise takes the position that responsibility for disciplining abusive soldiers who participate in UN peacekeeping operations remains with national authorities. In the wake of recent reports of abuses by troops participating in a UN operation in Somalia, a UN spokesman explained that "ultimately, when something goes wrong, the UN, under its arrangement with troop-contributing countries, does not have the authority to discipline troops." While the United Nations can investigate reports, if it found cause to believe violations had occurred it would ask the state contributing the forces to discipline those responsible for the abuses.[36]

States' insistence on retaining control over discipline of their soldiers who participate in multilateral operations is difficult to reconcile with the view, implicit in the argument that the "grave breaches" obligations of the Geneva Conventions of 1949 do not apply to SFOR or NATO because neither is a party to the conventions, that contributing states in effect cease to operate as national forces when they participate in multilateral operations.

The Duty to Comply with Arrest Orders and Requests for Assistance

Even if states contributing to SFOR were not parties to the Geneva Conventions, they would be bound to arrest at least some of the suspects indicted by the ICTY. The Security Council resolution establishing the tribunal, Resolution 827, requires states to comply with arrest orders and requests for assistance pursuant to Article 29 of the ICTY statute.[37] Article 29(2) of the statute provides that "states shall comply without undue delay with any request for assistance or an order issued by a Trial Chamber, including, but not limited to . . . the arrest or detention of persons."

As a decision of the Security Council, the duty imposed by Resolution 827 is legally binding on UN member states.[38] Thus, any member state that the tribunal either orders or requests to arrest suspects is legally bound to comply.

Generally the tribunal directs arrest warrants to the governmental authorities in the area where indicted suspects are believed to be located. But it also can issue international arrest warrants, and these are directed to all states.

The tribunal has issued such international warrants with regard to several of the suspects whom the prosecutor has indicted. In the cases of Radovan Karadzic and Ratko Mladic, a trial chamber directed "the authorities and officers and agents of all States to act promptly with all due diligence to secure the arrest, detention and transfer to the Tribunal" of the suspects. In light of this directive, it would be untenable for countries contributing to SFOR to claim that they have no duty to arrest these men when they have both the authority and opportunity to do so. In the case of Milan Martic, a trial chamber specifically "directed" IFOR (as well as "the authorities and all officers and agents of all States") "to act promptly with all due diligence to secure [his] arrest, detention and transfer to the Tribunal." By virtue of Security Council Resolution 1088 (1996), which establishes SFOR as the legal successor to IFOR, this directive now applies with continuing effect to SFOR.

As for indicted suspects who are not the subject of international arrest warrants, it appears that the ICTY's indictments and arrest warrants—at least those that are public—have been made available to NATO pursuant to arrangements between ICTY and NATO concerning IFOR/SFOR's detention of persons indicted by the tribunal.[39]

Far from disputing IFOR/SFOR's general duty to comply with UN Security Council resolutions regarding cooperation with the ICTY, NATO lawyers have recognized this obligation. Before the Security Council adopted Resolution 1031, which established IFOR's legal authority, the legal adviser to NATO's internal staff concluded that, in view of the operational control that NATO would have over IFOR, it had an obligation under Resolution 827 to cooperate with the ICTY and that this duty should be made clear in Resolution 1031.[40]

The Genocide Convention

Finally, the Convention on the Prevention and Punishment of the Crime of Genocide,[41] which the United States has ratified, requires parties to "prevent and punish" genocide.[42] When a state that has the power to arrest persons whom the ICTY has charged with genocide[43] stands aside and allows the suspects to evade arrest, it dishonors this solemn undertaking.

Significantly, in a decision on jurisdiction in a suit brought against the Federal Republic of Yugoslavia by Bosnia, the International Court of Justice rejected Yugoslavia's claim that its duties under the Genocide Convention stopped at its territorial borders. Instead, the court ruled, states parties' duties to prevent and punish genocide are not territorially limited.[44]

Conclusion

While Western countries have rejected calls for NATO forces in Bosnia to seek to arrest suspects indicted by the International Criminal Tribunal for the former Yugoslavia on the ground that SFOR has no mandate do so, their response is largely beside the point. States that have legal authority to arrest suspected war criminals also have defined obligations—moral and legal—to bring these men to the bar of justice.

NOTES

1. Article 29 of the Statute of the International Criminal Tribunal for the former Yugoslavia and Article 28 of the Statute of the International Criminal Tribunal for Rwanda require "States" to "comply without undue delay with any request for assistance or an order issued by a Trial Chamber," including requests and orders relating to the "arrest or detention of persons" and to the "surrender or the transfer of the accused" to the tribunal.

2. After elaborating specific powers of IFOR, Annex 1-A of the Dayton Peace Agreement provides, in Article VI:

> 4. The Parties understand and agree that further directives from the [North Atlantic Council] may establish additional duties and responsibilities for the IFOR in implementing this Annex.

Since Annex 1-A also requires parties to the agreement to cooperate fully with the ICTY, (see article X), Article VI(4) enables the North Atlantic Council to vest IFOR with authority to assist in implementing these obligations. A resolution adopted by the UN Security Council following conclusion of the Dayton Accords recognizes that the parties thereto are required to cooperate fully with the ICTY and have authorized IFOR "to take such actions as required, including the use of necessary force, to ensure compliance with Annex 1-A of the Peace Agreement." UN Security Council Resolution 1031, para. 5 (1995).

3. Geneva Convention for the Amelioration of the Condition of the Wounded and Sick in Armed Forces in the Field, August 12, 1949, 6 U.S.T. 3217, T.I.A.S. no. 3362, 75 U.N.T.S. 31; Geneva Convention for the Amelioration of the Condition of Wounded, Sick and Shipwrecked Members of Armed Forces at Sea, August 12, 1949, 6 U.S.T. 3217, T.I.A.S. no. 3363, 75 U.N.T.S. 85; Geneva Convention Relative to the Treatment

of Prisoners of War, August 12, 1949, 6 U.S.T. 3316, T.I.A.S. no. 3364, 75 U.N.T.S. 135; Geneva Convention Relative to the Protection of Civilian Persons in Time of War, August 12, 1949, 6 U.S.T. 3516, 75 U.N.T.S. 287 (hereafter *Fourth Geneva Convention*); hereafter these treaties will be referred to collectively as Geneva Conventions of 1949; Protocol Additional to the Geneva Conventions of 1949 and Relating to the Protection of Victims of International Armed Conflicts, opened for signature December 12, 1977, 1125 U.N.T.S. 3, 16 I.L.M. 1391 (1977) (hereafter Protocol I).

4. Although Article 3 common to the four Geneva Conventions of 1949 establishes obligations that apply in situations of noninternational armed conflict, the conventions generally apply "to all cases of declared war or of any other armed conflict which may arise between two or more of the High Contracting Parties, even if the state of war is not recognized by one of them," and to "all cases of partial or total occupation of the territory of a High Contracting Party, even if the said occupation meets with no armed resistance." Geneva Conventions of 1949, Common Article 2.

5. Fourth Geneva Convention, Article 147.

6. See Geneva Conventions of 1949, Articles 49/50/129/146; Protocol I, Article 86(1).

7. Geneva Conventions of 1949, Articles 49/50/129/146; see Protocol I, Article 85. Although these provisions contemplate prosecution by national courts, the drafting history of the 1949 conventions makes clear that the language establishing a duty to prosecute grave breaches "does not exclude handing over the accused to an international criminal court whose competence has been recognized by the Contracting Parties." International Committee of the Red Cross, IV Commentary on the Geneva Conventions of 12 August 1949: Geneva Convention Relative to the Protection of Civilian Persons in Time of War 593 (Jean S. Pictet, general ed., 1958) (hereafter Commentary on Fourth Geneva Convention). See also International Committee of the Red Cross, Commentary on the Additional Protocols of 8 June 1977 to the Geneva Conventions of 12 August 1949 at 975 n. 10 (Yves Sandoz et al., eds., 1987) (hereafter Commentary on Additional Protocols).

8. Articles 2–5 of the Statute of the International Criminal Tribunal on the former Yugoslavia establish the tribunal's subject matter jurisdiction over four categories, of which the first, set forth in Article 2, is "Grave breaches of the Geneva Conventions of 1949." Of seventy-eight suspects publicly indicted by the ICTY as of September 1997, at least seventy-two have been charged under Article 2, typically in conjunction with other charges.

9. See interview with Defense Department general counsel Judith A. Miller, *National Security Law Report* 1, 2 (Summer 1996). See also Col. John T. Burton, "'War Crimes' During Operations Other than War: Military Doctrine and Law 50 Years After Nuremberg and Beyond," 149 *Military Law Review* 199, 203 (1995).

10. Article 29 of the Vienna Convention on the Law of Treaties, May 23, 1969, U.N. Doc. A/CONF. 39/27 (entered into force January 27, 1990) provides: "Unless a different intention appears from the treaty or is otherwise established, a treaty is binding upon each party in respect of its entire territory."

11. See note 4.

12. See Ian Brownlie, *Principles of Public International Law,* 4th ed. (New York: Oxford University Press, 1990), p. 307.

13. More than half a century ago, the Supreme Court observed "An important incident to the conduct of war is the adoption of measures by the military command not only to repel and defeat the enemy, but to seize and subject to disciplinary measures those enemies who in their attempt to thwart or impede our military effort have violated the law of war." Ex parte Quirin, 317 U.S. 1, 28–29 (1942). See also In re Yamashita, 327 U.S. 1, 11–13 (1946); Johnson v. Eisentrager, 339 U.S. 763 (1950).

14. For provisions relating to the enforcement of penal law by an occupying power, see Fourth Geneva Convention, Articles 64–77. On various forms of military jurisdiction, see generally Robinson O. Everett and Scott L. Silliman, "Forums for Punishing Offenses Against the Law of Nations," 29 *Wake Forrest Law Review* 509 (1994); Elbridge Colby, "Occupation Under the Laws of War," 25 *Columbia Law Review* 904 (1925).

15. See Brownlie, *Principles of Public International Law, p.* 307.

16. Quoted in remarks of M. S. Johnson, Jr., legal adviser, Supreme Headquarters Allied Powers Europe, "NATO's Detention Policy Concerning Persons Indicted for War Crimes by the International Criminal Tribunal for the Former Yugoslavia," p. 5, presented at "Partnership for Peace Status of Forces Agreement Implementation, International Humanitarian Law/Law of War and War Crimes" conference, Garmisch-Partenkirchen, Germany, September 10–13, 1996 (hereafter Johnson Remarks).

17. Ibid., p. 5.

18. See note 2 and accompanying text.

19. Rule 59 bis(A) of the tribunal's rules of procedure and evidence, adopted in January 1996, authorizes the transmission to "an appropriate authority or international body or the Prosecutor" of an arrest warrant, "together with an order for his prompt transfer to the Tribunal in the event that he be taken into custody by that authority or international

body or the Prosecutor." This rule was adopted "to provide for the transmission of arrest warrants to, *inter alia,* the NATO-led International Implementation Force (IFOR), deployed in Bosnia and Herzegovina under the Dayton Accord." *The Practice of the International Criminal Tribunal for the former Yugoslavia and the International Criminal Tribunal for Rwanda* 134 (John R. W. D. Jones, ed., 3d ed., June 1997).

20. One passage in the commentary on the 1949 Geneva Conventions published by the ICRC seems to reflect this assumption. Concerning the "grave breaches" provisions, the commentary notes: "As soon as a Contracting Party realizes that there is *on its territory* a person who has committed a grave breach, its duty is to ensure that the person concerned is arrested and prosecuted with all speed." *Commentary on Fourth Geneva Convention,* p. 593 (emphasis added). But the principal thrust of this observation was to emphasize the "active" nature of the duty to arrest persons accused of ordering or committing a grave breach. Moreover, as noted in note 21 and accompanying text, the commentary on Protocol I published by the ICRC contemplates extraterritorial application of the "grave breaches" obligations of the 1949 conventions.

21. *Commentary on Additional Protocols,* p. 1026 (emphasis added). The commentary further asserts: "As long as the penal repression of grave breaches is ensured, the right of each Contracting Party to choose between prosecuting a person in its power or to hand him over to another Party interested in prosecuting him therefore remains absolute . . ." (p. 1029, emphasis added).

22. *Cf. Commentary on Fourth Geneva Convention,* p. 587 (noting that the "universality of jurisdiction" provided for in the grave breaches provisions "is some basis for the hope that they will not remain unpunished . . . "). Providing further indication of the breadth of the grave breaches duty, the Diplomatic Conference that drafted the 1949 conventions rejected an Italian proposal to limit these obligations to states that were parties to the armed conflict in which the grave breaches occurred. In response to this proposal, the Dutch delegate asserted that "each Contracting Party should be under this obligation, even if neutral in a conflict," and the president of the conference expressed the opinion that "a neutral State did not violate its neutrality by trying or handing over an accused, under an international obligation." Final Record of the Diplomatic Conference of Geneva of 1949, Vol. II, Section B, para. 5, p. 116. See also *Commentary on Additional Protocols,* p. 975 n. 8 (observing that the "Contracting Parties" referred to in the "grave breaches" provisions of the 1949 conventions include "neutral States or States not Parties to the conflict").

23. This does not necessarily preclude recognizing that some states—notably the host state—may have priority vis-à-vis other states with respect to the exercise of arrest power. Nor does it preclude making distinctions between the respective mandates of various forces participating in a multilateral operation. That SFOR as a whole is authorized to arrest persons indicted by the ICTY does not, for example, preclude SFOR commanders from designating and training special units to execute arrests. But these distinctions should not be made in a manner that defeats the "grave breaches" provisions by ensuring impunity or by causing undue delay in the capture and prosecution of persons alleged to have ordered or committed grave breaches.

24. See, e.g., Johnson Remarks, p. 6. Johnson continues: "[N]o single document or collection of documents have vested IFOR with plenary police powers to deal with alleged war criminals." See also Col. F. M. Lorenz, U.S. Marine Corps, "War Criminals: Testing the Limits of Military Force," *Joint Forces Quarterly* (Summer 1997): 61.

25. Letter from Max S. Johnson, Jr., legal adviser to the Supreme Allied Commander Europe (SACEUR), to Amnesty International, London, March 12, 1996.

26. Debate over the question whether multilateral operations are subject to the Geneva Conventions has focused on UN peacekeeping operations. The International Committee of the Red Cross has consistently taken the position that such operations are bound to comply with international humanitarian law whenever they become engaged in armed conflict, see, e.g., Final Declaration, International Conference for the Protection of War Victims, Geneva, August 30–September 1, 1993, while the United Nations has generally opposed this position. The UN's reasons include the fact that humanitarian law treaties make no provision for nonstate parties; the impossibility of classifying the United Nations as a "party to a conflict"; and the difficulty, if not impossibility, for a nonstate body to implement certain provisions, including those requiring prosecution and punishment of certain offenses. The UN has, however, declared that its forces should observe the principles and spirit of humanitarian law conventions. A clause to this effect now appears in the UN's model Status of Forces agreement for peacekeeping operations. See Antoine Bouvier, "Convention on the Safety of United Nations and Associated Personnel: Presentation and Analysis," *International Review of the Red Cross* 35 (1995): 651–52; Umesh Palwankar, "Applicability of International Humanitarian Law to United Nations Peace-keeping Forces," *International Review of the Red Cross* 33 (1993): 231–32. Moreover, the Convention on the Safety of United Nations and Associated

Personnel, adopted in 1994, implicitly recognizes the direct application of international humanitarian law to UN forces in some circumstances. UN General Assembly Resolution 49/59, Annex, Article 2(2) (1994).

27. See Palwankar, "Applicability of International Humanitarian Law," p. 230, citing a 1961 International Committee of the Red Cross memorandum entitled "Application and Dissemination of the Geneva Conventions."

28. Ibid., p. 231.

29. Cf. Kenneth S. Freeman, "Recent Developments: Punishing Attacks on United Nations Peacekeepers: A Case Study of Somalia," 8 *Emory International Law Review* 845, 847 (members of UN military contingents "remain subject to the laws and jurisdiction of their member state at all times"), citing *Peacekeeper's Handbook,* 3d ed. (New York: International Peace Academy, 1984), p. 365.

30. Ben Barber, "U.S. Officers Concede Knowing of Atrocities," *Washington Times,* July 27, 1997.

31. Ibid. (bracketed text in original article). This approach seems essentially consistent with a policy adopted by the chairman of the Joint Chiefs of Staff last year. An Instruction promulgated by the chairman in August 1996 sets forth the policy of the Department of Defense that U.S. Armed Forces will observe the law of war during the conduct of military operations in armed conflict, as well as during "all operations that are characterized as Military Operations Other Than War"; U.S. obligations under the law of war will be enforced by the U.S. Armed Forces; and violations of the law of war "alleged to have been committed by . . . allied military or civilian personnel will be reported through appropriate command channels for ultimate transmission to appropriate agencies of allied governments." CJCSI 5810.01, Office of the Chairman of the Joint Chiefs of Staff, August 12, 1996.

32. Barber, "U.S. Officers Concede Knowing of Atrocities."

33. There were three separate multinational operations in Somalia between 1992 and 1995. The first, UNOSOM I, was a UN peacekeeping operation. The second, the United Task Force (UNITAF), was a multinational coalition authorized by the UN Security Council but commanded by the U.S. military. The third, UNOSOM II, was a UN operation in which the United States participated by, inter alia, providing the deputy commander and other senior officers and contributing a thirteen-hundred-man Quick Reaction Force that served under the operational control of a U.S. general.

34. Barber, "U.S. Officers Concede Knowing of Atrocities."

35. See Jenny Kuper, "How to Stop the Massacre of Innocents," *The Independent* (London), July 15, 1997; Vera Haller, "Italy to Probe Army

Torture Allegations," *Washington Post,* June 18, 1997; "Somalia Welcomes Italian Decision to Reopen Torture Probe," Agence France-Press, August 26, 1997; Jennifer Gould, "UN Soldiers Acquitted: New Photos Emerge," *Village Voice,* July 15, 1997; *Dishonored Legacy: The Lessons of the Somalia Affair,* Report of the Somalia Commission of Inquiry, Government of Canada, Ottawa, July 1997.

36. "More Torture Allegations Investigated by UN," *Jane's Defense Weekly,* July 9, 1997.

37. UN Security Council Resolution 827, para. 4 (1993).

38. Article 25 of the UN Charter provides: "The Members of the United Nations agree to accept and carry out the decisions of the Security Council in accordance with the present Charter."

39. See Johnson Remarks, p. 4 (noting that, pursuant to an agreement reached between NATO and the ICTY shortly after the Dayton Accords were concluded, tribunal Judge Claude Jorda by special order made fifty-two indictments and arrest warrants available to the Supreme Headquarters Allied Powers Europe).

40. This opinion is summarized in Johnson Remarks, p. 3. In the opinion of Johnson, a Security Council resolution was not a sine qua non for IFOR's detention policy (pp. 3–4). This view seemingly implies that IFOR's authority to detain war criminals was or could be established on the basis of other authority, including the consent of the Bosnian government. Cf. Col. John T. Burton, "'War Crimes' During Operations Other than War," pp. 203–5 (expressing the opinion that the Yugoslavia tribunal has authority to issue orders that are binding on member states, including those participating in the NATO operation in Bosnia, but that implementation by soldiers requires a directive from the North Atlantic Council, and also expressing the view that if the then-anticipated peace accord were to require parties to comply with orders of the Yugoslavia tribunal, a military implementation force might, by virtue of its mandate to enforce the peace agreement, have authority to arrest indicted war criminals).

41. 78 U.N.T.S. 277, entered into force January 12, 1951.

42. Ibid., Article I.

43. At least seven suspects indicted by the Yugoslavia tribunal have been charged with genocide. Both of the suspects whom SFOR attempted to arrest in July 1997 had been charged with genocide. One, Simo Drljaca, was shot dead by SFOR soldiers when he resisted arrest. The other, Milan Kovacevic, was arrested by SFOR and transferred to The Hague to stand trial.

44. Although U.S. legislation enables American courts to prosecute genocide only when the crime was committed in U.S. territory or by a

U.S. national, 18 U.S.C. § 1091(d), this limitation does not apply to the United States' exercise of its authority to arrest persons indicted for genocide in Bosnia.

APPENDIXES

Appendixes 1–7
Sources of Authority

1. *UN Security Council Resolution 827 (1993) of 25 May 1993*

   This resolution legally establishes the International Criminal Tribunal for the former Yugoslavia.

2. *The Statute of the International Tribunal*

   This statute is the bedrock document of the tribunal. Much like a founding charter, it lays out the tribunal's structure, jurisdictional mandate, and procedural scope. Article 29 is particularly relevant to this report, in that it addresses the obligation of states to cooperate with the tribunal in all respects, including to cooperate with requests for assistance in arresting individuals.

3. Proximity Peace Talks, Wright-Patterson Air Force Base, Dayton, Ohio, November 1–21, 1995, *The General Framework Agreement for Peace in Bosnia and Herzegovina,* Article IX

   This agreement is the principal document in what is commonly called the Dayton Accords that provides the legal basis of the peace in Bosnia and imposes certain binding obligations on the parties. Article IX sets forth the obligation of the parties to Dayton to cooperate with the tribunal in its investigation and prosecution of war crimes.

4. *Constitution of Bosnia and Herzegovina,* Preamble and Article II, paragraph 8

   The Bosnian Constitution is incorporated in the Dayton Agreement as an annex. Article II, Paragraph 8 of the Constitution is important in that it explicitly sets forth the obligation to provide unrestricted access to the tribunal and comply with orders issued by the tribunal.

5. *Convention (IV) Relative to the Protection of Civilian Persons in Time of War,* Geneva, 12 August 1949 [selected provisions]

   This is one of the four General Conventions that codify many of the laws of war. The Fourth Convention is particularly relevant to this report in that it covers the protection of civilians. It has provided the basis for a number of the charges brought against the individuals indicted by the tribunal. The convention is long and quite detailed. The excerpts focus on provisions relevant to events in Bosnia.

6. *Protocol Additional to the Geneva Conventions of 12 August 1949, and Relating to the Protection of Victims of International Conflicts (Protocol I),* 8 June 1977 [selected provisions]

   This protocol supplements the Geneva Conventions of 1949. The excerpts of Protocol I included here focus on provisions relevant to events in Bosnia.

7. *Convention on the Prevention and Punishment of the Crime of Genocide,* 9 December 1948

   This is the primary international treaty addressing the crime of genocide. Seven individuals under indictment by the tribunal have been accused of genocide.

Appendix 1

UN Security Council Resolution 827 (1993) of 25 May 1993

The Security Council,

Reaffirming its resolution 713 (1991) of 25 September 1991 and all subsequent relevant resolutions,

Having considered the report of the Secretary-General (S/25704 and Add.1) pursuant to paragraph 2 of resolution 808 (1993),

Expressing once again its grave alarm at continuing reports of widespread and flagrant violations of international humanitarian law occurring within the territory of the former Yugoslavia, and especially in the Republic of Bosnia and Herzegovina, including reports of mass killings, massive, organized, and systematic detention and rape of women, and the continuance of the practice of "ethnic cleansing," including for the acquisition and the holding of territory,

Determining that this situation continues to constitute a threat to international peace and security,

Determined to put an end to such crimes and to take effective measures to bring to justice the persons who are responsible for them,

Convinced that in the particular circumstances of the former Yugoslavia the establishment as an ad hoc measure by the Council of an international tribunal and the prosecution of persons responsible for serious violations of international humanitarian law would enable this aim to be achieved and would contribute to the restoration and maintenance of peace,

Believing that the establishment of an international tribunal and the prosecution of persons responsible for the above-mentioned violations of international humanitarian law will contribute to ensuring that such violations are halted and effectively redressed,

Noting in this regard the recommendation by the Co-Chairmen of the Steering Committee of the International Conference on the Former Yugoslavia for the establishment of such a tribunal (S/25221),

Reaffirming in this regard its decision in resolution 808 (1993) that an international tribunal shall be established for the prosecution of persons responsible for serious violations of international humanitarian law committed in the territory of the former Yugoslavia since 1991,

Considering that, pending the appointment of the Prosecutor of the International Tribunal, the Commission of Experts established pursuant to resolution 780 (1992) should continue on an urgent basis the collection of information relating to evidence of grave breaches of the Geneva Conventions and other violations of international humanitarian law as proposed in its interim report (S/25274),

Acting under Chapter VII of the Charter of the United Nations,

1. *Approves* the report of the Secretary-General;

2. *Decides* hereby to establish an international tribunal for the sole purpose of prosecuting persons responsible for serious

violations of international humanitarian law committed in the territory of the former Yugoslavia between 1 January 1991 and a date to be determined by the Security Council upon the restoration of peace and to this end to adopt the Statute of the International Tribunal annexed to the above-mentioned report;

3. *Requests* the Secretary-General to submit to the judges of the International Tribunal, upon their election, any suggestions received from States for the rules of procedure and evidence called for in Article 15 of the Statute of the International Tribunal;

4. *Decides* that all States shall cooperate fully with the International Tribunal and its organs in accordance with the present resolution and the Statute of the International Tribunal and that consequently all States shall take any measures necessary under their domestic law to implement the provisions of the present resolution and the Statute, including the obligation of States to comply with requests for assistance or orders issued by a Trial Chamber under Article 29 of the Statute;

5. *Urges* States and intergovernmental and non-governmental organizations to contribute funds, equipment and services to the International Tribunal, including the offer of expert personnel;

6. *Decides* that the determination of the seat of the International Tribunal is subject to the conclusion of appropriate arrangements between the United Nations and the Netherlands acceptable to the Council, and that the International Tribunal may sit elsewhere when it considers it necessary for the efficient exercise of its functions;

7. *Decides* also that the work of the International Tribunal shall be carried out without prejudice to the right of the victims to seek, through appropriate means, compensation for damages incurred as a result of violations of international humanitarian law;

8. *Requests* the Secretary-General to implement urgently the present resolution and in particular to make practical arrangements for the effective functioning of the International Tribunal at the earliest time and to report periodically to the Council;

9. *Decides* to remain actively seized of the matter.

Appendix 2

Statute of the International Tribunal

Annex to the Report of the Secretary-General Pursuant to Paragraph 2 of Security Council Resolution 808 (1993)

Having been established by the Security Council acting under Chapter VII of the Charter of the United Nations, the International Tribunal for the Prosecution of Persons Responsible for Serious Violations of International Humanitarian Law Committed in the Territory of the Former Yugoslavia since 1991 (hereinafter referred to as "the International Tribunal") shall function in accordance with the provisions of the present Statute.

Article 1
Competence of the International Tribunal

The International Tribunal shall have the power to prosecute persons responsible for serious violations of international humanitarian law committed in the territory of the former Yugoslavia since 1991 in accordance with the provisions of the present Statute.

Article 2
Grave breaches of the Geneva Conventions of 1949

The International Tribunal shall have the power to prosecute persons committing or ordering to be committed grave breaches of the Geneva Conventions of 12 August 1949, namely the following acts against persons or property protected under the provisions of the relevant Geneva Convention:

(a) wilful killing;

(b) torture or inhuman treatment, including biological experiments;

(c) wilfully causing great suffering or serious injury to body or health;

(d) extensive destruction and appropriation of property, not justified by military necessity and carried out unlawfully and wantonly;

(e) compelling a prisoner of war or a civilian to serve in the forces of a hostile power;

(f) wilfully depriving a prisoner of war or a civilian of the rights of fair and regular trial;

(g) unlawful deportation or transfer or unlawful confinement of a civilian;

(h) taking civilians as hostages.

Article 3
Violations of the laws or customs of war

The International Tribunal shall have the power to prosecute persons violating the laws or customs of war. Such violations shall include, but not be limited to:

(a) employment of poisonous weapons or other weapons calculated to cause unnecessary suffering;

(b) wanton destruction of cities, towns or villages, or devastation not justified by military necessity;

(c) attack, or bombardment, by whatever means, of undefended towns, villages, dwellings, or buildings;

(d) seizure of, destruction or wilful damage done to institutions dedicated to religion, charity and education, the arts and sciences, historic monuments and works of art and science;

(e) plunder of public or private property.

Article 4
Genocide

1. The International Tribunal shall have the power to prosecute persons committing genocide as defined in paragraph 2 of

this article or of committing any of the other acts enumerated in paragraph 3 of this article.

2. Genocide means any of the following acts committed with intent to destroy, in whole or in part, a national, ethnical, racial or religious group, as such:

(a) killing members of the group;

(b) causing serious bodily or mental harm to members of the group;

(c) deliberately inflicting on the group conditions of life calculated to bring about its physical destruction in whole or in part;

(d) imposing measures intended to prevent births within the group;

(e) forcibly transferring children of the group to another group.

3. The following acts shall be punishable:

(a) genocide;

(b) conspiracy to commit genocide;

(c) direct and public incitement to commit genocide;

(d) attempt to commit genocide;

(e) complicity in genocide.

Article 5
Crimes against humanity

The International Tribunal shall have the power to prosecute persons responsible for the following crimes when committed in armed conflict, whether international or internal in character, and directed against any civilian population:

(a) murder;

(b) extermination;

(c) enslavement;

(d) deportation;

(e) imprisonment;

(f) torture;

(g) rape;

(h) persecutions on political, racial and religious grounds;

(i) other inhumane acts.

Article 6
Personal jurisdiction

The International Tribunal shall have jurisdiction over natural persons pursuant to the provisions of the present Statute.

Article 7
Individual criminal responsibility

1. A person who planned, instigated, ordered, committed or otherwise aided and abetted in the planning, preparation or execution of a crime referred to in articles 2 to 5 of the present Statute, shall be individually responsible for the crime.

2. The official position of any accused person, whether as Head of State or Government or as a responsible Government official, shall not relieve such person of criminal responsibility nor mitigate punishment.

3. The fact that any of the acts referred to in articles 2 to 5 of the present Statute was committed by a subordinate does not relieve his superior of criminal responsibility if he knew or had reason to know that the subordinate was about to commit such acts or had done so and the superior failed to take the necessary and reasonable measures to prevent such acts or to punish the perpetrators thereof.

4. The fact that an accused person acted pursuant to an order of a Government or of a superior shall not relieve him of criminal responsibility, but may be considered in mitigation of punishment if the International Tribunal determines that justice so requires.

Article 8
Territorial and temporal jurisdiction

The territorial jurisdiction of the International Tribunal shall extend to the territory of the former Socialist Federal Republic of Yugoslavia, including its land surface, airspace and territorial waters. The temporal jurisdiction of the International Tribunal shall extend to a period beginning on 1 January 1991.

Article 9
Concurrent jurisdiction

1. The International Tribunal and national courts shall have concurrent jurisdiction to prosecute persons for serious violations of international humanitarian law committed in the territory of the former Yugoslavia since 1 January 1991.

2. The International Tribunal shall have primacy over national courts. At any stage of the procedure, the International Tribunal may formally request national courts to defer to the competence of the International Tribunal in accordance with the present Statute and the Rules of Procedure and Evidence of the International Tribunal.

Article 10
Non-bis-in-idem

1. No person shall be tried before a national court for acts constituting serious violations of international humanitarian law under the present Statute, for which he or she has already been tried by the International Tribunal.

2. A person who has been tried by a national court for acts constituting serious violations of international humanitarian law may be subsequently tried by the International Tribunal only if:

(a) the act for which he or she was tried was characterized as an ordinary crime; or

(b) the national court proceedings were not impartial or independent, were designed to shield the accused from international criminal responsibility, or the case was not diligently prosecuted.

3. In considering the penalty to be imposed on a person convicted of a crime under the present Statute, the International Tribunal shall take into account the extent to which any penalty imposed by a national court on the same person for the same act has already been served.

Article 11
Organization of the International Tribunal

The International Tribunal shall consist of the following organs:

(a) The Chambers, comprising two Trial Chambers and an Appeals Chamber;

(b) The Prosecutor, and

(c) A Registry, servicing both the Chambers and the Prosecutor.

Article 12
Composition of the Chambers

The Chambers shall be composed of eleven independent judges, no two of whom may be nationals of the same State, who shall serve as follows:

(a) Three judges shall serve in each of the Trial Chambers;

(b) Five judges shall serve in the Appeals Chamber.

Article 13
Qualifications and election of judges

1 The judges shall be persons of high moral character, impartiality and integrity who possess the qualifications required in their respective countries for appointment to the highest judicial offices. In the overall composition of the Chambers due account shall be taken of the experience of the judges in criminal law, international law, including international humanitarian law and human rights law.

2. The judges of the International Tribunal shall be elected by the General Assembly from a list submitted by the Security Council, in the following manner:

(a) The Secretary-General shall invite nominations for judges of the International Tribunal from States Members of the United Nations and non-member States maintaining permanent observer missions at United Nations Headquarters;

(b) Within sixty days of the date of the invitation of the Secretary-General, each State may nominate up to two candidates meeting the qualifications set out in paragraph 1 above, no two of whom shall be of the same nationality;

(c) The Secretary-General shall forward the nominations received to the Security Council. From the nominations received the

Security Council shall establish a list of not less than twenty-two and not more than thirty-three candidates, taking due account of the adequate representation of the principal legal systems of the world;

(d) The President of the Security Council shall transmit the list of candidates to the President of the General Assembly. From that list the General Assembly shall elect the eleven judges of the International Tribunal. The candidates who receive an absolute majority of the votes of the States Members of the United Nations and of the non-Member States maintaining permanent observer missions at United Nations Headquarters, shall be declared elected. Should two candidates of the same nationality obtain the required majority vote, the one who received the higher number of votes shall be considered elected.

3. In the event of a vacancy in the Chambers, after consultation with the Presidents of the Security Council and of the General Assembly, the Secretary-General shall appoint a person meeting the qualifications of paragraph 1 above, for the remainder of the term of office concerned.

4. The judges shall be elected for a term of four years. The terms and conditions of service shall be those of the judges of the International Court of Justice. They shall be eligible for re-election.

Article 14
Officers and members of the Chambers

1. The judges of the International Tribunal shall elect a President.

2. The President of the International Tribunal shall be a member of the Appeals Chamber and shall preside over its proceedings.

3. After consultation with the judges of the International Tribunal, the President shall assign the judges to the Appeals Chamber and to the Trial Chambers. A judge shall serve only in the Chamber to which he or she was assigned.

4. The judges of each Trial Chamber shall elect a Presiding Judge, who shall conduct all of the proceedings of the Trial Chamber as a whole.

Article 15
Rules of procedure and evidence

The judges of the International Tribunal shall adopt rules of procedure and evidence for the conduct of the pre-trial phase of the proceedings, trials and appeals, the admission of evidence, the protection of victims and witnesses and other appropriate matters.

Article 16
The Prosecutor

1. The Prosecutor shall be responsible for the investigation and prosecution of persons responsible for serious violations of international humanitarian law committed in the territory of the former Yugoslavia since 1 January 1991.

2. The Prosecutor shall act independently as a separate organ of the International Tribunal. He or she shall not seek or receive instructions from any Government or from any other source.

3. The Office of the Prosecutor shall be composed of a Prosecutor and such other qualified staff as may be required.

4. The Prosecutor shall be appointed by the Security Council on nomination by the Secretary-General. He or she shall be of high moral character and possess the highest level of competence and experience in the conduct of investigations and prosecutions of criminal cases. The Prosecutor shall serve for a four-year term and be eligible for reappointment. The terms and conditions of service of the Prosecutor shall be those of an Under-Secretary-General of the United Nations.

5. The staff of the Office of the Prosecutor shall be appointed by the Secretary-General on the recommendation of the Prosecutor.

Article 17
The Registry

1. The Registry shall be responsible for the administration and servicing of the International Tribunal.

2. The Registry shall consist of a Registrar and such other staff as may be required.

3. The Registrar shall be appointed by the Secretary-General after consultation with the President of the International Tribunal. He or she shall serve for a four-year term and be eligible for reappointment. The terms and conditions of service of the Registrar shall be those of an Assistant Secretary-General of the United Nations.

4. The staff of the Registry shall be appointed by the Secretary-General on the recommendation of the Registrar.

Article 18
Investigation and preparation of indictment

1. The Prosecutor shall initiate investigations ex-officio or on the basis of information obtained from any source, particularly from Governments, United Nations organs, intergovernmental and non-governmental organizations. The Prosecutor shall assess the information received or obtained and decide whether there is sufficient basis to proceed.

2. The Prosecutor shall have the power to question suspects, victims and witnesses, to collect evidence and to conduct on-site investigations. In carrying out these tasks, the Prosecutor may, as appropriate, seek the assistance of the State authorities concerned.

3. If questioned, the suspect shall be entitled to be assisted by counsel of his own choice, including the right to have legal assistance assigned to him without payment by him in any such case if he does not have sufficient means to pay for it, as well as to necessary translation into and from a language he speaks and understands.

4. Upon a determination that a prima facie case exists, the Prosecutor shall prepare an indictment containing a concise statement of the facts and the crime or crimes with which the accused is charged under the Statute. The indictment shall be transmitted to a judge of the Trial Chamber.

Article 19
Review of the indictment

1. The judge of the Trial Chamber to whom the indictment has been transmitted shall review it. If satisfied that a prima facie

case has been established by the Prosecutor, he shall confirm the indictment. If not so satisfied, the indictment shall be dismissed.

2. Upon confirmation of an indictment, the judge may, at the request of the Prosecutor, issue such orders and warrants for the arrest, detention, surrender or transfer of persons, and any other orders as may be required for the conduct of the trial.

Article 20
Commencement and conduct of trial proceedings

1. The Trial Chambers shall ensure that a trial is fair and expeditious and that proceedings are conducted in accordance with the rules of procedure and evidence, with full respect for the rights of the accused and due regard for the protection of victims and witnesses.

2. A person against whom an indictment has been confirmed shall, pursuant to an order or an arrest warrant of the International Tribunal, be taken into custody, immediately informed of the charges against him and transferred to the International Tribunal.

3. The Trial Chamber shall read the indictment, satisfy itself that the rights of the accused are respected, confirm that the accused understands the indictment, and instruct the accused to enter a plea. The Trial Chamber shall then set the date for trial.

4. The hearings shall be public unless the Trial Chamber decides to close the proceedings in accordance with its rules of procedure and evidence.

Article 21
Rights of the accused

1. All persons shall be equal before the International Tribunal.

2. In the determination of charges against him, the accused shall be entitled to a fair and public hearing, subject to article 22 of the Statute.

3. The accused shall be presumed innocent until proved guilty according to the provisions of the present Statute.

4. In the determination of any charge against the accused pursuant to the present Statute, the accused shall be entitled to the following minimum guarantees, in full equality:

(a) to be informed promptly and in detail in a language which he understands of the nature and cause of the charge against him;

(b) to have adequate time and facilities for the preparation of his defence and to communicate with counsel of his own choosing;

(c) to be tried without undue delay;

(d) to be tried in his presence, and to defend himself in person or through legal assistance of his own choosing; to be informed, if he does not have legal assistance, of this right; and to have legal assistance assigned to him, in any case where the interests of justice so require, and without payment by him in any such case if he does not have sufficient means to pay for it;

(e) to examine, or have examined, the witnesses against him and to obtain the attendance and examination of witnesses on his behalf under the same conditions as witnesses against him;

(f) to have the free assistance of an interpreter if he cannot understand or speak the language used in the International Tribunal;

(g) not to be compelled to testify against himself or to confess guilt.

Article 22
Protection of victims and witnesses

The International Tribunal shall provide in its rules of procedure and evidence for the protection of victims and witnesses. Such protection measures shall include, but shall not be limited to, the conduct of in camera proceedings and the protection of the victim's identity.

Article 23
Judgement

1. The Trial Chambers shall pronounce judgements and impose sentences and penalties on persons convicted of serious violations of international humanitarian law.

2. The judgement shall be rendered by a majority of the judges of the Trial Chamber, and shall be delivered by the Trial Chamber in public. It shall be accompanied by a reasoned opinion in writing, to which separate or dissenting opinions may be appended.

Article 24
Penalties

1. The penalty imposed by the Trial Chamber shall be limited to imprisonment. In determining the terms of imprisonment, the Trial Chambers shall have recourse to the general practice regarding prison sentences in the courts of the former Yugoslavia.

2. In imposing the sentences, the Trial Chambers should take into account such factors as the gravity of the offence and the individual circumstances of the convicted person.

3. In addition to imprisonment, the Trial Chambers may order the return of any property and proceeds acquired by criminal conduct, including by means of duress, to their rightful owners.

Article 25
Appellate proceedings

1. The Appeals Chamber shall hear appeals from persons convicted by the Trial Chambers or from the Prosecutor on the following grounds:

(a) an error on a question of law invalidating the decision; or

(b) an error of fact which has occasioned a miscarriage of justice.

2. The Appeals Chamber may affirm, reverse or revise the decisions taken by the Trial Chambers.

Article 26
Review proceedings

Where a new fact has been discovered which was not known at the time of the proceedings before the Trial Chambers or the Appeals Chamber and which could have been a decisive factor in reaching the decision, the convicted person or the Prosecutor may submit to the International Tribunal an application for review of the judgement.

Article 27
Enforcement of sentences

Imprisonment shall be served in a State designated by the International Tribunal from a list of States which have indicated to the Security Council their willingness to accept convicted persons. Such imprisonment shall be in accordance with the applicable law of the State concerned, subject to the supervision of the International Tribunal.

Article 28
Pardon or commutation of sentences

If, pursuant to the applicable law of the State in which the convicted person is imprisoned, he or she is eligible for pardon or commutation of sentence, the State concerned shall notify the International Tribunal accordingly. The President of the International Tribunal, in consultation with the judges, shall decide the matter on the basis of the interests of justice and the general principles of law.

Article 29
Cooperation and judicial assistance

1. States shall cooperate with the International Tribunal in the investigation and prosecution of persons accused of committing serious violations of international humanitarian law.

2. States shall comply without undue delay with any request for assistance or an order issued by a Trial Chamber, including, but not limited to:

(a) the identification and location of persons;

(b) the taking of testimony and the production of evidence;

(c) the service of documents;

(d) the arrest or detention of persons;

(e) the surrender or the transfer of the accused to the International Tribunal.

Article 30
The status, privileges and immunities of the International Tribunal

1. The Convention on the Privileges and Immunities of the United Nations of 13 February 1946 shall apply to the International Tribunal, the judges, the Prosecutor and his staff, and the Registrar and his staff.

2. The judges, the Prosecutor and the Registrar shall enjoy the privileges and immunities, exemptions and facilities accorded to diplomatic envoys, in accordance with international law.

3. The staff of the Prosecutor and of the Registrar shall enjoy the privileges and immunities accorded to officials of the United Nations under articles V and VII of the Convention referred to in paragraph 1 of this article.

4. Other persons, including the accused, required at the seat of the International Tribunal shall be accorded such treatment as is necessary for the proper functioning of the International Tribunal.

Article 31
Seat of the International Tribunal

The International Tribunal shall have its seat at The Hague.

Article 32
Expenses of the International Tribunal

The expenses of the International Tribunal shall be borne by the regular budget of the United Nations in accordance with Article 17 of the Charter of the United Nations.

Article 33
Working languages

The working languages of the International Tribunal shall be English and French.

Article 34
Annual report

The President of the International Tribunal shall submit an annual report of the International Tribunal to the Security Council and to the General Assembly.

Appendix 3

Proximity Peace Talks
Wright-Patterson Air Force Base, Dayton, Ohio, November 1–21, 1995

General Framework Agreement for Peace in Bosnia and Herzegovina

Article IX

The Parties shall cooperate fully with all entities involved in implementation of this peace settlement, as described in the Annexes to this Agreement, or which are otherwise authorized by the United Nations Security Council, pursuant to the obligation of all Parties to cooperate in the investigation and prosecution of war crimes and other violations of international humanitarian law.

APPENDIX 4

CONSTITUTION OF BOSNIA AND HERZEGOVINA

PREAMBLE

Based on respect for human dignity, liberty, and equality,

Dedicated to peace, justice, tolerance, and reconciliation,

Convinced that democratic governmental institutions and fair procedures best produce peaceful relations within a pluralist society,

Desiring to promote the general welfare and economic growth through the protection of private property and the promotion of a market economy,

Guided by the Purposes and Principles of the Charter of the United Nations,

Committed to the sovereignty, territorial integrity, and political independence of Bosnia and Herzegovina in accordance with international law,

Determined to ensure full respect for international humanitarian law,

Inspired by the Universal Declaration of Human Rights, the International Covenants on Civil and Political Rights and on Economic, Social and Cultural Rights, and the Declaration on the Rights of Persons Belonging to National or Ethnic, Religious and Linguistic Minorities, as well as other human rights instruments,

Recalling the Basic Principles agreed in Geneva on September 8, 1995, and in New York on September 26, 1995,

Bosniacs, Croats, and Serbs, as constituent peoples (along with Others), and citizens of Bosnia and Herzegovina hereby determine that the Constitution of Bosnia and Herzegovina is as follows: . . .

Article II

Human Rights and Fundamental Freedoms

8. *Cooperation.* All competent authorities in Bosnia and Herzegovina shall cooperate with and provide unrestricted access to: any international human rights monitoring mechanisms established for Bosnia and Herzegovina; the supervisory bodies established by any of the international agreements listed in Annex I to this Constitution; the International Tribunal for the Former Yugoslavia (and in particular shall comply with orders issued pursuant to Article 29 of the Statute of the Tribunal); and any other organization authorized by the United Nations Security Council with a mandate concerning human rights or humanitarian law.

Appendix 5

Convention (IV) Relative to the Protection of Civilian Persons in Time of War Geneva, 12 August 1949

Part I. General Provisions

Article 1.

The High Contracting Parties undertake to respect and to ensure respect for the present Convention in all circumstances.

Article 2.

In addition to the provisions which shall be implemented in peace-time, the present Convention shall apply to all cases of declared war or of any other armed conflict which may arise between two or more of the High Contracting Parties, even if the state of war is not recognized by one of them.The Convention shall also apply to all cases of partial or total occupation of the territory of a High Contracting Party, even if the said occupation meets with no armed resistance.Although one of the Powers in conflict may not be a party to the present Convention, the Powers who are parties thereto shall remain bound by it in their mutual relations. They shall furthermore be bound by the Convention in relation to the said Power, if the latter accepts and applies the provisions thereof.

Article 3.

In the case of armed conflict not of an international character occurring in the territory of one of the High Contracting Parties, each Party to the conflict shall be bound to apply, as a minimum, the following provisions:

1. Persons taking no active part in the hostilities, including members of armed forces who have laid down their arms and those placed hors de combat by sickness, wounds, detention, or any other cause, shall in all circumstances be treated humanely, without any adverse distinction founded on race, colour, religion or faith, sex, birth or wealth, or any other similar criteria.To this end the following acts are and shall remain prohibited at any time and in any place whatsoever with respect to the above-mentioned persons:

(a) violence to life and person, in particular murder of all kinds, mutilation, cruel treatment and torture;

(b) taking of hostages;

(c) outrages upon personal dignity, in particular humiliating and degrading treatment;

(d) the passing of sentences and the carrying out of executions without previous judgment pronounced by a regularly constituted court, affording all the judicial guarantees which are recognized as indispensable by civilized peoples.

2. The wounded and sick shall be collected and cared for.

An impartial humanitarian body, such as the International Committee of the Red Cross, may offer its services to the Parties to the conflict.

The Parties to the conflict should further endeavor to bring into force, by means of special agreements, all or part of the other provisions of the present Convention.

The application of the preceding provisions shall not affect the legal status of the Parties to the conflict.

Article 4.

Persons protected by the Convention are those who, at a given moment and in any manner whatsoever, find themselves, in case of a conflict or occupation, in the hands of a Party to the conflict or Occupying Power of which they are not nationals.

Nationals of a State which is not bound by the Convention are not protected by it. Nationals of a neutral State who find themselves in the territory of a belligerent State, and nationals of a co-belligerent State, shall not be regarded as protected persons while the State of which they are nationals has normal diplomatic representation in the State in whose hands they are.

The provisions of Part II are, however, wider in application, as defined in Article 13.

Persons protected by the Geneva Convention for the Amelioration of the Condition of the Wounded and Sick in Armed Forces in the Field of 12 August 1949, or by the Geneva Convention for the Amelioration of the Condition of Wounded, Sick and Shipwrecked Members of Armed Forces at Sea of 12 August 1949, or by the Geneva Convention relative to the Treatment of Prisoners of War of 12 August 1949, shall not be considered as protected persons within the meaning of the present Convention.

Article 5.

Where in the territory of a Party to the conflict, the latter is satisfied that an individual protected person is definitely suspected of or engaged in activities hostile to the security of the State, such individual person shall not be entitled to claim such rights and privileges under the present Convention as would, if exercised in the favour of such individual person, be prejudicial to the security of such State.

Where in occupied territory an individual protected person is detained as a spy or saboteur, or as a person under definite suspicion of activity hostile to the security of the Occupying Power, such person shall, in those cases where absolute military security so requires, be regarded as having forfeited rights of communication under the present Convention.

In each case, such persons shall nevertheless be treated with humanity and, in case of trial, shall not be deprived of the rights of fair and regular trial prescribed by the present Convention. They shall also be granted the full rights and privileges of a protected person under the present Convention at the earliest date consistent with the security of the State or Occupying Power, as the case may be.

Article 6.

The present Convention shall apply from the outset of any conflict or occupation mentioned in Article 2.

In the territory of Parties to the conflict, the application of the present Convention shall cease on the general close of military operations.

In the case of occupied territory, the application of the present Convention shall cease one year after the general close of military operations; however, the Occupying Power shall be bound, for the duration of the occupation, to the extent that such Power exercises the functions of government in such territory, by the provisions of the following Articles of the present Convention: 1 to 12, 27, 29 to 34, 47, 49, 51, 52, 53, 59, 61 to 77, 143.

Protected persons whose release, repatriation or re-establishment may take place after such dates shall meanwhile continue to benefit by the present Convention. . . .

Article 9.

The present Convention shall be applied with the cooperation and under the scrutiny of the Protecting Powers whose duty it is to safeguard the interests of the Parties to the conflict. For this purpose, the Protecting Powers may appoint, apart from their diplomatic or consular staff, delegates from amongst their own nationals or the nationals of other neutral Powers. The said delegates shall be subject to the approval of the Power with which they are to carry out their duties. The Parties to the conflict shall facilitate to the greatest extent possible the task of the representatives or delegates of the Protecting Powers.

The representatives or delegates of the Protecting Powers shall not in any case exceed their mission under the present Convention.

They shall, in particular, take account of the imperative necessities of security of the State wherein they carry out their duties.

Article 10.

The provisions of the present Convention constitute no obstacle to the humanitarian activities which the International Committee of the Red Cross or any other impartial humanitarian organization may, subject to the consent of the Parties to the conflict concerned, undertake for the protection of civilian persons and for their relief.

Article 11.

The High Contracting Parties may at any time agree to entrust to an international organization which offers all guarantees of impartiality and efficacy the duties incumbent on the Protecting Powers by virtue of the present Convention.

When persons protected by the present Convention do not benefit or cease to benefit, no matter for what reason, by the activities of a Protecting Power or of an organization provided for in the first paragraph above, the Detaining Power shall request a neutral State, or such an organization, to undertake the functions performed under the present Convention by a Protecting Power designated by the Parties to a conflict.

If protection cannot be arranged accordingly, the Detaining Power shall request or shall accept, subject to the provisions of this Article, the offer of the services of a humanitarian organization, such as the International Committee of the Red Cross, to assume the humanitarian functions performed by Protecting Powers under the present Convention.

Any neutral Power or any organization invited by the Power concerned or offering itself for these purposes, shall be required to act with a sense of responsibility towards the Party to the conflict on which persons protected by the present Convention depend, and shall be required to furnish sufficient assurances that it is in a position to undertake the appropriate functions and to discharge them impartially.

No derogation from the preceding provisions shall be made by special agreements between Powers one of which is restricted, even temporarily, in its freedom to negotiate with the other Power or its allies by reason of military events, more particularly where the whole, or a substantial part, of the territory of the said Power is occupied.

Whenever in the present Convention mention is made of a Protecting Power, such mention applies to substitute organizations in the sense of the present Article.

The provisions of this Article shall extend and be adapted to cases of nationals of a neutral State who are in occupied territory or who find themselves in the territory of a belligerent State in which the State of which they are nationals has not normal diplomatic representation. . . .

Part II. General Protection of Populations Against Certain Consequences of War

Article 13.

The provisions of Part II cover the whole of the populations of the countries in conflict, without any adverse distinction based, in particular, on race, nationality, religion or political opinion, and are intended to alleviate the sufferings caused by war.

Article 14.

In time of peace, the High Contracting Parties and, after the outbreak of hostilities, the Parties thereto, may establish in their own territory and, if the need arises, in occupied areas, hospital and safety zones and localities so organized as to protect from the effects of war, wounded, sick and aged persons, children under fifteen, expectant mothers and mothers of children under seven.

Upon the outbreak and during the course of hostilities, the Parties concerned may conclude agreements on mutual recognition of the zones and localities they have created. They may for this purpose implement the provisions of the Draft Agreement annexed to the present Convention, with such amendments as they may consider necessary.

The Protecting Powers and the International Committee of the Red Cross are invited to lend their good offices in order to facilitate the institution and recognition of these hospital and safety zones and localities.

Article 15.

Any Party to the conflict may, either direct or through a neutral State or some humanitarian organization, propose to the adverse Party to establish, in the regions where fighting is taking place, neutralized zones intended to shelter from the effects of war the following persons, without distinction:

(a) wounded and sick combatants or non-combatants;
(b) civilian persons who take no part in hostilities, and who, while they reside in the zones, perform no work of a military character.

When the Parties concerned have agreed upon the geographical position, administration, food supply and supervision of the proposed neutralized zone, a written agreement shall be concluded and signed by the representatives of the Parties to the conflict. The agreement shall fix the beginning and the duration of the neutralization of the zone.

Article 16.

The wounded and sick, as well as the infirm, and expectant mothers, shall be the object of particular protection and respect.

As far as military considerations allow, each Party to the conflict shall facilitate the steps taken to search for the killed and wounded, to assist the shipwrecked and other persons exposed to grave danger, and to protect them against pillage and ill-treatment.

Article 17.

The Parties to the conflict shall endeavour to conclude local agreements for the removal from besieged or encircled areas, of wounded, sick, infirm, and aged persons, children and maternity cases, and for the passage of ministers of all religions, medical personnel and medical equipment on their way to such areas.

Article 18.

Civilian hospitals organized to give care to the wounded and sick, the infirm and maternity cases, may in no circumstances be the object of attack but shall at all times be respected and protected by the Parties to the conflict.

Article 19.

The protection to which civilian hospitals are entitled shall not cease unless they are used to commit, outside their humanitarian duties, acts harmful to the enemy. Protection may, however, cease only after due warning has been given, naming, in all appropriate cases, a reasonable time limit and after such warning has remained unheeded. The fact that sick or wounded members of the armed forces are nursed in these hospitals, or the presence of small arms and ammunition taken from such combatants which have not yet been handed to the proper service, shall not be considered to be acts harmful to the enemy.

Article 20.

Persons regularly and solely engaged in the operation and administration of civilian hospitals, including the personnel engaged in the search for, removal and transporting of and caring for wounded and sick civilians, the infirm and maternity cases shall be respected and protected. . . .

Article 23.

Each High Contracting Party shall allow the free passage of all consignments of medical and hospital stores and objects necessary for religious worship intended only for civilians of another High Contracting Party, even if the latter is its adversary. It shall likewise permit the free passage of all consignments of essential foodstuffs, clothing and tonics intended for children under fifteen, expectant mothers and maternity cases. . . .

Article 26.

Each Party to the conflict shall facilitate enquiries made by members of families dispersed owing to the war, with the object of renewing contact with one another and of meeting, if possible. It shall encourage, in particular, the work of organizations engaged on this task provided they are acceptable to it and conform to its security regulations.

Part III. Status and Treatment of Protected Persons

Section I. Provisions common to the territories of the parties to the conflict and to occupied territories

Article 27.

Protected persons are entitled, in all circumstances, to respect for their persons, their honour, their family rights, their religious convictions and practices, and their manners and customs. They shall at all times be humanely treated, and shall be protected especially against all acts of violence or threats thereof and against insults and public curiosity.

Women shall be especially protected against any attack on their honour, in particular against rape, enforced prostitution, or any form of indecent assault.

Without prejudice to the provisions relating to their state of health, age and sex, all protected persons shall be treated with the same consideration by the Party to the conflict in whose power they are, without any adverse distinction based, in particular, on race, religion or political opinion.

However, the Parties to the conflict may take such measures of control and security in regard to protected persons as may be necessary as a result of the war. . . .

Article 29.

The Party to the conflict in whose hands protected persons may be, is responsible for the treatment accorded to them by its agents, irrespective of any individual responsibility which may be incurred.

Article 30.

Protected persons shall have every facility for making application to the Protecting Powers, the International Committee of the Red Cross, the National Red Cross (Red Crescent, Red Lion and Sun) Society of the country where they may be, as well as to any organization that might assist them.

These several organizations shall be granted all facilities for that purpose by the authorities, within the bounds set by military or security considerations.

Apart from the visits of the delegates of the Protecting Powers and of the International Committee of the Red Cross, provided for by Article 143, the Detaining or Occupying Powers shall facilitate, as much as possible, visits to protected persons by the representatives of other organizations whose object is to give spiritual aid or material relief to such persons.

Article 31.

No physical or moral coercion shall be exercised against protected persons, in particular to obtain information from them or from third parties.

Article 32.

The High Contracting Parties specifically agree that each of them is prohibited from taking any measure of such a character as to cause the physical suffering or extermination of protected persons in their hands. This prohibition applies not only to murder, torture, corporal punishments, mutilation and medical or scientific experiments not necessitated by the medical treatment of a protected person, but also to any other measures of brutality whether applied by civilian or military agents.

Article 33.

No protected person may be punished for an offense he or she has not personally committed. Collective penalties and likewise all measures of intimidation or of terrorism are prohibited. Pillage is prohibited.

Reprisals against protected persons and their property are prohibited.

Article 34.

The taking of hostages is prohibited.

SECTION II. ALIENS IN THE TERRITORY OF A PARTY TO THE CONFLICT

Article 35.

All protected persons who may desire to leave the territory at the outset of, or during a conflict, shall be entitled to do so, unless their departure is contrary to the national interests of the State. The applications of such persons to leave shall be decided in accordance with regularly established procedures and the decision shall be taken as rapidly as possible. Those persons permitted to leave may provide themselves with the necessary funds for their journey and take with them a reasonable amount of their effects and articles of personal use. . . .

Article 37.

Protected persons who are confined pending proceedings or subject to a sentence involving loss of liberty, shall during their confinement be humanely treated.

As soon as they are released, they may ask to leave the territory in conformity with the foregoing Articles.

Article 38.

With the exception of special measures authorized by the present Convention, in particularly by Article 27 and 41 thereof, the situation of protected persons shall continue to be regulated, in principle, by the provisions concerning aliens in time of peace. In any case, the following rights shall be granted to them:

(1) they shall be enabled to receive the individual or collective relief that may be sent to them.

(2) they shall, if their state of health so requires, receive medical attention and hospital treatment to the same extent as the nationals of the State concerned.

(3) they shall be allowed to practice their religion and to receive spiritual assistance from ministers of their faith.

(4) if they reside in an area particularly exposed to the dangers of war, they shall be authorized to move from that area to the same extent as the nationals of the State concerned.

(5) children under fifteen years, pregnant women and mothers of children under seven years shall benefit by any preferential treatment to the same extent as the nationals of the State concerned. . . .

Article 40.

Protected persons may be compelled to work only to the same extent as nationals of the Party to the conflict in whose territory they are.

If protected persons are of enemy nationality, they may only be compelled to do work which is normally necessary to ensure the feeding, sheltering, clothing, transport and health of human beings and which is not directly related to the conduct of military operations. . . .

Article 42.

The internment or placing in assigned residence of protected persons may be ordered only if the security of the Detaining Power makes it absolutely necessary.

Article 43.

Unless the protected persons concerned object, the Detaining Power shall, as rapidly as possible, give the Protecting Power the names of any protected persons who have been interned or subjected to assigned residence, or who have been released from internment or assigned residence. . . .

Article 45.

In no circumstances shall a protected person be transferred to a country where he or she may have reason to fear persecution for his or her political opinions or religious beliefs. . . .

Article 49.

Individual or mass forcible transfers, as well as deportations of protected persons from occupied territory to the territory of the Occupying Power or to that of any other country, occupied or not, are prohibited, regardless of their motive.

Nevertheless, the Occupying Power may undertake total or partial evacuation of a given area if the security of the population or imperative military reasons so demand. Such evacuations may not involve the displacement of protected persons outside the bounds of the occupied territory except when for material reasons it is impossible to avoid such displacement. Persons thus evacuated shall be transferred back to their homes as soon as hostilities in the area in question have ceased.

The Occupying Power undertaking such transfers or evacuations shall ensure, to the greatest practicable extent, that proper accommodation is provided to receive the protected persons, that the removals are effected in satisfactory conditions of hygiene, health, safety and nutrition, and that members of the same family are not separated.

The Protecting Power shall be informed of any transfers and evacuations as soon as they have taken place.

The Occupying Power shall not detain protected persons in an area particularly exposed to the dangers of war unless the security of the population or imperative military reasons so demand.

The Occupying Power shall not deport or transfer parts of its own civilian population into the territory it occupies.

Article 50.

The Occupying Power shall, with the cooperation of the national and local authorities, facilitate the proper working of all institutions devoted to the care and education of children.

The Occupying Power shall take all necessary steps to facilitate the identification of children and the registration of their parentage. It may not, in any case, change their personal status, nor enlist them in formations or organizations subordinate to it.

Should the local institutions be inadequate for the purpose, the Occupying Power shall make arrangements for the maintenance and education, if possible by persons of their own nationality, language and religion, of children who are orphaned or separated from their parents as a result of the war and who cannot be adequately cared for by a near relative or friend.

A special section of the Bureau set up in accordance with Article 136 shall be responsible for taking all necessary steps to identify children whose identity is in doubt. Particulars of their parents or other near relatives should always be recorded if available.

The Occupying Power shall not hinder the application of any preferential measures in regard to food, medical care and protection against the effects of war which may have been adopted prior to the occupation in favour of children under fifteen years, expectant mothers, and mothers of children under seven years.

Article 51.

The Occupying Power may not compel protected persons to serve in its armed or auxiliary forces. No pressure or propaganda which aims at securing voluntary enlistment is permitted.

The Occupying Power may not compel protected persons to work unless they are over eighteen years of age, and then only on work which is necessary either for the needs of the army of occupation, or for the public utility services, or for the feeding, sheltering, clothing, transportation or health of the population of the occupied country. Protected persons may not be compelled to undertake any work which would involve them in the obligation of taking part in military operations. . . .

Article 53.

Any destruction by the Occupying Power of real or personal property belonging individually or collectively to private persons, or to the State, or to other public authorities, or to social or cooperative organizations, is prohibited, except where such destruction is rendered absolutely necessary by military operations. . . .

Article 55.

To the fullest extent of the means available to it, the Occupying Power has the duty of ensuring the food and medical supplies of the population; it should, in particular, bring in the necessary foodstuffs, medical stores and other articles if the resources of the occupied territory are inadequate.

The Occupying Power may not requisition foodstuffs, articles or medical supplies available in the occupied territory, except for use by the occupation forces and administration personnel, and then only if the requirements of the civilian population have been taken into account. Subject to the provisions of other international Conventions, the Occupying Power shall make arrangements to ensure that fair value is paid for any requisitioned goods. . . .

Article 58.

The Occupying Power shall permit ministers of religion to give spiritual assistance to the members of their religious communities.

Article 59.

If the whole or part of the population of an occupied territory is inadequately supplied, the Occupying Power shall agree to relief schemes on behalf of the said population, and shall facilitate them by all the means at its disposal.

Such schemes, which may be undertaken either by States or by impartial humanitarian organizations such as the International Committee of the Red Cross, shall consist, in particular, of the provision of consignments of foodstuffs, medical supplies and clothing.

All Contracting Parties shall permit the free passage of these consignments and shall guarantee their protection. . . .

Article 62.

Subject to imperative reasons of security, protected persons in occupied territories shall be permitted to receive the individual relief consignments sent to them.

Article 63.

Subject to temporary and exceptional measures imposed for urgent reasons of security by the Occupying Power:

(a) recognized National Red Cross (Red Crescent, Red Lion and Sun) Societies shall be able to pursue their activities in accordance with Red Cross principles, as defined by the International Red Cross Conferences. Other relief societies shall be permitted to continue their humanitarian activities under similar conditions;

(b) the Occupying Power may not require any changes in the personnel or structure of these societies, which would prejudice the aforesaid activities.

The same principles shall apply to the activities and personnel of special organizations of a non-military character, which already exist or which may be established, for the purpose of ensuring the living conditions of the civilian population by the maintenance of the essential public utility services, by the distribution of relief and by the organization of rescues.

Article 64.

The penal laws of the occupied territory shall remain in force, with the exception that they may be repealed or suspended by the Occupying Power in cases where they constitute a threat to its security or an obstacle to the application of the present Convention.

Subject to the latter consideration and to the necessity for ensuring the effective administration of justice, the tribunals of the occupied territory shall continue to function in respect of all offences covered by the said laws.

The Occupying Power may, however, subject the population of the occupied territory to provisions which are essential to enable the Occupying Power to fulfil its obligations under the present Convention, to maintain the orderly government of the territory, and to ensure the security of the Occupying Power, of the members and property of the occupying forces or administration, and likewise of the establishments and lines of communication used by them.

Article 65.

The penal provisions enacted by the Occupying Power shall not come into force before they have been published and brought to the knowledge of the inhabitants in their own language. The effect of these penal provisions shall not be retroactive.

Article 66.

In case of a breach of the penal provisions promulgated by it by virtue of the second paragraph of Article 64 the Occupying Power may hand over the accused to its properly constituted, non-political military courts, on condition that the said courts sit in the occupied country. Courts of appeal shall preferably sit in the occupied country.

Article 67.

The courts shall apply only those provisions of law which were applicable prior to the offence, and which are in accordance with general principles of law, in particular the principle that the penalty shall be proportionate to the offence. They shall take into consideration the fact the accused is not a national of the Occupying Power.

Article 68.

Protected persons who commit an offence which is solely intended to harm the Occupying Power, but which does not constitute an attempt on the life or limb of members of the occupying forces or administration, nor a grave collective danger, nor seriously damage the property of the occupying forces or administration or the installations used by them, shall be liable to internment or simple imprisonment, provided the duration of such internment or imprisonment is proportionate to the offence committed. Furthermore, internment or imprisonment shall, for such offences, be the only measure adopted for depriving protected persons of liberty. The courts provided for under Article 66 of the present Convention may at their discretion convert a sentence of imprisonment to one of internment for the same period.

The penal provisions promulgated by the Occupying Power in accordance with Articles 64 and 65 may impose the death penalty on a protected person only in cases where the person is guilty of espionage, of serious acts of sabotage against the military installations of the Occupying Power or of intentional offences which have caused the death of one or more persons, provided that such offences were punishable by death under the law of the occupied territory in force before the occupation began.

The death penalty may not be pronounced on a protected person unless the attention of the court has been particularly called to the fact that since the accused is not a national of the Occupying Power, he is not bound to it by any duty of allegiance. In any case, the death penalty may not be pronounced on a protected person who was under eighteen years of age at the time of the offence.

Article 69.

In all cases the duration of the period during which a protected person accused of an offence is under arrest awaiting trial or punishment shall be deducted from any period of imprisonment of awarded.

Article 70.

Protected persons shall not be arrested, prosecuted or convicted by the Occupying Power for acts committed or for opinions expressed before the occupation, or during a temporary interruption thereof, with the exception of breaches of the laws and customs of war.

Nationals of the occupying Power who, before the outbreak of hostilities, have sought refuge in the territory of the occupied State, shall not be arrested, prosecuted, convicted or deported from the occupied territory, except for offences committed after the outbreak of hostilities, or for offences under common law committed before the outbreak of hostilities which, according to the law of the occupied State, would have justified extradition in time of peace.

Article 71.

No sentence shall be pronounced by the competent courts of the Occupying Power except after a regular trial.

Accused persons who are prosecuted by the Occupying Power shall be promptly informed, in writing, in a language which they understand, of the particulars of the charges preferred against them, and shall be brought to trial as rapidly as possible. The Protecting Power shall be informed of all proceedings instituted by the Occupying Power against protected persons in respect of charges involving the death penalty or imprisonment for two years or more; it shall be enabled, at any time, to obtain information regarding the state of such proceedings. Furthermore, the Protecting Power shall be entitled, on request, to be furnished with all particulars of these and of any other proceedings instituted by the Occupying Power against protected persons.

The notification to the Protecting Power, as provided for in the second paragraph above, shall be sent immediately, and shall in any case reach the Protecting Power three weeks before the date of the first hearing. Unless, at the opening of the trial, evidence is submitted that the provisions of this Article are fully complied with, the trial shall not proceed. The notification shall include the following particulars:

(a) description of the accused;
(b) place of residence or detention;
(c) specification of the charge or charges (with mention of the penal provisions under which it is brought);
(d) designation of the court which will hear the case;
(e) place and date of the first hearing.

Article 72.

Accused persons shall have the right to present evidence necessary to their defence and may, in particular, call witnesses. They shall have the right to be assisted by a qualified advocate or counsel of their own choice, who shall be able to visit them freely and shall enjoy the necessary facilities for preparing the defence.

Failing a choice by the accused, the Protecting Power may provide him with an advocate or counsel. When an accused person has to meet a serious charge and the Protecting Power is not functioning, the Occupying Power, subject to the consent of the accused, shall provide an advocate or counsel.

Accused persons shall, unless they freely waive such assistance, be aided by an interpreter, both during preliminary investigation and during the hearing in court. They shall have at any time the right to object to the interpreter and to ask for his replacement.

Article 73.

A convicted person shall have the right of appeal provided for by the laws applied by the court. He shall be fully informed of his right to appeal or petition and of the time limit within which he may do so.

The penal procedure provided in the present Section shall apply, as far as it is applicable, to appeals. Where the laws applied by the Court make no provision for appeals, the convicted person shall have the right to petition against the finding and sentence to the competent authority of the Occupying Power.

Article 74.

Representatives of the Protecting Power shall have the right to attend the trial of any protected person, unless the hearing has, as an exceptional measure, to be held in camera in the interests of the security of the Occupying Power, which shall then notify the Protecting Power. A notification in respect of the date and place of trial shall be sent to the Protecting Power.

Any judgment involving a sentence of death, or imprisonment for two years or more, shall be communicated, with the relevant grounds, as rapidly as possible to the Protecting Power. The notification shall contain a reference to the notification made under Article 71 and, in the case of sentences of imprisonment, the name of the place where the sentence is to be served. A record of judgments other than those referred to above shall be kept by the court and shall be open to inspection by representatives of the

Protecting Power. Any period allowed for appeal in the case of sentences involving the death penalty, or imprisonment of two years or more, shall not run until notification of judgement has been received by the Protecting Power.

Article 75.

In no case shall persons condemned to death be deprived of the right of petition for pardon or reprieve.

No death sentence shall be carried out before the expiration of a period of a least six months from the date of receipt by the Protecting Power of the notification of the final judgment confirming such death sentence, or of an order denying pardon or reprieve.

The six months period of suspension of the death sentence herein prescribed may be reduced in individual cases in circumstances of grave emergency involving an organized threat to the security of the Occupying Power or its forces, provided always that the Protecting Power is notified of such reduction and is given reasonable time and opportunity to make representations to the competent occupying authorities in respect of such death sentences.

Article 76.

Protected persons accused of offences shall be detained in the occupied country, and if convicted they shall serve their sentences therein. They shall, if possible, be separated from other detainees and shall enjoy conditions of food and hygiene which will be sufficient to keep them in good health, and which will be at least equal to those obtaining in prisons in the occupied country.

They shall receive the medical attention required by their state of health.

They shall also have the right to receive any spiritual assistance which they may require.

Women shall be confined in separate quarters and shall be under the direct supervision of women.

Proper regard shall be paid to the special treatment due to minors.

Protected persons who are detained shall have the right to be visited by delegates of the Protecting Power and of the International Committee of the Red Cross, in accordance with the provisions of Article 143.

Such persons shall have the right to receive at least one relief parcel monthly.

Article 77.

Protected persons who have been accused of offences or convicted by the courts in occupied territory, shall be handed over at the close of occupation, with the relevant records, to the authorities of the liberated territory.

Article 78.

If the Occupying Power considers it necessary, for imperative reasons of security, to take safety measures concerning protected persons, it may, at the most, subject them to assigned residence or to internment.

Decisions regarding such assigned residence or internment shall be made according to a regular procedure to be prescribed by the Occupying Power in accordance with the provisions of the present Convention. This procedure shall include the right of appeal for the parties concerned. Appeals shall be decided with the least possible delay. In the event of the decision being upheld, it shall be subject to periodical review, if possible every six months, by a competent body set up by the said Power.

Section IV. Regulations for the treatment of internees

Chapter I. General provisions

Article 79.

The Parties to the conflict shall not intern protected persons, except in accordance with the provisions of Articles 41, 42, 43, 68 and 78. . . .

Chapter III. Food and Clothing

Article 89.

Daily food rations for internees shall be sufficient in quantity, quality and variety to keep internees in a good state of health and prevent the development of nutritional deficiencies. Account shall also be taken of the customary diet of the internees. . . .

Article 91.

Every place of internment shall have an adequate infirmary, under the direction of a qualified doctor, where internees may have the attention they require, as well as appropriate diet. Isolation wards shall be set aside for cases of contagious or mental diseases. . . .

Chapter V. Religious, Intellectual and Physical Activities

Article 93.

Internees shall enjoy complete latitude in the exercise of their religious duties, including attendance at the services of their faith, on condition that they comply with the disciplinary routine prescribed by the detaining authorities. . . .

Article 95.

The Detaining Power shall not employ internees as workers, unless they so desire. Employment which, if undertaken under compulsion by a protected person not in internment, would involve a breach of Articles 40 or 51 of the present Convention, and employment on work which is of a degrading or humiliating character are in any case prohibited.

After a working period of six weeks, internees shall be free to give up work at any moment, subject to eight days' notice. . . .

Chapter VI. Personal Property and Financial Resources

Article 97.

Internees shall be permitted to retain articles of personal use. Monies, cheques, bonds, etc., and valuables in their possession may not be taken from them except in accordance with established procedure. Detailed receipts shall be given therefor.

On release or repatriation, internees shall be given all articles, monies or other valuables taken from them during internment and shall receive in currency the balance of any credit to their accounts kept in accordance with Article 98, with the exception of any articles or amounts withheld by the

Detaining Power by virtue of its legislation in force. If the property of an internee is so withheld, the owner shall receive a detailed receipt.

Family or identity documents in the possession of internees may not be taken away without a receipt being given. At no time shall internees be left without identity documents. If they have none, they shall be issued with special documents drawn up by the detaining authorities, which will serve as their identity papers until the end of their internment. . . .

Chapter VII. Administration and Discipline

Article 100.

The disciplinary regime in places of internment shall be consistent with humanitarian principles, and shall in no circumstances include regulations imposing on internees any physical exertion dangerous to their health or involving physical or moral victimization. Identification by tattooing or imprinting signs or markings on the body, is prohibited.

In particular, prolonged standing and roll-calls, punishment drill, military drill and maneuvers, or the reduction of food rations, are prohibited. . . .

Chapter VIII. Relations with the Exterior

Article 105.

Immediately upon interning protected persons, the Detaining Powers shall inform them, the Power to which they owe allegiance and their Protecting Power of the measures taken for executing the provisions of the present Chapter. The Detaining Powers shall likewise inform the Parties concerned of any subsequent modifications of such measures. . . .

Article 107.

Internees shall be allowed to send and receive letters and cards. . . .

Article 116.

Every internee shall be allowed to receive visitors, especially near relatives, at regular intervals and as frequently as possible. . . .

Chapter X. Transfers of Internees

Article 127.

The transfer of internees shall always be effected humanely. As a general rule, it shall be carried out by rail or other means of transport, and under conditions at least equal to those obtaining for the forces of the Detaining Power in their changes of station. If, as an exceptional measure, such removals have to be effected on foot, they may not take place unless the internees are in a fit state of health, and may not in any case expose them to excessive fatigue.

Sick, wounded or infirm internees and maternity cases shall not be transferred if the journey would be seriously detrimental to them, unless their safety imperatively so demands.

If the combat zone draws close to a place of internment, the internees in the said place shall not be transferred unless their removal can be carried out in adequate conditions of safety, or unless they are exposed to greater risks by remaining on the spot than by being transferred.

When making decisions regarding the transfer of internees, the Detaining Power shall take their interests into account and, in particular, shall not do anything to increase the difficulties of repatriating them or returning them to their own homes. . . .

Chapter XI. Deaths

Article 129.

The wills of internees shall be received for safe-keeping by the responsible authorities; and if the event of the death of an internee his will shall be transmitted without delay to a person whom he has previously designated.

Deaths of internees shall be certified in every case by a doctor, and a death certificate shall be made out, showing the causes of death and the conditions under which it occurred.

An official record of the death, duly registered, shall be drawn up in accordance with the procedure relating thereto in force in the territory where the place of internment is situated, and a duly certified copy of such record shall be transmitted without delay to the Protecting Power as well as to the Central Agency referred to in Article 140.

Article 130.

The detaining authorities shall ensure that internees who die while interned are honorably buried, if possible according to the rites of the religion to which they belonged and that their graves are respected, properly maintained, and marked in such a way that they can always be recognized.

As soon as circumstances permit, and not later than the close of hostilities, the Detaining Power shall forward lists of graves of deceased internees to the Powers on whom deceased internees depended, through the Information Bureaux provided for in Article 136. Such lists shall include all particulars necessary for the identification of the deceased internees, as well as the exact location of their graves. . . .

Article 134.

The High Contracting Parties shall endeavour, upon the Repatriation close of hostilities or occupation, to ensure the return of all internees to their last place of residence, or to facilitate their residence repatriation. . . .

Article 138.

The information received by the national Bureau and transmitted by it shall be of such a character as to make it possible to identify the protected person exactly and to advise his next of kin quickly. The information in respect of each person shall include at least his surname, first names, place and date of birth, nationality, last residence and distinguishing characteristics, the first name of the father and the maiden name of the mother, the date, place and nature of the action taken with regard to the individual, the address at which correspondence may be sent to him and the name and address of the person to be informed. Likewise, information regarding the state of health of internees who are seriously ill or seriously wounded shall be supplied regularly and if possible every week. . . .

Part IV. Execution of the Convention

Section I. General Provisions

Article 142.

Subject to the measures which the Detaining Powers may consider essential to ensure their security or to meet any other reasonable need, the representatives of religious organizations, relief societies, or any other organizations assisting the protected persons, shall receive from these Powers, for themselves or their duly accredited agents, all facilities for visiting the protected persons, for distributing relief supplies and material from any source, intended for educational, recreational or religious purposes, or for assisting them in organizing their leisure time within the places of internment. Such societies or organizations may be constituted in the territory of the Detaining Power, or in any other country, or they may have an international character.

The Detaining Power may limit the number of societies and organizations whose delegates are allowed to carry out their activities in its territory and under its supervision, on condition, however, that such limitation shall not hinder the supply of effective and adequate relief to all protected persons.

The special position of the International Committee of the Red Cross in this field shall be recognized and respected at all times.

Article 143.

Representatives or delegates of the Protecting Powers shall have permission to go to all places where protected persons are, particularly to places of internment, detention and work.

They shall have access to all premises occupied by protected persons and shall be able to interview the latter without witnesses, personally or through an interpreter.

Such visits may not be prohibited except for reasons of imperative military necessity, and then only as an exceptional and temporary measure. Their duration and frequency shall not be restricted.

Such representatives and delegates shall have full liberty to select the places they wish to visit. The Detaining or Occupying Power, the Protecting Power and when occasion arises the Power of origin of the persons to be visited, may agree that compatriots of the internees shall be permitted to participate in the visits.

The delegates of the International Committee of the Red Cross shall also enjoy the above prerogatives. The appointment of such delegates shall be submitted to the approval of the Power governing the territories where they will carry out their duties. . . .

Article 146.

The High Contracting Parties undertake to enact any legislation necessary to provide effective penal sanctions for persons committing, or ordering to be committed, any of the grave breaches of the present Convention defined in the following Article.

Each High Contracting Party shall be under the obligation to search for persons alleged to have committed, or to have ordered to be committed, such grave breaches, and shall bring such persons, regardless of their nationality, before its own courts. It may also, if it prefers, and in accordance with the provisions of its own legislation, hand such persons over for trial to another High Contracting Party concerned, provided such High Contracting Party has made out a prima facie case.

Each High Contracting Party shall take measures necessary for the suppression of all acts contrary to the provisions of the present Convention other than the grave breaches defined in the following Article.

In all circumstances, the accused persons shall benefit by safeguards of proper trial and defence, which shall not be less favourable than those provided by Article 105 and those following of the Geneva Convention relative to the Treatment of Prisoners of War of 12 August 1949.

Article 147.

Grave breaches to which the preceding Article relates shall be those involving any of the following acts, if committed against persons or property protected by the present Convention: willful killing, torture or inhuman treatment, including biological experiments, willfully causing great suffering or serious injury to body or health, unlawful deportation or transfer or unlawful confinement of a protected person, compelling a protected person to serve in the forces of a hostile Power, or willfully depriving a protected person of the rights of fair and regular trial prescribed in the present Convention, taking of hostages and extensive destruction and appropriation of property, not justified by military necessity and carried out unlawfully and wantonly.

Article 148.

No High Contracting Party shall be allowed to absolve itself or any other High Contracting Party of any liability incurred by itself or by another High Contracting Party in respect of breaches referred to in the preceding Article.

Done at Geneva this twelfth day of August 1949, in the English and French languages. The original shall be deposited in the Archives of the Swiss Confederation. The Swiss Federal Council shall transmit certified copies thereof to each of the signatory and acceding States.

Appendix 6

Protocol Additional to the Geneva Conventions of 12 August 1949, and Relating to the Protection of Victims of International Armed Conflicts (Protocol I), 8 June 1977

PREAMBLE

The High Contracting Parties,

Proclaiming their earnest wish to see peace prevail among peoples,

Recalling that every State has the duty, in conformity with the Charter of the United Nations, to refrain in its international relations from the threat or use of force against the sovereignty, territorial integrity or political independence of any State, or in any other manner inconsistent with the purposes of the United Nations,

Believing it necessary nevertheless to reaffirm and develop the provisions protecting the victims of armed conflicts and to supplement measures intended to reinforce their application,

Expressing their conviction that nothing in this Protocol or in the Geneva Conventions of 12 August 1949 can be construed as legitimizing or authorizing any act of aggression or any other use of force inconsistent with the Charter of the United Nations,

Reaffirming further that the provisions of the Geneva Conventions of 12 August 1949 and of this Protocol must be fully applied in all circumstances to all persons who are protected by those instruments, without any adverse distinction based on the nature or origin of the armed conflict or on the causes espoused by or attributed to the Parties to the conflict,

Have agreed on the following:

Part I. General Provisions

Article 1. General principles and scope of application

1. The High Contracting Parties undertake to respect and to ensure respect for this Protocol in all circumstances.

2. In cases not covered by this Protocol or by other international agreements, civilians and combatants remain under the protection and authority of the principles of international law derived from established custom, from the principles of humanity and from dictates of public conscience.

3. This Protocol, which supplements the Geneva Conventions of 12 August 1949 for the protection of war victims, shall apply in the situations referred to in Article 2 common to those Conventions.

4. The situations referred to in the preceding paragraph include armed conflicts which peoples are fighting against colonial domination and alien occupation and against racist regimes in the exercise of their right of self-determination, as enshrined in the Charter of the United Nations and the Declaration on Principles of International Law concerning Friendly Relations and Co-operation among States in accordance with the Charter of the United Nations.

Article 2. Definitions

For the purposes of this Protocol

(a) "First Convention," "Second Convention," "Third Convention," and "Fourth Convention" mean, respectively, the Geneva Convention for the Amelioration of the Condition of the Wounded and Sick in Armed Forces in the Field of 12 August 1949; the Geneva Convention for the Amelioration of the Condition of Wounded, Sick and Ship-wrecked Members of Armed Forces at Sea of 12 August 1949; the Geneva Convention relative to the Treatment of Prisoners of War of 12 August 1949; the Geneva Convention relative to the Protection of Civilian Persons in Time of War of 12 August 1949; "the Conventions" means the four Geneva Conventions of 12 August 1949 for the protection of war victims;

(b) "Rules of international law applicable in armed conflict" means the rules applicable in armed conflict set forth in international agreements to which the Parties to the conflict are Parties and the generally recognized principles and rules of international law which are applicable to armed conflict;

(c) "Protecting Power" means a neutral or other State not a Party to the conflict which has been designated by a Party to the conflict and accepted by the adverse Party and has agreed to carry out the functions assigned to a Protecting Power under the Conventions and this Protocol;

(d) "Substitute" means an organization acting in place of a Protecting Power in accordance with Article 5.

Article 3. Beginning and end of application

Without prejudice to the provisions which are applicable at all times:

(a) the Conventions and this Protocol shall apply from the beginning of any situation referred to in Article 1 of this Protocol.

(b) the application of the Conventions and of this Protocol shall cease, in the territory of Parties to the conflict, on the general close of military operations and, in the case of occupied territories, on the termination of the occupation, except, in either circumstance, for those persons whose final release, repatriation or re-establishment takes place thereafter. These persons shall continue to benefit from the relevant provisions of the Conventions and of this Protocol until their final release repatriation or re-establishment.

Article 4. Legal status of the Parties to the conflict

The application of the Conventions and of this Protocol, as well as the conclusion of the agreements provided for therein, shall not affect the legal status of the Parties to the conflict. Neither the occupation of a territory nor the application of the Conventions and this Protocol shall affect the legal status of the territory in question.

Article 5. Appointment of Protecting Powers and of their substitute

1. It is the duty of the Parties to a conflict from the beginning of that conflict to secure the supervision and implementation of the Conventions and of this Protocol by the application of the system of Protecting Powers, including inter alia the designation and acceptance of those Powers, in accordance with the following paragraphs. Protecting Powers shall have the duty of safeguarding the interests of the Parties to the conflict.

2. From the beginning of a situation referred to in Article 1, each Party to the conflict shall without delay designate a Protecting Power for the purpose of applying the Conventions and this Protocol and shall, likewise without delay and for the same purpose, permit the activities or a Protecting Power which has been accepted by it as such after designation by the adverse Party.

3. If a Protecting Power has not been designated or accepted from the beginning of a situation referred to in Article 1, the

International Committee of the Red Cross, without prejudice to the right of any other impartial humanitarian organization to do likewise, shall offer its good offices to the Parties to the conflict with a view to the designation without delay of a Protecting Power to which the Parties to the conflict consent. . . .

4. If, despite the foregoing, there is no Protecting Power, the Parties to the conflict shall accept without delay an offer which may be made by the International Committee of the Red Cross or by any other organization which offers all guarantees of impartiality and efficacy, after due consultations with the said Parties and taking into account the result of these consultations, to act as a substitute. The functioning of such a substitute is subject to the consent of the Parties to the conflict; every effort shall be made by the Parties to the conflict to facilitate the operations of the substitute in the performance of its tasks under the Conventions and this Protocol. . . .

Part II: Wounded, Sick and Shipwrecked

Section I. General Protection

Article 8. Terminology

For the purposes of this Protocol:

1. "Wounded" and "sick" mean persons, whether military or civilian, who, because of trauma, disease or other physical or mental disorder or disability, are in need of medical assistance or care and who refrain from any act of hostility. These terms also cover maternity cases, new-born babies and other persons who may be in need of immediate medical assistance or care, such as the infirm or expectant mothers, and who refrain from any act of hostility; . . . .

3. "Medical personnel" means those persons assigned, by a Party to the conflict, exclusively to the medical purposes enumerated under (5) or to the administration of medical units or to

the operation or administration of medical transports. Such assignments may be either permanent or temporary. The term includes:

(a) medical personnel of a Party to the conflict, whether military or civilian, including those described in the First and Second Conventions, and those assigned to civil defense organizations;

(b) medical personnel of national Red Cross (Red Crescent, Red Lion and Sun) Societies and other national voluntary aid societies duly recognized and authorized by a Party to the conflict;

(c) medical personnel or medical units or medical transports described in Article 9, paragraph 2.

4. "Religious personnel" means military or civilian persons, such as chaplains, who are exclusively engaged in the work of their ministry and attached:

(a) to the armed forces of a Party to the conflict;

(b) to medical units or medical transports of a Party to the conflict;

(c) to medical units or medical transports described in Article 9, Paragraph 2; or

(d) to civil defense organizations of a Party to the conflict.

The attachment of religious personnel may be either permanent or temporary, and the relevant provisions mentioned under (11) apply to them;

5. "Medical units" means establishments and other units, whether military or civilian, organized for medical purposes, namely the search for, collection, transportation, diagnosis or treatment—including first-aid treatment—of the wounded, sick and shipwrecked, or for the prevention of disease. The term includes for example, hospitals and other similar units, blood transfusion centres, preventive medicine centres and institutes, medical depots and the medical and pharmaceutical stores of such units. Medical units may be fixed or mobile, permanent or temporary; . . . .

Article 9. Field of application

1. This Part, the provisions of which are intended to ameliorate the condition of the wounded, sick and shipwrecked, shall apply to all those affected by a situation referred to in Article 1, without any adverse distinction founded on race, colour, sex, language, religion or belief political or other opinion, national or social origin, wealth, birth or other status, or on any other similar criteria. . . .

Article 10. Protection and care

1. All the wounded, sick and shipwrecked, to whichever Party they belong, shall be respected and protected.

2. In all circumstances they shall be treated humanely and shall receive, to the fullest extent practicable and with the least possible delay, the medical care and attention required by their condition. There shall be no distinction among them founded on any grounds other than medical ones.

Article 11. Protection of persons

1. The physical or mental health and integrity of persons who are in the power of the adverse Party or who are interned, detained or otherwise deprived of liberty as a result of a situation referred to in Article 1 shall not be endangered by any unjustified act or omission. Accordingly, it is prohibited to subject the persons described in this Article to any medical procedure which is not indicated by the state of health of the person concerned and which is not consistent with generally accepted medical standards which would be applied under similar medical circumstances to persons who are nationals of the Party conducting the procedure and who are in no way deprived of liberty.

2. It is, in particular, prohibited to carry out on such persons, even with their consent:

(a) physical mutilations;

(b) medical or scientific experiments;

(c) removal of tissue or organs for transplantation, except where these acts are justified in conformity with the conditions provided for in paragraph 1. . . .

4. Any willful act or omission which seriously endangers the physical or mental health or integrity of any person who is in the power of a Party other than the one on which he depends and which either violates any of the prohibitions in paragraphs 1 and 2 or fails to comply with the requirements of paragraph 3 shall be a grave breach of this Protocol. . . .

Article 12. Protection of medical units

1. Medical units shall be respected and protected at all times and shall not be the object of attack. . . .

Article 15. Protection of civilian medical and religious personnel

1. Civilian medical personnel shall be respected and protected. . . .

5. Civilian religious personnel shall be respected and protected. The provisions of the Conventions and of this Protocol concerning the protection and identification of medical personnel shall apply equally to such persons.

Article 17. Role of the civilian population and of aid societies

1. The civilian population shall respect the wounded, sick and shipwrecked, even if they belong to the adverse Party, and shall commit no act of violence against them. The civilian population and aid societies, such as national Red Cross (Red Crescent, Red Lion and Sun) Societies, shall be permitted, even on their own initiative, to collect and care for the wounded, sick and shipwrecked, even in invaded or occupied areas. No one shall be harmed, prosecuted, convicted or punished for such humanitarian acts. . . .

Article 19. Neutral and other States not Parties to the conflict

Neutral and other States not Parties to the conflict shall apply the relevant provisions of this Protocol to persons protected by this Part who may be received or interned within their territory, and to any dead of the Parties to that conflict whom they may find.

Article 20. Prohibition of reprisals

Reprisals against the persons and objects protected by this Part are prohibited. . . .

SECTION III: MISSING AND DEAD PERSONS

Article 32. General principle

In the implementation of this Section, the activities of the High Contracting Parties, of the Parties to the conflict and of the international humanitarian organizations mentioned in the Conventions and in this Protocol shall be prompted mainly by the right of families to know the fate of their relatives.

Article 33. Missing persons

1. As soon as circumstances permit, and at the latest from the end of active hostilities, each Party to the conflict shall search for the persons who have been reported missing by an adverse Party. Such adverse Party shall transmit all relevant information concerning such persons in order to facilitate such searches.

2. In order to facilitate the gathering of information pursuant to the preceding paragraph, each Party to the conflict shall, with respect to persons who would not receive more favourable consideration under the Conventions and this Protocol:

(a) record the information specified in Article 138 of the Fourth Convention in respect of such persons who have been detained, imprisoned or otherwise held in captivity for more than two weeks as a result of hostilities or occupation, or who have died during any period of detention;

(b) to the fullest extent possible, facilitate and, if need be, carry out the search for and the recording of information concerning such persons if they have died in other circumstances as a result of hostilities or occupation.

3. Information concerning persons reported missing pursuant to paragraph 1 and requests for such information shall be transmitted either directly or through the Protecting Power or the Central Tracing Agency of the International Committee of the Red Cross or national Red Cross (Red Crescent, Red Lion and Sun) Societies. Where the information is not transmitted through the International Committee of the Red Cross and its Central Tracing Agency, each Party to the conflict shall ensure that such information is also supplied to the Central Tracing Agency.

4. The Parties to the conflict shall endeavour to agree on arrangements for teams to search for, identify and recover the dead from battlefield areas, including arrangements, if appropriate, for such teams to be accompanied by personnel of the adverse Party while carrying out these missions in areas controlled by the adverse Party. Personnel of such teams shall be respected and protected while exclusively carrying out these duties.

Article 34. Remains of deceased

1. The remains of persons who have died for reasons related to occupation or in detention resulting from occupation or hostilities and those or persons not nationals of the country in which they have died as a result of hostilities shall be respected, and the gravesites of all such persons shall be respected, maintained and marked as provided for in Article 130 of the Fourth Convention, where their remains or gravesites would not receive more favourable consideration under the Conventions and this Protocol.

2. As soon as circumstances and the relations between the adverse Parties permit, the High Contracting Parties in whose territories graves and, as the case may be, other locations of the remains of persons who have died as a result of hostilities or during occupation or in detention are situated, shall conclude agreements in order:

(a) to facilitate access to the gravesites by relatives of the deceased and by representatives of official graves registration services and to regulate the practical arrangements for such access;
(b) to protect and maintain such gravesites permanently;
(c) to facilitate the return of the remains of the deceased and of personal effects to the home country upon its request or, unless that country objects, upon the request of the next of kin.

3. In the absence of the agreements provided for in paragraph 2 (b) or (c) and if the home country or such deceased is not willing to arrange at its expense for the maintenance of such gravesites, the High Contracting Party in whose territory the gravesites are situated may offer to facilitate the return of the remains of the deceased to the home country. Where such an offer has not been accepted the High Contracting Party may, after the expiry of five years from the date of the offer and upon due notice to the home country, adopt the arrangements laid down in its own laws relating to cemeteries and graves.

4. A High Contracting Party in whose territory the grave sites referred to in this Article are situated shall be permitted to exhume the remains only:

(a) in accordance with paragraphs 2 (c) and 3, or
(b) where exhumation is a matter or overriding public necessity, including cases of medical and investigative necessity, in which case the High Contracting Party shall at all times respect the remains, and shall give notice to the home country or its intention to exhume the remains together with details of the intended place of reinterment.

Part III. Methods and Means of Warfare Combatant and Prisoners-of-War

Section I. Methods and Means of Warfare

Article 35. Basic rules

1. In any armed conflict, the right of the Parties to the conflict to choose methods or means of warfare is not unlimited.

2. It is prohibited to employ weapons, projectiles and material and methods of warfare of a nature to cause superfluous injury or unnecessary suffering. . . .

Article 37. Prohibition of Perfidy

1. It is prohibited to kill, injure or capture an adversary by resort to perfidy. Acts inviting the confidence of an adversary to lead him to believe that he is entitled to, or is obliged to accord, protection under the rules of international law applicable in armed conflict, with intent to betray that confidence, shall constitute perfidy. . . .

Article 38. Recognized emblems

1. It is prohibited to make improper use of the distinctive emblem of the red cross, red crescent or red lion and sun or of other emblems, signs or signals provided for by the Conventions or by this Protocol. It is also prohibited to misuse deliberately in an armed conflict other internationally recognized protective emblems, signs or signals, including the flag of truce, and the protective emblem of cultural property.

2. It is prohibited to make use of the distinctive emblem of the United Nations, except as authorized by that Organization. . . .

Article 40. Quarter

It is prohibited to order that there shall be no survivors, to threaten an adversary therewith or to conduct hostilities on this basis.

Article 41. Safeguard of an enemy hors de combat

1. A person who is recognized or who, in the circumstances should be recognized to be hors de combat shall not be made the object of attack. . . .

Section II. Combatants and Prisoners of War

Article 43. Armed forces

1. The armed forces of a Party to a conflict consist of all organized armed forces, groups and units which are under a command responsible to that Party for the conduct or its subordinates, even if that Party is represented by a government or an authority not recognized by an adverse Party. Such armed forces shall be subject to an internal disciplinary system which, inter alia, shall enforce compliance with the rules of international law applicable in armed conflict.

2. Members of the armed forces of a Party to a conflict (other than medical personnel and chaplains covered by Article 33 of the Third Convention) are combatants, that is to say, they have the right to participate directly in hostilities. . . .

Article 44. Combatants and prisoners of war

1. Any combatant, as defined in Article 43, who falls into the power of an adverse Party shall be a prisoner of war.

2. While all combatants are obliged to comply with the rules of international law applicable in armed conflict, violations of these rules shall not deprive a combatant of his right to be a combatant or, if he falls into the power of an adverse Party, of his right to be a prisoner of war, except as provided in paragraphs 3 and 4.

3. In order to promote the protection of the civilian population from the effects of hostilities, combatants are obliged to distinguish themselves from the civilian population while they are engaged in an attack or in a military operation preparatory to an attack.

Recognizing, however, that there are situations in armed conflicts where, owing to the nature of the hostilities an armed combatant cannot so distinguish himself, he shall retain his status as a combatant, provided that, in such situations, he carries his arms openly:

(a) during each military engagement, and

(b) during such time as he is visible to the adversary while he is engaged in a military deployment preceding the launching of an attack in which he is to participate.

Acts which comply with the requirements of this paragraph shall not be considered as perfidious within the meaning of Article 37, paragraph 1 (c).

4. A combatant who falls into the power of an adverse Party while failing to meet the requirements set forth in the second sentence of paragraph 3 shall forfeit his right to be a prisoner of war, but he shall, nevertheless, be given protections equivalent in all respects to those accorded to prisoners of war by the Third Convention and by this Protocol. This protection includes protections equivalent to those accorded to prisoners of war by the Third Convention in the case where such a person is tried and punished for any offenses he has committed.

5. Any combatant who falls into the power of an adverse Party while not engaged in an attack or in a military operation preparatory to an attack shall not forfeit his rights to be a combatant and a prisoner of war by virtue of his prior activities.

6. This Article is without prejudice to the right of any person to be a prisoner of war pursuant to Article 4 of the Third Convention. . . .

8. In addition to the categories of persons mentioned in Article 13 of the First and Second Conventions, all members of the armed forces of a Party to the conflict, as defined in Article 43 of this Protocol, shall be entitled to protection under those Conventions if they are wounded or sick or, in the case of the Second Convention, shipwrecked at sea or in other waters.

Article 45. Protection of persons who have taken part in hostilities

1. A person who takes part in hostilities and falls into the power of an adverse Party shall be presumed to be a prisoner of war, and therefore shall be protected by the Third Convention, if he claims the status of prisoner of war, or if he appears to be entitled to such status, or if the Party on which he depends claims such status on his behalf by notification to the detaining Power or to the Protecting Power. Should any doubt arise as to whether any such person is entitled to the status of prisoner of war, he shall continue to have such status and, therefore, to be protected by the Third Convention and this Protocol until such time as his status has been determined by a competent tribunal. . . .

Part IV. Civilian Population

Section I. General Protection Against Effects of Hostilities

Chapter I. Basic rule and field of application

Article 48. Basic rule

In order to ensure respect for and protection of the civilian population and civilian objects, the Parties to the conflict shall at all times distinguish between the civilian population and combatants and between civilian objects and military objectives and accordingly shall direct their operations only against military objectives.

Article 49. Definition of attacks and scope of application

1. "Attacks" means acts of violence against the adversary, whether in offense or in defense.

2. The provisions of this Protocol with respect to attacks apply to all attacks in whatever territory conducted, including the national territory belonging to a Party to the conflict but under the control of an adverse Party.

3. The provisions of this section apply to any land, air or sea warfare which may affect the civilian population, individual civilians or civilian objects on land. They further apply to all attacks from the sea or from the air against objectives on land but do not otherwise affect the rules of international law applicable in armed conflict at sea or in the air.

4. The provisions of this section are additional to the rules concerning humanitarian protection contained in the Fourth Convention, particularly in part II thereof, and in other international agreements binding upon the High Contracting Parties, as well as to other rules of international law relating to the protection of civilians and civilian objects on land, at sea or in the air against the effects of hostilities.

Chapter II. Civilians and civilian population

Article 50. Definition of civilians and civilian population

1. A civilian is any person who does not belong to one of the categories of persons referred to in Article 4 (A) (1), (2), (3) and (6) of the Third Convention and in Article 43 of this Protocol. In case of doubt whether a person is a civilian, that person shall be considered to be a civilian.

2. The civilian population comprises all persons who are civilians.

3. The presence within the civilian population of individuals who do not come within the definition of civilians does not deprive the population of its civilian character.

Article 51. Protection of the civilian population

1. The civilian population and individual civilians shall enjoy general protection against dangers arising from military operations. To give effect to this protection, the following rules, which are additional to other applicable rules of international law, shall be observed in all circumstances.

2. The civilian population as such, as well as individual civilians, shall not be the object of attack. Acts or threats of violence the primary purpose of which is to spread terror among the civilian population are prohibited.

3. Civilians shall enjoy the protection afforded by this section, unless and for such time as they take a direct part in hostilities.

4. Indiscriminate attacks are prohibited. Indiscriminate attacks are:

(a) those which are not directed at a specific military objective;
(b) those which employ a method or means of combat which cannot be directed at a specific military objective; or
(c) those which employ a method or means of combat the effects of which cannot be limited as required by this Protocol; and consequently, in each such case, are of a nature to strike military objectives and civilians or civilian objects without distinction.

5. Among others, the following types of attacks are to be considered as indiscriminate:

(a) an attack by bombardment by any methods or means which treats as a single military objective a number of clearly separated and distinct military objectives located in a city, town, village or other area containing a similar concentration of civilians or civilian objects; and
(b) an attack which may be expected to cause incidental loss of civilian life, injury to civilians, damage to civilian objects, or a combination thereof, which would be excessive in relation to the concrete and direct military advantage anticipated.

6. Attacks against the civilian population or civilians by way of reprisals are prohibited. . . .

8. Any violation of these prohibitions shall not release the Parties to the conflict from their legal obligations with respect to the civilian population and civilians, including the obligation to take the precautionary measures provided for in Article 57.

Chapter III. Civilian objects

Article 52. General Protection of civilian objects

1. Civilian objects shall not be the object of attack or of reprisals. Civilian objects are all objects which are not military objectives as defined in paragraph 2.

2. Attacks shall be limited strictly to military objectives. In so far as objects are concerned, military objectives are limited to those objects which by their nature, location, purpose or use make an effective contribution to military action and whose total or partial destruction, capture or neutralization, in the circumstances ruling at the time, offers a definite military advantage.

3. In case of doubt whether an object which is normally dedicated to civilian purposes, such as a place of worship, a house or other dwelling or a school, is being used to make an effective contribution to military action, it shall be presumed not to be so used.

Article 53. Protection of cultural objects and of places of worship

Without prejudice to the provisions of the Hague Convention for the Protection of Cultural Property in the Event of Armed Conflict of 14 May 1954, and of other relevant international instruments, it is prohibited:

(a) to commit any acts of hostility directed against the historic monuments, works of art or places of worship which constitute the cultural or spiritual heritage of peoples;
(b) to use such objects in support of the military effort;
(c) to make such objects the object of reprisals.

Article 54. Protection of objects indispensable to the survival of the civilian population

1. Starvation of civilians as a method of warfare is prohibited. . . .

Chapter IV. Precautionary measures

Article 57. Precautions in attack

1. In the conduct of military operations, constant care shall be taken to spare the civilian population, civilians and civilian objects.

2. With respect to attacks, the following precautions shall be taken:

(a) those who plan or decide upon an attack shall:

(i) do everything feasible to verify that the objectives to be attacked are neither civilians nor civilian objects and are not subject to special protection but are military objectives within the meaning of paragraph 2 of Article 52 and that it is not prohibited by the provisions of this Protocol to attack them;

(ii) take all feasible precautions in the choice of means and methods of attack with a view to avoiding, and in any event to minimizing, incidental loss or civilian life, injury to civilians and damage to civilian objects;

(iii) refrain from deciding to launch any attack which may be expected to cause incidental loss of civilian life, injury to civilians, damage to civilian objects, or a combination thereof, which would be excessive in relation to the concrete and direct military advantage anticipated;

(b) an attack shall be canceled or suspended if it becomes apparent that the objective is not a military one or is subject to special protection or that the attack may be expected to cause incidental loss of civilian life, injury to civilians, damage to civilian objects, or a combination thereof, which would be excessive in relation to the concrete and direct military advantage anticipated;

(c) effective advance warning shall be given of attacks which may affect the civilian population, unless circumstances do not permit.

3. When a choice is possible between several military objectives for obtaining a similar military advantage, the objective to be selected shall be that the attack on which may be expected to cause the least danger to civilian lives and to civilian objects. . . .

5. No provision of this article may be construed as authorizing any attacks against the civilian population, civilians or civilian objects.

Article 58. Precautions against the effects of attacks

The Parties to the conflict shall, to the maximum extent feasible:

(a) without prejudice to Article 49 of the Fourth Convention, endeavour to remove the civilian population, individual civilians and civilian objects under their control from the vicinity of military objectives;

(b) avoid locating military objectives within or near densely populated areas;

(c) take the other necessary precautions to protect the civilian population, individual civilians and civilian objects under their control against the dangers resulting from military operations.

Chapter V. Localities and zones under special protection

Article 59. Non-defended localities

1. It is prohibited for the Parties to the conflict to attack, by any means whatsoever, non-defended localities.

2. The appropriate authorities of a Party to the conflict may declare as a non-defended locality any inhabited place near or in a zone where armed forces are in contact which is open for occupation by an adverse Party. Such a locality shall fulfill the following conditions:

(a) all combatants, as well as mobile weapons and mobile military equipment must have been evacuated;

(b) no hostile use shall be made of fixed military installations or establishments;

(c) no acts of hostility shall be committed by the authorities or by the population; and

(d) no activities in support of military operations shall be undertaken.

3. The presence, in this locality, of persons specially protected under the Conventions and this Protocol, and of police forces retained for the sole purpose of maintaining law and order, is not contrary to the conditions laid down in paragraph 2. . . .

5. The Parties to the conflict may agree on the establishment of non-defended localities even if such localities do not fulfill the conditions laid down in paragraph 2. The agreement should define and describe, as precisely as possible, the limits of the non-defended locality; if necessary, it may lay down the methods of supervision. . . .

Article 60. Demilitarized zones

1. It is prohibited for the Parties to the conflict to extend their military operations to zones on which they have conferred by agreement the status of demilitarized zone, if such extension is contrary to the terms of this agreement. . . .

3. The subject of such an agreement shall normally be any zone which fulfills the following conditions:

(a) all combatants, as well as mobile weapons and mobile military equipment, must have been evacuated;

(b) no hostile use shall be made of fixed military installations or establishments;

(c) no acts of hostility shall be committed by the authorities or by the population; and

(d) any activity linked to the military effort must have ceased. . . .

7. If one of the Parties to the conflict commits a material breach of the provisions of paragraphs 3 or 6, the other Party shall be released from its obligations under the agreement conferring

upon the zone the status of demilitarized zone. In such an eventuality, the zone loses its status but shall continue to enjoy the protection provided by the other provisions of this Protocol and the other rules of international law applicable in armed conflict.

Chapter VI. Civil defense

Article 61. Definitions and scope

For the purpose of this Protocol:

1. "Civil defense" means the performance of some or all of the undermentioned humanitarian tasks intended to protect the civilian population against the dangers, and to help it to recover from the immediate effects, of hostilities or disasters and also to provide the conditions necessary for its survival. These tasks are:

(a) warning;
(b) evacuation;
(c) management of shelters;
(d) management of blackout measures;
(e) rescue;
(f) medical services, including first aid, and religious assistance;
(g) fire-fighting;
(h) detection and marking of danger areas;
(i) decontamination and similar protective measures;
(j) provision of emergency accommodation and supplies;
(k) emergency assistance in the restoration and maintenance of order in distressed areas;
(l) emergency repair of indispensable public utilities;
(m) emergency disposal of the dead;
(n) assistance in the preservation of objects essential for survival;
(o) complementary activities necessary to carry out any of the tasks mentioned above, including, but not limited to, planning and organization; . . .

Article 62. General protection

1. Civilian civil defense organizations and their personnel shall be respected and protected, subject to the provisions of this Protocol, particularly the provisions of this section. They shall be entitled to perform their civil defense tasks except in case of imperative military necessity. . . .

Article 64. Civilian civil defense organizations of neutral or other States not Parties to the conflict and international co-ordinating organizations

1. Articles 62, 63, 65 and 66 shall also apply to the personnel and materiel of civilian civil defense organizations of neutral or other States not Parties to the conflict which perform civil defense tasks mentioned in Article 61 in the territory of a Party to the conflict, with the consent and under the control of that Party. Notification of such assistance shall be given as soon as possible to any adverse Party concerned. In no circumstances shall this activity be deemed to be an interference in the conflict. This activity should, however, be performed with due regard to the security interests of the Parties to the conflict concerned.

Article 65. Cessation of protection

1. The protection to which civilian civil defense organizations, their personnel, buildings, shelters and materiel are entitled shall not cease unless they commit or are used to commit, outside their proper tasks, acts harmful to the enemy. Protection may, however, cease only after a warning has been given setting, whenever appropriate, a reasonable time-limit, and after such warning has remained unheeded.

2. The following shall not be considered as acts harmful to the enemy:

(a) that civil defense tasks are carried out under the direction or control of military authorities;

(b) that civilian civil defense personnel co-operate with military personnel in the performance of civil defense tasks, or that some military personnel are attached to civilian civil defense organizations;

(c) that the performance of civil defense tasks may incidentally benefit military victims, particularly those who are hors de combat.

3. It shall also not be considered as an act harmful to the enemy that civilian civil defense personnel bear light individual weapons for the purpose of maintaining order or for self-defense. However, in areas where land fighting is taking place or is likely to take place, the Parties to the conflict shall undertake the appropriate measures to limit these weapons to handguns, such as pistols or revolvers, in order to assist in distinguishing between civil defense personnel and combatants. Although civil defense personnel bear other light individual weapons in such areas, they shall nevertheless be respected and protected as soon as they have been recognized as such.

4. The formation of civilian civil defense organizations along military lines, and compulsory service in them, shall also not deprive them of the protection conferred by this Chapter.

Article 67. Members of the armed forces and military units assigned to civil defense organizations

1. Members of the armed forces and military units assigned to civil defense organizations shall be respected and protected, provided that:

(a) such personnel and such units are permanently assigned and exclusively devoted to the performance of any of the tasks mentioned in Article 61;

(b) if so assigned, such personnel do not perform any other military duties during the conflict;

(c) such personnel are clearly distinguishable from the other members of the armed forces by prominently displaying the international distinctive sign of civil defense, which shall be as large as appropriate, and such personnel are provided with the identity card referred to in Chapter V of Annex I to this Protocol certifying their status;

(d) such personnel and such units are equipped only with light individual weapons for the purpose of maintaining order or for self-defense. The provisions of Article 65, paragraph 3 shall also apply in this case;

(e) such personnel do not participate directly in hostilities, and do not commit, or are not used to commit, outside their civil defense tasks, acts harmful to the adverse Party

(f) such personnel and such units perform their civil defense tasks only within the national territory of their Party.

The non-observance of the conditions stated in (e) above by any member of the armed forces who is bound by the conditions prescribed in (a) and (b) above is prohibited.

2. Military personnel serving within civil defense organizations shall, if they fall into the power of an adverse Party, be prisoners of war. In occupied territory they may, but only in the interest of the civilian population of that territory, be employed on civil defense tasks in so far as the need arises, provided however that, if such work is dangerous, they volunteer for such tasks. . . .

Section II. Relief in Favour of the Civilian Population

Article 68. Field of application

The provisions of this Section apply to the civilian population as defined in this Protocol and are supplementary to Articles 23, 55, 59, 60, 61 and 62 and other relevant provisions of the Fourth Convention.

Article 69. Basic needs in occupied territories

1. In addition to the duties specified in Article 55 of the Fourth Convention concerning food and medical supplies, the Occupying Power shall, to the fullest extent of the means available to it and without any adverse distinction, also ensure the provision

of clothing, bedding, means of shelter, other supplies essential to the survival of the civilian population of the occupied territory and objects necessary for religious worship.

2. Relief actions for the benefit of the civilian population of occupied territories are governed by Articles 59, 60, 61, 62, 108, 109, 110 and 111 of the Fourth Convention, and by Article 71 of this Protocol, and shall be implemented without delay.

Article 70. Relief actions

1. If the civilian population of any territory under the control of a Party to the conflict, other than occupied territory, is not adequately provided with the supplies mentioned in Article 69, relief actions which are humanitarian and impartial in character and conducted without any adverse distinction shall be undertaken, subject to the agreement of the Parties concerned in such relief actions. Offers of such relief shall not be regarded as interference in the armed conflict or as unfriendly acts. In the distribution of relief consignments, priority shall be given to those persons, such as children, expectant mothers, maternity cases and nursing mothers, who, under the Fourth Convention or under this Protocol, are to be accorded privileged treatment or special protection.

2. The Parties to the conflict and each High Contracting Party shall allow and facilitate rapid and unimpeded passage of all relief consignments, equipment and personnel provided in accordance with this Section, even if such assistance is destined for the civilian population of the adverse Party. . . .

Article 71. Personnel participating in relief actions

1. Where necessary, relief personnel may form part of the assistance provided in any relief action, in particular for the transportation and distribution of relief consignments; the participation of such personnel shall be subject to the approval of the Party in whose territory they will carry out their duties.

2. Such personnel shall be respected and protected. . . .

Section III. Treatment of Persons in the Power of a Party to the Conflict

Chapter I. Field of application and protection of persons and objects

Article 72. Field of application

The provisions of this Section are additional to the rules concerning humanitarian protection of civilians and civilian objects in the power of a Party to the conflict contained in the Fourth Convention, particularly Parts I and III thereof, as well as to other applicable rules of international law relating to the protection of fundamental human rights during international armed conflict. . . .

Article 74. Reunion of dispersed families

The High Contracting Parties and the Parties to the conflict shall facilitate in every possible way the reunion of families dispersed as a result of armed conflicts and shall encourage in particular the work of the humanitarian organizations engaged in this task in accordance with the provisions of the Conventions and of this Protocol and in conformity with their respective security regulations.

Article 75. Fundamental guarantees

1. In so far as they are affected by a situation referred to in Article 1 of this Protocol, persons who are in the power of a Party to the conflict and who do not benefit from more favourable treatment under the Conventions or under this Protocol shall be treated humanely in all circumstances and shall enjoy, as a minimum, the protection provided by this Article without any adverse distinction based upon race, colour, sex, language, religion or belief, political or other opinion, national or social origin, wealth, birth or other status, or on any other similar criteria. Each Party shall respect the person, honour, convictions and religious practices of all such persons.

2. The following acts are and shall remain prohibited at any time and in any place whatsoever, whether committed by civilian or by military agents:

(a) violence to the life, health, or physical or mental well-being of persons, in particular:

(i) murder;
(ii) torture of all kinds, whether physical or mental;
(iii) corporal punishment; and
(iv) mutilation;

(b) outrages upon personal dignity, in particular humiliating and degrading treatment, enforced prostitution and any form or indecent assault;
(c) the taking of hostages;
(d) collective punishments; and
(e) threats to commit any of the foregoing acts.

3. Any person arrested, detained or interned for actions related to the armed conflict shall be informed promptly, in a language he understands, of the reasons why these measures have been taken. Except in cases of arrest or detention for penal offenses, such persons shall be released with the minimum delay possible and in any event as soon as the circumstances justifying the arrest, detention or internment have ceased to exist. . . .

5. Women whose liberty has been restricted for reasons related to the armed conflict shall be held in quarters separated from men's quarters. They shall be under the immediate supervision of women. Nevertheless, in cases where families are detained or interned, they shall, whenever possible, be held in the same place and accommodated as family units.

6. Persons who are arrested, detained or interned for reasons related to the armed conflict shall enjoy the protection provided by this Article until their final release, repatriation or re-establishment, even after the end of the armed conflict.

7. In order to avoid any doubt concerning the prosecution and trial of persons accused of war crimes or crimes against humanity, the following principles shall apply:

(a) persons who are accused or such crimes should be submitted for the purpose of prosecution and trial in accordance with the applicable rules of international law; and

(b) any such persons who do not benefit from more favourable treatment under the Conventions or this Protocol shall be accorded the treatment provided by this Article, whether or not the crimes of which they are accused constitute grave breaches of the Conventions or of this Protocol.

8. No provision of this Article may be construed as limiting or infringing any other more favourable provision granting greater protection, under any applicable rules of international law, to persons covered by paragraph 1.

Chapter II. Measures in favour of women and children

Article 76. Protection of women

1. Women shall be the object of special respect and shall be protected in particular against rape, forced prostitution and any other form of indecent assault. . . .

Article 77. Protection of children

1. Children shall be the object of special respect and shall be protected against any form of indecent assault. The Parties to the conflict shall provide them with the care and aid they require, whether because of their age or for any other reason. . . .

Part V. Execution of the Conventions and of its Protocols

Section I. General Provisions

Article 80. Measures for execution

1. The High Contracting Parties and the Parties to the conflict shall without delay take all necessary measures for the

execution of their obligations under the Conventions and this Protocol.

2. The High Contracting Parties and the Parties to the conflict shall give orders and instructions to ensure observance of the Conventions and this Protocol, and shall supervise their execution.

Article 81. Activities of the Red Cross and other humanitarian organizations

1. The Parties to the conflict shall grant to the International Committee of the Red Cross all facilities, within their power so as to enable it to carry out the humanitarian functions assigned to it by the Conventions and this Protocol in order to ensure protection and assistance to the victims of conflicts; the International Committee of the Red Cross may also carry out any other humanitarian activities in favour of these victims, subject to the consent of the Parties to the conflict concerned.

2. The Parties to the conflict shall grant to their respective Red Cross (Red Crescent, Red Lion and Sun) organizations the facilities necessary for carrying out their humanitarian activities in favour of the victims of the conflict, in accordance with the provisions of the Conventions and this Protocol and the fundamental principles of the Red Cross as formulated by the International Conferences of the Red Cross. . . .

4. The High Contracting Parties and the Parties to the conflict shall, as far as possible, make facilities similar to those mentioned in paragraphs 2 and 3 available to the other humanitarian organizations referred to in the Conventions and this Protocol which are duly authorized by the respective Parties to the conflict and which perform their humanitarian activities in accordance with the provisions of the Conventions and this Protocol.

Article 82. Legal advisers in armed forces

The High Contracting Parties at all times, and the Parties to the conflict in time of armed conflict, shall ensure that legal advisers are available, when necessary, to advise military commanders at the appropriate level on the application of the Conventions and this Protocol and on the appropriate instruction to be given to the armed forces on this subject.

Article 83. Dissemination

1. The High Contracting Parties undertake, in time of peace as in time of armed conflict, to disseminate the Conventions and this Protocol as widely as possible in their respective countries and, in particular, to include the study thereof in their programmes of military instruction and to encourage the study thereof by the civilian population, so that those instruments may become known to the armed forces and to the civilian population.

2. Any military or civilian authorities who, in time of armed conflict, assume responsibilities in respect of the application of the Conventions and this Protocol shall be fully acquainted with the text thereof. . . .

Section II. Repression of Breaches of the Conventions and of This Protocol

Article 85. Repression of breaches of this Protocol

1. The provisions of the Conventions relating to the repression of breaches and grave breaches, supplemented by this Section, shall apply to the repression of breaches and grave breaches of this Protocol.

2. Acts described as grave breaches in the Conventions are grave breaches of this Protocol if committed against persons in the power of an adverse Party protected by Articles 44, 45 and 73 of this Protocol, or against the wounded, sick and shipwrecked of the adverse Party who are protected by this Protocol, or against those medical or religious personnel, medical units or medical transports which are under the control of the adverse Party and are protected by this Protocol.

3. In addition to the grave breaches defined in Article 11, the following acts shall be regarded as grave breaches of this Protocol,

when committed willfully, in violation of the relevant provisions of this Protocol, and causing death or serious injury to body or health:

(a) making the civilian population or individual civilians the object of attack;

(b) launching an indiscriminate attack affecting the civilian population or civilian objects in the knowledge that such attack will cause excessive loss of life, injury to civilians or damage to civilian objects, as defined in Article 57, paragraph 2 (a) (iii);

(c) launching an attack against works or installations containing dangerous forces in the knowledge that such attack will cause excessive loss of life, injury to civilians or damage to civilian objects, as defined in Article 57, paragraph 2 (a) (iii);

(d) making non-defended localities and demilitarized zones the object of attack;

(e) making a person the object of attack in the knowledge that he is hors de combat;

(f) the perfidious use, in violation of Article 37, of the distinctive emblem of the red cross, red crescent or red lion and sun or of other protective signs recognized by the Conventions or this Protocol.

4. In addition to the grave breaches defined in the preceding paragraphs and in the Conventions, the following shall be regarded as grave breaches of this Protocol, when committed willfully and in violation of the Conventions or the Protocol:

(a) the transfer by the occupying Power of parts of its own civilian population into the territory it occupies, or the deportation or transfer of all or parts of the population of the occupied territory within or outside this territory, in violation of Article 49 of the Fourth Convention;

(b) unjustifiable delay in the repatriation of prisoners of war or civilians;

(c) practices of apartheid and other inhuman and degrading practices involving outrages upon personal dignity, based on racial discrimination;

(d) making the clearly-recognized historic monuments, works of art or places of worship which constitute the cultural or spiritual heritage of peoples and to which special protection has been given by special arrangement, for example, within the framework of a competent international organization, the object of attack, causing as a result extensive destruction thereof, where there is no evidence of the violation by the adverse Party of Article 53, subparagraph (b), and when such historic monuments, works of art and places of worship are not located in the immediate proximity of military objectives;

(e) depriving a person protected by the Conventions or referred to in paragraph 2 or this Article of the rights of fair and regular trial.

5. Without prejudice to the application of the Conventions and of this Protocol, grave breaches of these instruments shall be regarded as war crimes.

Article 86. Failure to act

1. The High Contracting Parties and the Parties to the conflict shall repress grave breaches, and take measures necessary to suppress all other breaches, of the Conventions or of this Protocol which result from a failure to act when under a duty to do so.

2. The fact that a breach of the Conventions or of this Protocol was committed by a subordinate does not absolve his superiors from penal disciplinary responsibility, as the case may be, if they knew, or had information which should have enabled them to conclude in the circumstances at the time, that he was committing or was going to commit such a breach and if they did not take all feasible measures within their power to prevent or repress the breach.

Article 87. Duty of commanders

1. The High Contracting Parties and the Parties to the conflict shall require military commanders, with respect to members of the armed forces under their command and other persons under their control, to prevent and, where necessary, to suppress and to report to competent authorities breaches of the Conventions and of this Protocol.

2. In order to prevent and suppress breaches, High Contracting Parties and Parties to the conflict shall require that, commensurate with their level of responsibility, commanders ensure that members of the armed forces under their command are aware of their obligations under the Conventions and this Protocol.

3. The High Contracting Parties and Parties to the conflict shall require any commander who is aware that subordinates or other persons under his control are going to commit or have committed a breach of the Conventions or of this Protocol, to initiate such steps as are necessary to prevent such violations of the Conventions or this Protocol, and, where appropriate, to initiate disciplinary or penal action against violators thereof.

Article 88. Mutual assistance in criminal matters

1. The High Contracting Parties shall afford one another the greatest measure of assistance in connection with criminal proceedings brought in respect of grave breaches of the Conventions or of this Protocol.

2. Subject to the rights and obligations established in the Conventions and in Article 85, paragraph 1 of this Protocol, and when circumstances permit, the High Contracting Parties shall co-operate in the matter of extradition. They shall give due consideration to the request of the State in whose territory the alleged offense has occurred.

3. The law of the High Contracting Party requested shall apply in all cases. The provisions of the preceding paragraphs shall not, however, affect the obligations arising from the provisions of any other treaty of a bilateral or multilateral nature which governs or will govern the whole or part the subject of mutual assistance in criminal matters.

Article 89. Co-operation

In situations of serious violations or the Conventions or of this Protocol, the High Contracting Parties undertake to act jointly or individually, in co-operation with the United Nations and in conformity with the United Nations Charter. . . .

Article 91. Responsibility

A Party to the conflict which violates the provisions of the Conventions or of this Protocol shall, if the case demands, be liable to pay compensation. It shall be responsible for all acts committed by persons forming part of its armed forces. . . .

Part IV. Final Resolutions

Article 95. Entry into force

1. This Protocol shall enter into force six months after two instruments of ratification or accession have been deposited.

2. For each Party to the Conventions thereafter ratifying or acceding to this Protocol, it shall enter into force six months after the deposit by such Party of its instrument of ratification or accession.

Article 96. Treaty relations upon entry into force of this Protocol

1. When the Parties to the Conventions are also Parties to this Protocol, the Conventions shall apply as supplemented by this Protocol.

2. When one of the Parties to the conflict is not bound by this Protocol, the Parties to the Protocol shall remain bound by it in their mutual relations. They shall furthermore be bound by this Protocol in relation to each of the Parties which are not bound by it, if the latter accepts and applies the provisions thereof.

3. The authority representing a people engaged against a High Contracting Party in an armed conflict of the type referred to in Article 1, paragraph 4, may undertake to apply the Conventions and this Protocol in relation to that conflict by means of

a unilateral declaration addressed to the depositary. Such declaration shall, upon its receipt by the depositary, have in relation to that conflict the following effects:

(a) the Conventions and this Protocol are brought into force for the said authority as a Party to the conflict with immediate effect;

(b) the said authority assumes the same rights and obligations as those which have been assumed by a High Contracting Party to the Conventions and this Protocol; and

(c) the Conventions and this Protocol are equally binding upon all Parties to the conflict.

Appendix 7

Convention on the Prevention and Punishment of the Crime of Genocide, 9 December 1948

The Contracting Parties,

Having considered the declaration made by the General Assembly of the United Nations in its resolution 96 (I) dated 11 December 1946 that genocide is a crime under international law, contrary to the spirit and aims of the United Nations and condemned by the civilized world,

Recognizing that at all periods of history genocide has inflicted great losses on humanity, and

Being convinced that, in order to liberate mankind from such an odious scourge, international co-operation is required,

Hereby agree as hereinafter provided:

Article 1

The Contracting Parties confirm that genocide, whether committed in time of peace or in time of war, is a crime under international law which they undertake to prevent and to punish.

Article 2

In the present Convention, genocide means any of the following acts committed with intent to destroy, in whole or in part, a national, ethnical, racial or religious group, as such:

(a) Killing members of the group;
(b) Causing serious bodily or mental harm to members of the group;
(c) Deliberately inflicting on the group conditions of life calculated to bring about its physical destruction in whole or in part;
(d) Imposing measures intended to prevent births within the group;
(e) Forcibly transferring children of the group to another group.

Article 3

The following acts shall be punishable:

(a) Genocide;
(b) Conspiracy to commit genocide;
(c) Direct and public incitement to commit genocide;
(d) Attempt to commit genocide;
(e) Complicity in genocide.

Article 4

Persons committing genocide or any of the other acts enumerated in article III shall be punished, whether they are constitutionally responsible rulers, public officials or private individuals.

Article 5

The Contracting Parties undertake to enact, in accordance with their respective Constitutions, the necessary legislation to give effect to the provisions of the present Convention, and, in particular, to provide effective penalties for persons guilty of genocide or any of the other acts enumerated in article III.

Article 6

Persons charged with genocide or any of the other acts enumerated in article III shall be tried by a competent tribunal of the State in the territory of which the act was committed, or by such international penal tribunal as may have jurisdiction with respect to those Contracting Parties which shall have accepted its jurisdiction.

Article 7

Genocide and the other acts enumerated in article III shall not be considered as political crimes for the purpose of extradition.

The Contracting Parties pledge themselves in such cases to grant extradition in accordance with their laws and treaties in force.

Article 8

Any Contracting Party may call upon the competent organs of the United Nations to take such action under the Charter of the United Nations as they consider appropriate for the prevention and suppression of acts of genocide or any of the other acts enumerated in article III.

Article 9

Disputes between the Contracting Parties relating to the interpretation, application or fulfillment of the present Convention, including those relating to the responsibility of a State for genocide or for any of the other acts enumerated in article III, shall be submitted to the International Court of Justice at the request of any of the parties to the dispute.

Article 10

The present Convention, of which the Chinese, English, French, Russian and Spanish texts are equally authentic, shall bear the date of 9 December 1948.

Article 11

The present Convention shall be open until 31 December 1949 for signature on behalf of any Member of the United Nations and of any nonmember State to which an invitation to sign has been addressed by the General Assembly.

The present Convention shall be ratified, and the instruments of ratification shall be deposited with the Secretary-General of the United Nations.

After 1 January 1950, the present Convention may be acceded to on behalf of any Member of the United Nations and of any non-member State which has received an invitation as aforesaid. Instruments of accession shall be deposited with the Secretary-General of the United Nations.

Article 12

Any Contracting Party may at any time, by notification addressed to the Secretary-General of the United Nations, extend the application of the present Convention to all or any of the territories for the conduct of whose foreign relations that Contracting Party is responsible.

Article 13

On the day when the first twenty instruments of ratification or accession have been deposited, the Secretary-General shall draw up a proces-verbal and transmit a copy thereof to each Member of the United Nations and to each of the non-member States contemplated in article 11.

The present Convention shall come into force on the ninetieth day following the date of deposit of the twentieth instrument of ratification or accession.

Any ratification or accession effected, subsequent to the latter date shall become effective on the ninetieth day following the deposit of the instrument of ratification or accession.

Article 14

The present Convention shall remain in effect for a period of ten years as from the date of its coming into force.

It shall thereafter remain in force for successive periods of five years for such Contracting Parties as have not denounced it at least six months before the expiration of the current period.

Denunciation shall be effected by a written notification addressed to the Secretary-General of the United Nations.

Article 15

If, as a result of denunciations, the number of Parties to the present Convention should become less than sixteen, the Convention shall cease to be in force as from the date on which the last of these denunciations shall become effective.

Article 16

A request for the revision of the present Convention may be made at any time by any Contracting Party by means of a notification in writing addressed to the Secretary-General.

The General Assembly shall decide upon the steps, if any, to be taken in respect of such request.

Article 17

The Secretary-General of the United Nations shall notify all Members of the United Nations and the non-member States contemplated in article XI of the following:

(a) Signatures, ratifications and accessions received in accordance with article 11;
(b) Notifications received in accordance with article 12;
(c) The date upon which the present Convention comes into force in accordance with article 13;

(d) Denunciations received in accordance with article 14;

(e) The abrogation of the Convention in accordance with article 15;

(f) Notifications received in accordance with article 16.

Article 18

The original of the present Convention shall be deposited in the archives of the United Nations.

A certified copy of the Convention shall be transmitted to each Member of the United Nations and to each of the non-member States contemplated in article XI.

Article 19

The present Convention shall be registered by the Secretary-General of the United Nations on the date of its coming into force.

Appendixes 8–12
Indictments and Other Materials

8. *Indictment of 25 July* 1995 *for Radovan Karadzic and Ratko Mladic*

   This indictment against Radovan Karadzic and Ratko Mladic sets forth the formal written charges against the two men for their actions during the war, including ethnic cleansing in Bosnia.

9. *Indictment of 16 November 1995 for Radovan Karadzic and Ratko Mladic (The "Srebrenica Indictment")*

   This indictment against Radovan Karadzic and Ratko Mladic is the formal written charges against the two men for their roles in the fall of Srebrenica, the UN protected safe area in eastern Bosnia. Thousands of Muslim men from the safe area were rounded up by Serb soldiers and taken off to be executed during the Serb takeover of the safe haven.

10. *International Arrest Warrants and Orders for Surrender: Radovan Karadzic and Ratko Mladic*

    These arrest warrants and orders for surrender for Radovan Karadzic and Ratko Mladic are the result of Rule 61 proceedings. The tribunal is authorized to conduct Rule 61 proceedings when an initial arrest warrant has not been executed against the accused. There have been Rule 61 proceedings against eight indictees who are still at large.

11. *Indictment of 26 June 1996 for Gagovic and Others (the "Foca Indictment")*

    This indictment is included for several reasons. First, it contains precedent-setting charges in which rape and sexual assault are identified as crimes against humanity. Second, it provides insight into some of the indictments against individuals other than Radovan Karadzic and Ratko Mladic, the two people who have received the most international press attention. Finally, the Foca indictment is relevant because a number of the indictees are still living openly in Foca, with little apparent fear of being arrested.

12. *Coalition for International Justice Whereabouts List*

    This is a chart listing the individuals for whom there is information concerning their present whereabouts. It also contains all available identifying information, including items such as addresses and distinguishing physical characteristics. One of the claims sometimes made by individuals explaining why so few arrests have occurred is that the whereabouts of the indictees are unknown. This chart provides evidence to the contrary.

UNITED NATIONS | NATIONS UNIES

INTERNATIONAL CRIMINAL TRIBUNAL FOR THE FORMER YUGOSLAVIA
CHURCHILLPLEIN, 1. P.O. BOX 13888
2501 EW THE HAGUE, NETHERLANDS
TELEPHONE: 31 70 416-5343
FAX: 31 70 416-5355
PRESS AND INFORMATION OFFICE

TRIBUNAL PÉNAL INTERNATIONAL POUR L'EX-YOUGOSLAVIE
CHURCHILLPLEIN, 1. B.P. 13888
2501 EW LA HAYE, PAYS-BAS
TÉLÉPHONE: 31 70 416-5343
FAX: 31 70 416-5355
BUREAU DE PRESSE ET D'INFORMATION

INDICTMENT
ACTE D'ACCUSATION

Karadzic & Mladic

(25 July 1995 / 25 Juillet 1995)

PRESS AND INFORMATION OFFICE
BUREAU DE PRESSE ET D'INFORMATION

TEL.: (31) 70 - 416 5343
FAX : (31) 70 - 416 5355

ICTY, The Hague,
25 July 1995

THIS PRESS FOLDER CONTAINS:

- **Press Release of 25 July 1995 - English version.**
- **Statement by Justice R. Goldstone - 25 July 1995 - English version.**
- **The Indictment/Acte d'Accusation.**

*****

CC/PIO/013 - E
The Hague, 25 July 1995

PRESS RELEASE
(Exclusively for the use of media. **Not an official record**)

MILAN MARTIĆ, RADOVAN KARADŽIĆ AND RATKO MLADIĆ INDICTED ALONG WITH 21 OTHER ACCUSED.
Warrants of arrest have been issued.

MILAN MARTIĆ, president of the Croatian Serb administration of Knin, **RADOVAN KARADŽIĆ**, president of the Bosnian Serb administration of Pale, and **RATKO MLADIĆ**, commander of the army of the Bosnian Serb administration, are among the 24 accused whose indictments are announced today by the International Criminal Tribunal for the former Yugoslavia (ICTY). Warrants for the arrest of the 24 accused have been issued.

MILAN MARTIĆ is charged with war crimes in connection with the firing of cluster-bombs into the central part of Zagreb on 2 and 3 May 1995.

RADOVAN KARADŽIĆ and RATKO MLADIĆ are charged with genocide and crimes against humanity, among others, arising from atrocities perpetrated against the civilian population throughout Bosnia-Herzegovina, for the sniping campaign against civilians in Sarajevo, and for the taking of UN-peacekeepers as hostages and their use as human shields.

21 other individuals are indicted in relation to three specific investigations :

1) Prijedor: Keraterm camp (13 accused): the commander **DUŠKO SIKIRICA**; three shift commanders, **DAMIR DOŠEN, DRAGAN FUŠTAR, DRAGAN KULUNDŽIJA**; four guards or interrogators, **NENAD BANOVIĆ, PREDRAG BANOVIĆ, GORAN LAJIĆ, DRAGAN KONDIĆ**; and five frequent visitors of the camp **NIKICA JANJIĆ, DUŠAN KNEŽEVIĆ, DRAGOMIR ŠAPONJA, NEDJELJKO TIMARAC, ZORAN ŽIGIC**.

2) Bosanski Šamac (6 accused): the Deputy Commander of the "Grey Wolves", a paramilitary unit from Serbia, **SLOBODAN MILJKOVIĆ**; the president of the local Serbian Democratic Party **BLAGOJE SIMIĆ**, and two other local politicians **MILAN SIMIĆ, MIROSLAV TADIĆ**; the Chief of Police for Bosanski Šamac, **STEVAN TODOROVIĆ**; the Supervisor of a Serb territorial defence unit, **SIMO ZARIĆ**.

3) Brčko (2 accused): the commander of Luka camp, **GORAN JELISIĆ**; and **RANKO ČEŠIĆ**, a person in a position of authority at Luka camp.

CONFIRMATION OF THE INDICTMENTS

The indictments "Sikirica and others" (Keraterm investigation), "Miljković and others" (Bosanski Šamac), and "Jelisić and Češić" (Brčko) were confirmed, and the warrants of arrest were signed, by Judge Vohrah on Friday 21 July 1995.

The indictments "Martić", and "Karadžić and Mladić" were confirmed, and the warrants of arrest were signed, by Judge Jorda on Tuesday 25 July 1995.

FULL MOBILIZATION OF OTP'S RESOURCES

Those five indictments bring up to **46** the number of individuals **accused** of serious violations of international humanitarian law **by the Office of the Prosecutor (OTP) within its first year of operation.**

They are the result of extensive investigations by several teams of investigators, attorneys, analysts and translators from the Office of the Prosecutor.

FULL PICTURE OF OTP'S STRATEGY

As stated by Justice Richard Goldstone (see attached), those five indictments illustrate the strategy of the Office of the Prosecutor :

1) they are related to events which occurred in both Croatia and Bosnia, and to atrocities committed against Bosnian Muslims, Bosnian Croats and Croatians

2) they cover events which took place in 1992 (Keraterm, Bosanski Šamac, Brčko), and in 1995 (Zagreb, Tuzla), as well as to the conduct of some leaders throughout this period of time (Karadžić and Mladić)

3) they indicate a wide range of crimes : the setting-up of "death camps" (Keraterm, Bosanski Šamac and Luka), the campaigns of terror following the take-over by Serb military forces of areas or towns (Prijedor, Bosanski Šamac, Brčko), the firing of rockets into cities (Zagreb,Tuzla), the deportation of civilians, the shelling of civilian gatherings, the plunder and destruction of property, the destruction of sacred sites, the sniping campaign in Sarajevo, the targetting of UN-peacekeepers.

4) Lastly, they illustrate the variety of those accused, in terms of rank and degree of participation.

THE CRIMES

A number of accused have been indicted on the basis of their superior authority and control in respect of the crimes committed by their subordinates. They are: MILAN MARTIĆ; RADOVAN KARADŽIĆ and RATKO MLADIĆ; DUŠKO SIKIRICA, DAMIR DOŠEN, DRAGAN FUŠTAR and DRAGAN KULUNDŽICA (Keraterm); BLAGOJE SIMIC (Bosanski Šamac).

The crimes charged in the five indictments, either on the basis of superior authority or on the basis of direct responsability, are:

1. Genocide, being prohibited acts (such as, among others, killing members of a group or causing serious bodily or mental harm to members of a group) committed with intent to destroy, in whole or in part, a national, ethnic or religious group.

Indicted for genocide are : RADOVAN KARADŽIC and RATKO MLADIĆ; DUŠKO SIKIRICA (Keraterm), GORAN JELISIĆ (Brčko).

2. Crimes against humanity, being prohibited acts (such as, among others, murder, rape, sexual assault, torture or persecution on political, racial, or religious grounds) committed in armed conflict, international or national in character, and as a part of a widespread or systematic attack directed against a civilian population.

Indicted for crimes against humanity are : all the accused in the indictments "Karadžić and Mladić", "Sikirica and others"(Keraterm), "Miljković and others" (Bosanski Šamac), "Jelisić and Češić"(Brčko).

3. Violations of the laws or customs of war, against persons who took no active part in the hostilities, in particular violence to life and person, murder, rape and sexual assault, cruel treatment and torture, as well as outrages upon personal dignity (in particular humiliating and degrading treatment).

Indicted for violations of the laws or customs of war are : all the accused in all indictments.

4. Grave breaches of the Geneva Conventions of 1949, relative to the protection of civilian persons in time of war, including forcible sexual intercourse.

Indicted for grave breaches of the Geneva Conventions of 1949 are : all the accused in the indictments "Karadžić and Mladić", "Sikirica and others" (Keraterm), "Miljković and others" (Bosanski Šamac), "Jelisić and Češić" (Brčko).

THE FACTS

The following details appear from the indictments:

UNITED NATIONS NATIONS UNIES

INTERNATIONAL TRIBUNAL FOR THE PROSECUTION OF PERSONS RESPONSIBLE FOR SERIOUS VIOLATIONS OF INTERNATIONAL HUMANITARIAN LAW COMMITTED IN THE TERRITORY OF THE FORMER YUGOSLAVIA SINCE 1991

TRIBUNAL INTERNATIONAL CHARGE DE POURSUIVRE LES PERSONNES PRESUMEES RESPONSABLES DE VIOLATIONS GRAVES DU DROIT INTERNATIONAL HUMANITAIRE COMMISES SUR LE TERRITOIRE DE L'EX-YOUGOSLAVIE DEPUIS 1991

Aegon Building, Churchillplein 1, 2501 EW The Hague, The Netherlands Telephone: 31 70 416-5347 Fax: 31-70 416-5325

Press Statement by the Prosecutor, Justice Richard Goldstone,
in Conjunction with the Announcement of Indictments on 25 July 1995

The five indictments announced today are the result of investigations begun in 1994, and in the case of the indictment in respect of Ratko Mladic and Radovan Karadzic, follows the deferral application granted in May. The indictments are illustrative of a consistent prosecution strategy; namely, the investigation and indictment of leaders in the former Yugoslavia who are suspected of being criminally responsible, either directly or indirectly, for wide-spread and serious violations of international humanitarian law.

That strategy includes the investigation of lower-level persons directly involved in carrying out the crimes in order to build effective cases against the military and civilian leaders who were party to the overall planning and organization of those crimes.

It is in this context that the indictments relating to specific locations and events in Bosnia-Herzegovina are incorporated in the indictment against the two Bosnian Serb leaders, Radovan Karadzic and Ratko Mladic, now indicted. Today's indictments cover a wide variety of criminal offenses and demonstrate the different degrees of participation of the accused persons. Our investigations show that the methods used in Bosanski Samac, Brcko, and Prijedor to take control of the non-Serb population are typical of the methods used in many other places throughout Bosnia-Herzegovina.

It is important to recall statements of the Secretary-General and the Security Council that a primary objective of the Tribunal is to establish individual responsibility for the crimes committed in the former Yugoslavia in order to avoid the attribution of collective guilt. In this regard, the reference in the indictments to "Bosnian Serb" pertains to the Bosnian Serbs who are in the military or civilian service of the authorities in Pale. No reference is intended to those Bosnian Serbs who neither support nor associate themselves with the commission of the crimes charged.

I would like to stress that the availability of evidence determines which suspects we investigate and indict. The identity of the accused in the indictments issued to date is in no way attributable to nationality, ethnic origin, or religion. However, investigations into allegations of serious violations of humanitarian law committed against Serb victims are being materially hampered by the low level of cooperation by the government of the Federal Republic of Yugoslavia and the authorities in Knin and Pale. I sincerely hope that this policy will change.

Further, consistent with my policy of impartiality and following from the deferral application, the investigation into serious humanitarian law violations allegedly committed by Bosnian-Croat perpetrators in the Lasva River Valley is making good progress. The indictment or indictments which will flow from this investigation will be issued and made public before the end of this year.

With regard to the events in April and May, 1995, in Western Slavonia, allegations of war crimes committed by members of the Croatian Army have been received by the Office of the Prosecutor. The investigation into those allegations is still in progress and a decision as to whether any crimes falling within the jurisdiction of the Tribunal have been committed and can be charged against identifiable accused will be taken as soon as possible.

Investigations into alleged serious humanitarian law violations committed by Bosnian Muslim perpetrators are still in progress. However, we are not yet in a position to state when indictments will be issued.

That serious violations of international humanitarian law have taken place in Bosnia-Herzegovina over the past three weeks is manifest. Once again, the media have brought us the vivid portrayal of the human tragedies which have resulted from the unlawful attacks by Bosnian Serbs on United Nations designated "safe areas." Those events are under investigation by my Office. The criminal responsibility of Dr. Karadzic and General Mladic with regard to those and other crimes committed since the outbreak of hostilities throughout Bosnia-Herzegovina is also under investigation and, if warranted, indictments against them will be appropriately amended. The investigation in respect of Dr. Karadzic and General Mladic is not limited to the matters discussed in the indictment announced today and is still ongoing.

Pursuant to the deferral order granted on 16 May 1995 by a Trial Chamber of the Tribunal in respect of the investigation by the Government of Bosnia-Herzegovina into the alleged criminal conduct of Mico Stanisic, the investigation by the Office of the Prosecutor concerning Mico Stanisic and other senior Bosnian Serb military and civilian officials is still proceeding. We are not yet in a position to state when indictments will be issued.

The indictments are the result of many months of effort by the staff of the Office of the Prosecutor. My staff, drawn from 35 nations, have shown extraordinary dedication and commitment to the task which has been entrusted to the Office of the Prosecutor by the Security Council. ***

IT-95-5-I 337
D337 - D315
24 JULY 1995

INDICTMENT

THE INTERNATIONAL CRIMINAL TRIBUNAL
FOR THE FORMER YUGOSLAVIA

THE PROSECUTOR
OF THE TRIBUNAL

AGAINST

RADOVAN KARADŽIĆ
RATKO MLADIĆ

INDICTMENT

Richard J. Goldstone, Prosecutor of the International Criminal Tribunal for the Former Yugoslavia, pursuant to his authority under Article 18 of the Statute of the International Criminal Tribunal for the Former Yugoslavia ("The Statute of the Tribunal"), charges:

THE ACCUSED

1. **RADOVAN KARADŽIĆ** was born on 19 June 1945 in the municipality of Šavnik of the Republic of Montenegro. From on or about 13 May 1992 to the present, he has been president of the Bosnian Serb administration in Pale.

2. **RATKO MLADIĆ** was born on 12 March 1943 in the municipality of Kalinovik of the Republic of Bosnia and Herzegovina. He is a career military officer and holds the rank of general in the Bosnian Serb armed forces. From on or about 14 May 1992 to the present, he has been the commander of the army of the Bosnian Serb administration.

IT-95-5-I 18/337bis
D 1/337bis - D 18/337bis
25 JULY 1995

ACTE D'ACCUSATION

LE TRIBUNAL PENAL INTERNATIONAL
POUR L'EX-YOUGOSLAVIE

LE PROCUREUR
DU TRIBUNAL

CONTRE

RADOVAN KARADŽIĆ
RATKO MLADIĆ

ACTE D'ACCUSATION

Richard J. Goldstone, Procureur du Tribunal pénal international pour l'ex-Yougoslavie, en vertu des pouvoirs que lui confère l'article 18 du Statut du Tribunal pénal international pour l'ex-Yougoslavie ("le Statut du Tribunal"), accuse :

LES ACCUSES

1. **RADOVAN KARADŽIĆ**, né le 19 juin 1945 dans la municipalité de Savnik, République du Monténégro. Il est le président de l'administration des Serbes de Bosnie à Pale depuis le 13 mai 1992 environ.

2. **RATKO MLADIĆ**, né le 12 mars 1943 dans la municipalité de Kalinovik, en République de Bosnie-Herzégovine. Il est officer de carrière dans l'armée des Serbes de Bosnie avec le rang de Général. Il occupe les fonctions de Commandant de l'armée de l'administration des Serbes de Bosnie depuis le 14 mai 1992 environ.

RESPONSABILITE DES SUPERIEURS HIERARCHIQUES

RADOVAN KARADŽIĆ

3. **RADOVAN KARADŽIĆ** est l'un des membres fondateurs et le président du Parti démocratique serbe (SDS) de ce qui était alors la République socialiste de Bosnie-Herzégovine. Le SDS était le principal parti politique des Serbes en Bosnie-Herzégovine. En sa qualité de président du SDS, Karadžić était et reste le plus puissant dirigeant officiel du parti. Ses

IT-95-5-I 336

SUPERIOR AUTHORITY

RADOVAN KARADŽIĆ

3. **RADOVAN KARADŽIĆ** was a founding member and president of the Serbian Democratic Party (SDS) of what was then the Socialist Republic of Bosnia and Herzegovina. The SDS was the main political party among the Serbs in Bosnia and Herzegovina. As president of the SDS, he was and is the most powerful official in the party. His duties as president include representing the party, co-ordinating the work of party organs and ensuring the realisation of the programmatic tasks and goals of the party. He continues to hold this post.

4. **RADOVAN KARADŽIĆ** became the first president of the Bosnian Serb administration in Pale on or about 13 May 1992. At the time he assumed this position, his *de jure* powers, as described in the constitution of the Bosnian Serb administration, included, but were not limited to, commanding the army on the Bosnian Serb administration in times of war and peace and having the authority to appoint, promote and discharge officers of the army.

5. In addition to his powers described in the constitution, **RADOVAN KARADŽIĆ'S** powers as president of the Bosnian Serb administration are augmented by Article 6 of the Bosnian Serb Act on People's Defence which vested in him, among other powers, the authority to supervise the Territorial Defence both in peace and war and the authority to issue orders for the utilisation of the police in case of war, immediate threat and other emergencies. Article 39 of the same Act empowered him, in cases of imminent threat of war and other emergencies, to deploy Territorial Defence units for the maintenance of law and order.

6. **RADOVAN KARADŽIĆ'S** powers are further augmented by Article 33 of the Bosnian Serb Act on Internal Affairs, which authorised him to activate reserve police in emergency situations.

7. **RADOVAN KARADŽIĆ** has exercised the powers described above and has acted and been dealt with internationally as the president of the Bosnian Serb administration in Pale. In that capacity, he has, *inter alia*, participated in international negotiations and has personally made agreements on such matters as cease-fires and humanitarian relief that have been implemented.

IT-95-5-I 17/337bis

fonctions de président comprennent la représentation du parti, la coordination des activités de ses différents organes et l'exécution de ses tâches et objectifs programmatiques. Il continue d'occuper ce poste.

4. **RADOVAN KARADŽIĆ** est devenu le premier président de l'administration des Serbes de Bosnie à Pale vers le 13 mai 1992. A l'époque à laquelle il est entré en fonction, ses pouvoirs *de jure*, décrits dans la constitution de l'administration des Serbes de Bosnie, comprenaient, sans y être limités, le commandement de l'armée de ladite administration en temps de guerre et de paix et le pouvoir de nommer, promouvoir et limoger les officiers de ladite armée.

5. En plus de ses pouvoirs constitutionnels, les pouvoirs de **RADOVAN KARADŽIĆ** en qualité de président de l'administration des Serbes de Bosnie sont renforcés par les dispositions de l'article 6 de la Loi serbe bosniaque sur la défense populaire, qui l'habilite notamment à superviser la Défense du territoire en temps de paix et de guerre et à donnere des ordres pour l'utilisation des forces de police en cas de guerre, de menace immédiate ou de toute autre urgence. L'article 39 de la même Loi l'habilite, en cas de menaces imminentes de guerre ou autres urgences, à déployer des unités de Défense du territoire en vue de maintenir l'ordre.

6. Les pouvoirs de **RADOVAN KARADŽIĆ** sont encore renforcés par l'article 33 de la Loi serbe bosniaque sur les affaires intérieures, qui l'autorise à mobiliser les forces de réserve de la police en cas d'urgence.

7. **RADOVAN KARADŽIĆ** exerce les pouvoirs décrits ci-avant, agit et est traité à l'échelon international comme le président de l'administration des Serbes de Bosnie à Pale. En cette capacité, il a, *inter alia*, participé à des négociations internationales et conclu personnellement des accords sur des questions comme des cessez-le-feu et l'aide humanitaire, lesquels accords ont été appliqués.

RATKO MLADIĆ

8. **RATKO MLADIĆ** a été nommé Commandant du 9e corps de l'armée populaire yougoslave (JNA) à Knin, en République de Croatie, en 1991. En mai 1992, il a pris le commandement des forces du Deuxième district militaire de la JNA, qui est alors devenue effectivement l'armée des Serbes de Bosnie. Il a le rang de Général et est, depuis le 14 mai 1992 environ, le Commandant de l'armée de l'administration des Serbes de Bosnie.

9. **RATKO MLADIĆ** a démontré sa maîtrise des questions militaires en négociant, *inter alia*, des accords de cessez-le-feu et d'échanges de prisonniers; des accords relatifs à l'ouverture de l'aéroport de Sarajevo; des accords relatifs à l'accès des convois d'aide humanitaire; et des accords contre le recours à des tireurs isolés. Tous les accords précités ont été appliqués.

CONTEXTE GENERAL

10. A toutes les époques concernées dans le présent acte d'accusation, le territoire de la République de Bosnie-Herzégovine, en ex-Yougoslavie, était le théatre d'un conflit armé et se trouvait sous occupation partielle.

IT-95-5-I 335

RATKO MLADIĆ

8. **RATKO MLADIĆ** was, in 1991, appointed commander of the 9th Corps of the Yugoslav People's Army (JNA) in Knin in the Republic of Croatia. Subsequently, in May 1992, he assumed command of the forces of the Second Military District of the JNA which then effectively became the Bosnian Serb army. He holds the rank of general and from about 14 May 1992 to the present, has been the commander of the army of the Bosnian Serb administration.

9. **RATKO MLADIĆ** has demonstrated his control in military matters by negotiating, *inter alia*, cease-fire and prisoner exchange agreements; agreements relating to the opening of Sarajevo airport; agreements relating to access for humanitarian aid convoys; and anti-sniping agreements, all of which have been implemented.

GENERAL ALLEGATIONS

10. At all times relevant to this indictment, a state of armed conflict and partial occupation existed in the Republic of Bosnia and Herzegovina in the territory of the former Yugoslavia.

11. All acts or omissions herein set forth as grave breaches of the Geneva Conventions of 1949 (hereafter "grave breaches") recognised by Article 2 of the Statute of the Tribunal occurred during that armed conflict and partial occupation.

12. In each paragraph charging crimes against humanity, crimes recognised by Article 5 of the Statute of the Tribunal, the alleged acts or omissions were part of a widespread, systematic or large-scale attack directed against a civilian population.

13. The term "UN peacekeepers" used throughout this indictment includes UN military observers of the United Nations.

14. The UN peacekeepers and civilians referred to in this indictment were, at all relevant times, persons protected by the Geneva Conventions of 1949.

15. The accused in this indictment were required to abide by the laws and customs governing the conduct of war, including the Geneva Conventions of 1949.

IT-95-5-I 16/337 bis

11. Tous les actes ou omissions présentés comme des infractions graves aux Conventions de Genève visées à l'article 2 du Statut du Tribunal se sont produits durant ce conflit armé et cette occupation partielle.

12. Dans chacun des paragraphes relatifs au chef d'accusation de crimes contre l'humanité, lequel est sanctionné par l'article 5 du Statut du Tribunal, les actes ou omissions allégués faisaient partie d'une offensive généralisée, à grande échelle ou systématique, dirigée contre une population civile.

13. L'expression "membres des forces de maintien de la paix des Nations Unies", utilisée à travers tout le présent acte d'accusation, comprend les observateurs militaires des Nations Unies.

14. Les membres des forces de maintien de la paix des Nations Unies et les civils visés dans le présent acte d'accusation étaient, à toutes les époques concernées, des personnes protégées par les Conventions de Genève de 1949.

15. Les accusés visés par le présent acte d'accusation étaient tenus de se conformer aux prescriptions des lois ou coutumes de la guerre, y compris des Conventions de Genève de 1949.

CHEFS D'ACCUSATION

16. Les chefs d'accusation figurant dans le présent acte d'accusation sont répartis en trois parties:

La Partie I de l'acte d'accusation - chefs 1 à 9 - un crime de génocide, des crimes contre l'humanité et des crimes perpétrés contre les populations civiles et contre les édifices du culte sur l'ensemble du territoire de la République de Bosnie-Herzégovine.

La Partie II de l'acte d'accusation - chefs d'accusation 10 à 12 - des crimes relatifs à la campagne de tirs isolés contre des civils à Sarajevo.

La Partie III de l'acte d'accusation - chefs d'accusation 13 à 16 - des crimes relatifs à la prise en otages de membres des forces du maintien de la paix des Nations Unies.

PARTIE I

CHEFS D'ACCUSATION 1-2
(GENOCIDE)
(CRIME CONTRE L'HUMANITE)

17. RADOVAN KARADŽIĆ et RATKO MLADIĆ ont, depuis avril 1992, par leurs actes et omissions sur le territoire de la République de Bosnie-Herzégovine, commis un génocide.

18. Des civils musulmans bosniaques et croates bosniaques ont été persécutés pour des raisons nationales, politiques et religieuses sur tout le territoire de la République de Bosnie-Herzégovine. Des milliers d'entre-eux ont été internés dans des camps de détention, où ils ont fait l'objet de violences physiques et psychologiques généralisées et où ils ont été soumis à des conditions inhumaines. Le personnel des camps de détention qui administrait les camps

IT-95-5-I 334

CHARGES

16. The charges set forth in this indictment are in three parts:

Part I of the indictment, Counts 1 to 9, charges a crime of genocide, crimes against humanity and crimes that were perpetrated against the civilian population and against places of worship throughout the territory of the Republic of Bosnia and Herzegovinia.

Part II of the indictment, Counts 10 to 12, charges crimes relating to the sniping campaign against civilians in Sarajevo.

Part III of the indictment, Counts 13 to 16, charges crimes relating to the taking of UN peacekeepers as hostages.

PART I

COUNTS 1-2
(GENOCIDE)
(CRIME AGAINST HUMANITY)

17. **RADOVAN KARADŽIĆ** and **RATKO MLADIĆ**, from April 1992, in the territory of the Republic of Bosnia and Herzegovina, by their acts and omissions, committed genocide.

18. Bosnian Muslim and Bosnian Croat civilians were persecuted on national, political and religious grounds throughout the Republic of Bosnia and Herzegovina. Thousands of them were interned in detention facilities where they were subjected to widespread acts of physical and psychological abuse and to inhumane conditions. Detention facility personnel who ran and operated the Omarska, Keraterm and Luka detention facilities, among others, including, but not limited to Željko Meakić (Omarska), Duško Sikirica (Keraterm) and Goran Jelisić (Luka), intended to destroy Bosnian Muslim and Bosnian Croat people as national, ethnic, or religious groups and killed, seriously injured and deliberately inflicted upon them conditions intended to bring about their physical destruction. The conditions in the detention facilities, which are described in paragraphs 20-22 hereunder, are incorporated in full herein.

d'Omarska, Keraterm et Luka, entre autres, y compris mais sans y être limité, Željko Meakić (Omarska), Duško Sikirica (Keraterm) et Goran Jelisić (Luka), avaient l'intention de détruire des civils musulmans bosniaques et croates bosniaques en tant que groupe national, ethnique ou religieux et ont tué, gravement blessé et délibérément infligé auxdits civils des conditions visant à leur destruction physique. Les conditions prévalant dans les camps de détention, décrites aux paragraphes 20 à 22 ci-après, sont ici intégralement incorporées.

19. **RADOVAN KARADŽIĆ** et **RATKO MLADIĆ** ont, entre avril 1992 et juillet 1995, sur le territoire de la République de Bosnie-Herzégovine, par leurs actes et omissions, et de concert avec d'autres, commis un crime contre l'humanité en persécutant des civils musulmans bosniaques et croates bosniaques pour des raisons nationales, politiques et religieuses. Ainsi qu'il est précisé ci-après, ils sont pénalement responsables de la détention illégale, du meurtre, du viol, des violences sexuelles, de la torture, des coups et blessures, des vols et des traitements inhumains infligés à des civils; la prise pour cible de dirigeants politiques, d'intellectuels et de professionnels; l'expulsion et le transfert illégaux de civils; le pillonnage illégal de civils; l'appropriation illégale et le pillage de biens meubles et immeubles; la destruction de maisons et d'établissements industriels et commerciaux; et la destruction d'édifices du culte.

CAMPS D'INTERNEMENT

20. Dès que des forces militaires de Bosnie et d'ailleurs en ex-Yougoslavie ont commencé à attaquer des villes et villages dans la République de Bosnie-Herzégovine, des milliers de civils musulmans bosniaques et croates bosniaques ont été systématiquement choisis et rassemblés pour des raisons nationales, ethniques, politiques ou religieuses et incarcérés dans des camps d'internement répartis sur l'ensemble du territoire occupé par les Serbes de Bosnie. Ces camps comprennent, sans y être limités :

Camps d'internement	**Dates d'existence**
Omarska	mai-août 1992
Keraterm	mai-août 1992
Trnopolje	mai-décembre 1992
Luka	mai-juillet 1992
Manjača	été 1991-décembre 1992
Sušica	juin 1992-septembre 1992
KP Dom Foča	avril-milieu de 1993

21. Bon nombre de ces camps d'internement étaient dotés d'un personnel militaire et policier et de leurs agents qui en assuraient l'administration, sous le contrôle de **RADOVAN KARADŽIĆ** et **RATKO MLADIĆ**. De plus, des interrogateurs appartenant aux forces policières et militaires serbes bosniaques pouvaient accéder sans entrave à tous les camps d'internement et opéraient en conjonction avec le personnel chargé du contrôle desdits camps. Ces camps et ce personnel comprennent, sans y être limités :

IT-95-5-I 333

19. **RADOVAN KARADŽIĆ** and **RATKO MLADIĆ**, between April 1992 and July 1995, in the territory of the Republic of Bosnia and Herzegovina, by their acts and omissions, and in concert with others, committed a crime against humanity by persecuting Bosnian Muslim and Bosnian Croat civilians on national, political and religious grounds. As set forth below, they are criminally responsible for the unlawful confinement, murder, rape, sexual assault, torture, beating, robbery and inhumane treatment of civilians; the targeting of political leaders, intellectuals and professionals; the unlawful deportation and transfer of civilians; the unlawful shelling of civilians; the unlawful appropriation and plunder of real and personal property; the destruction of homes and businesses; and the destruction of places of worship.

DETENTION FACILITIES

20. As soon as military forces from Bosnia and elsewhere in the former Yugoslavia began to attack towns and villages in the Republic of Bosnia and Herzegovina, thousands of Bosnian Muslim and Bosnian Croat civilians were systematically selected and rounded up on national, ethnic, political or religious grounds and interned in detention facilities throughout the territory occupied by the Bosnian Serbs. These facilities include, but are not limited to:

Detention Facility	Dates of existence
Omarska:	May - August 1992
Keraterm:	May - August 1992
Trnopolje:	May - December 1992
Luka	May - July 1992
Manjača:	Summer 1991 - December 1992
Sušica:	June 1992 - September 1992
KP Dom Foča:	April - mid-1993

21. Many of these detention facilities were staffed and operated by military and police personnel and their agents, under the control of **RADOVAN KARADŽIĆ** and **RATKO MLADIĆ**. In addition, Bosnian Serb police and military interrogators had unfettered access to all of the detention facilities and operated in conjunction with the personnel in control of these detention facilities. These facilities and personnel include, but are not limited to:

IT-95-5-I 14/337bis

Camp	Commandant	Gardiens
Omarska	Željko Meakić (police)	police/milit.
Keraterm	Duško Sikirica (police)	police/milit.
Trnopolje	Slobodon Kuruzović (milit.)	police/milit.
Luka	Goran Jelisić	paramilitaire
Manjača	Božidar Popović (milit.)	militaires
Sušica	Dragan Nikolić (milit.)	militaires
KP Dom Foča	Milorad Krnojelac	militaires

22. Des milliers de civils musulmans bosniaques et croates bosniaques, y compris des femmes, enfants et personnes âgées, ont été détenus dans ces camps pendant de longues périodes. Ils ont été privés des garanties d'une procédure judiciaire, et leur internement n'était pas justifié par des impératifs militaires. Ils ont été détenus, dans une grande mesure, du fait de leur identité nationale, religieuse et politique. Les conditions de vie dans les camps d'internement étaient inhumaines et exécrables. Le personnel militaire et policier serbe bosniaque chargé de ces camps, y compris Dragan Nikolić (Sušica), Željko Meakić (Omarska), Duško Sikirica (Keraterm) et d'autres personnes d'un rang hiérarchique inférieur, ont infligé aux détenus civils des atteintes à leur intégrité physique et mentale, des menaces et des mauvais traitements. Le personnel des camps d'internement, ayant l'intention de détruire les Musulmans bosniaques et les Croates bosniaques en tant que groupe national, ethnique, ou religieux, ont tué, gravement blessé et infligé délibérément à ces personnes des conditions visant à leur destruction physique. Des détenus ont à maintes reprises assisté et/ou fait l'objet d'actes inhumains, y compris les suivants : meurtre, viol, violences sexuelles, torture, coups et blessures, vol, ainsi que d'autres formes d'atteintes à l'intégrité mentale et physique. Dans de nombreux cas, des femmes et des filles détenues ont été violées dans les camps ou ont été retirées de ces camps et fait l'objet de viols et autres violences sexuelles en d'autres endroits. Les rations alimentaires quotidiennes fournies aux détenus étaient insuffisantes et correspondaient souvent à des rations de famine. Les soins médicaux dispensés aux détenus étaient insuffisants ou inexistants et les conditions générales d'hygiène étaient totalement inadéquates.

PRISE POUR CIBLE DE DIRIGEANTS POLITIQUES, INTELLECTUELS ET PROFESSIONNELS

23. Les dirigeants politiques et les membres du parti politique essentiellement musulman bosniaque, le Parti d'action démocratique (SDA) ainsi que du principal parti politique croate bosniaque, l'Union démocrate croate (HDZ), des villes de Prijedor, Vlasenica, Bosanski Šamac et Foča, notamment, ont été particulièrement ciblés aux fins de persécution par le personnel militaire et policier serbe bosniaque et leurs agents, sous la direction et le contrôle de **RADOVAN KARADŽIĆ** et **RATKO MLADIĆ**. Dans de nombreux cas, des listes identifiant les dirigeants du SDA et du HDZ ont été fournies par le SDS au personnel militaire et policier serbe bosniaque et à leurs agents. Sur la base de ces listes, des dirigeants politiques musulmans bosniaques et croates bosniaques ont été arrêtés, internés, ont fait l'objet de violences physiques et ont, dans de nombreux cas, été exécutés. Certains dirigeants locaux du SDA qui ont été persécutés en raison de leurs convictions politiques comprennent, sans y être limités, Muhamed Čehajić (Prijedor), Suleman Tihić (Bosanki Šamac) et Ahmet Hadžić (Brčko).

IT-95-5-I 332

Detention Facility	Commander	Guards
Omarska:	Željko Meakić (police)	police/military
Keraterm:	Duško Sikirica (police)	police/military
Trnopolje:	Slobodon Kuruzović (military)	police/military
Luka	Goran Jelisić (police)	paramilitary
Manjača:	Božidar Popović (military)	military
Sušica:	Dragan Nikolić (military)	military
KP Dom Foča:	Milorad Krnojelac	military

22. Thousands of Bosnian Muslim and Bosnian Croat civilians, including women, children and elderly persons, were detained in these facilities for protracted periods of time. They were not afforded judicial process and their internment was not justified by military necessity. They were detained, in large measure, because of their national, religious and political identity. The conditions in the detention facilities were inhumane and brutal. Bosnian Serb military and police personnel in charge of these facilities, including Dragan Nikolić (Sušica), Željko Meakić (Omarska), Duško Sikirica (Keraterm) and other persons over whom they had control, subjected the civilian detainees to physical and psychological abuse, intimidation and maltreatment. Detention facility personnel, intending to destroy Bosnian Muslim and Bosnian Croat people as national, ethnic or religious groups, killed, seriously injured and deliberately inflicted upon them conditions intended to bring about their physical destruction. Detainees were repeatedly subjected to and/or witnessed inhumane acts, including murder, rape, sexual assault, torture, beatings, robbery as well as other forms of mental and physical abuse. In many instances, women and girls who were detained were raped at the camps or taken from the detention centres and raped or otherwise sexually abused at other locations. Daily food rations provided to detainees were inadequate and often amounted to starvation rations. Medical care for the detainees was insufficient or non-existent and the general hygienic conditions were grossly inadequate.

IT-95-5-I 13/337 bis

24. En plus des persécutions de dirigeants politiques musulmans bosniaques et croates bosniaques, les forces militaires et policières serbes bosniaques et leurs agents ont systématiquement pris comme cibles aux fins de persécution pour des raisons nationales ou religieuses, les intellectuels et professionnels musulmans bosniaques et croates bosniaques dans de nombreuses villes et villages, y compris notamment Prijedor, Vlasenica, Bosanski Šamac et Foča. Les personnes persécutées comprennent, sans y être limitées, Abdullah Puškar (universitaire), Žiko Crnalić (homme d'affaires) et Esad Mehmedalija (avocat) de Prijedor; Osman Vatić (avocat) de Brčko.

25. Des milliers de Musulmans bosniaques et de Croates bosniaques des régions de Vlasenica, Prijedor, Bosanski Šamac, Brčko et Foča, notamment, ont été systématiquement arrêtés et mis en détention dans des camps d'internement établis et administrés par les forces militaires et policières serbes bosniaques et leurs agents, puis expulsés ou déportés illégalement vers des endroits à l'intérieur et à l'extérieur de la République de Bosnie-Herzégovine. De plus, des civils musulmans bosniaques et croates bosniaques, y compris des femmes, enfants et personnes âgées, ont été enlevés directement de leurs domiciles et utilisés dans le cadre d'échanges de prisonniers par les forces militaires et policières serbes bosniaques et leurs agents sous le contrôle et la direction de RADOVAN KARADŽIĆ et RATKO MLADIĆ. Ces expulsions et autres n'étaient pas des évacuations motivées par des raisons de sécurité ou des exigences militaires ou pour toute autre raison légale, et elles ont, en conjonction avec d'autres actions dirigées contre la population musulmane bosniaque et croate bosniaque, résulté en une réduction significative ou en l'élimination des Musulmans bosniaques et des Croates bosniaques de certaines régions occupées.

PILLONNAGE DE RASSEMBLEMENTS CIVILS

26. A compter de juillet 1992 et jusqu'en juillet 1995, les forces militaires serbes bosniaques, sous la direction et le contrôle de RADOVAN KARADŽIĆ et RATKO MLADIĆ, ont tiré illégalement sur des rassemblements civils sans signification militaire dans le but de tuer, terroriser et démoraliser la population civile musulmane bosniaque et croate bosniaque. Ces incidents comprennent, sans y être limités :

Lieu/type de rassemblement	Municipalité	Date	Victimes
Sarajevo (pique-nique)	Sarajevo	03/07/92	10
Sarajevo (aéroport)	Sarajevo	11/02/93	4
Srebenica (terrain de jeu)	Srebrenica	12/4/93	15
Dobrinja (match de football)	Sarajevo	01/06/93	146
Dobrinja (approvisionnement)	Sarajevo	12/07/93	27
Sarajevo (rue résidentielle)	Sarajevo	28/11/93	11
Ciglane Market (marché aux fruits)	Sarajevo	06/12/93	20
Alipašino Polje (enfants jouant)	Sarajevo	22/01/94	10
Cetinjska St (enfants jouant)	Sarajevo	26/10/94	7
Sarajevo (Livanjska Street)	Sarajevo	08/11/94	7
Sarajevo (marché aux puces)	Sarajevo	22/12/94	9
Tuzla (place)	Tuzla	24/05/95	195

IT-95-5-I 331

TARGETING OF POLITICAL LEADERS, INTELLECTUALS AND PROFESSIONALS

23. Particularly singled out for persecution by the Bosnian Serb military, Bosnian Serb police and their agents, under the direction and control of **RADOVAN KARADŽIĆ** and **RATKO MLADIĆ**, were civilian political leaders and members of the primary Bosnian Muslim political party, the Party for Democratic Action (SDA), and the principal Bosnian Croat political party, the Croatian Democratic Union (HDZ), from the cities of Prijedor, Vlasenica, Bosanski Šamac and Foča, amongst others. In many instances, lists identifying leaders of the SDA and the HDZ were provided by the SDS to personnel of the Bosnian Serb military, police and their agents. Using these lists, Bosnian Muslim and Bosnian Croat political leaders were arrested, interned, physically abused and, in many instances, murdered. Some local SDA leaders who were persecuted because of their political beliefs include, but are not limited to, Muhamed Čehajić (Prijedor), Sulejman Tihić (Bosanski Šamac), and Ahmet Hadžić (Brčko).

24. In addition to persecutions of Bosnian Muslim and Bosnian Croat political leaders, the Bosnian Serb military, police and their agents systematically targeted for persecution on national or religious grounds, Bosnian Muslim and Bosnian Croat intellectuals and professionals in many towns and villages including Prijedor, Vlasenica, Bosanski Šamac and Foča, among others. Individuals who were persecuted include, but are not limited to Abdulah Puškar (academic), Žiko Crnalić (businessman) and Esad Mehmedalija (attorney) from Prijedor; Osman Vatić (attorney) from Brčko.

DEPORTATION

25. Thousands of Bosnian Muslims and Bosnian Croats from the areas of Vlasenica, Prijedor, Bosanski Šamac, Brčko and Foča, among others, were systematically arrested and interned in detention facilities established and maintained by the Bosnian Serb military, police and their agents and thereafter unlawfully deported or transferred to locations inside and outside of the Republic of Bosnia and Herzegovina. In addition, Bosnian Muslim and Bosnian Croat civilians, including women, children and elderly persons, were taken directly from their homes and eventually used in prisoner exchanges by Bosnian Serb military and police and their agents under the control and direction of

IT-95-5-I 12/337bis

APPROPRIATION ET PILLAGE DE BIENS

27. Peu de temps après l'ouverture des hostilités armées en République de Bosnie-Herzégovine, les forces serbes bosniaques ont rapidement éliminé la résistance armée dans la plupart des villes et des villages. Durant et après la consolidation de leurs gains, le personnel militaire et policier serbe bosniaque et d'autres agents de l'administration serbe bosniaque, sous la direction et le contrôle de **RADOVAN KARADŽIĆ** et **RATKO MLADIĆ**, se sont appropriés et ont pillé systématiquement et arbitrairement les biens meubles et immeubles de civils musulmans bosniaques et croates bosniaques. L'appropriation des biens a eu lieu sur une grande échelle, sans être justifiée par des nécessités militaires. Elle a été observée d'avril 1992 à janvier 1993 dans les municipalités de Prijedor, Vlasenica et Bosanski Šamac, notamment.

28. L'appropriation et le pillage desdits biens se sont déroulés de la manière et sous les formes suivantes, notamment :

A. Des milliers de civils musulmans bosniaques et croates bosniaques ont été jetés dans des camps d'internement où ils sont restés pendant de longues périodes. Lors de leur arrivée dans ces camps d'internement, le personnel administrant lesdits camps a systématiquement volé les biens personnels des détenus, y compris bijoux, montres, fonds en espèces et autres objets de valeur. Des reçus ont rarement été remis aux détenus pour les biens confisqués et ils ont rarement retrouvé leurs biens lors de leur élargissement.

B. Des civils internés dans ces camps ont été les témoins et/ou ont fait l'objet d'atteintes à leur intégrité physique et mentale. Après avoir assisté et fait l'objet de mauvais traitements, des milliers de détenus ont été transférés de force de ces camps dans des endroits situés à l'intérieur et à l'extérieur de la République de Bosnie-Herzégovine. Avant ce transfert forcé, de nombreux détenus ont été contraints de signer des documents officiels serbes bosniaques par lesquels ils abandonnaient "volontairement" à l'administration serbe bosniaque le titre de propriété et la possession de leurs biens meubles et immeubles.

C. Dans de nombreux cas, des détenus civils musulmans bosniaques et croates bosniaques ont été emmenés des camps d'internement à leur domicile et à leur établissement industriel ou commercial et contraints de remettre à leurs escortes leurs fonds et autres biens de valeur. Dans d'autres cas, ils ont servi à charger dans des camions, pour des destinations inconnues, les biens confisqués dans des maisons et des établissements industriels ou commerciaux musulmans bosniaques et croates bosniaques. Ces évènements se sont déroulés avec le consentement et l'approbation des responsables du contrôle des camps d'internement.

D. De nombreux civils musulmans bosniaques et croates bosniaques, qui n'ont pas été internés dans des camps, ont été contraints de rester dans leurs collectivités, où ils ont fait l'objet d'atteintes à leur intégrité physique et mentale de la part du personnel militaire et policier serbe bosniaque et de leurs agents, des forces paramilitaires et d'éléments criminels de la communauté serbe bosniaque. Les conditions sont devenues intolérables pour beaucoup d'entre-eux et ils sont partis. Avant de partir, de nombreux civils ont été contraints de signer des documents officiels serbes bosniaques par lesquels ils abandonnaient "volontairement" à l'administration serbe bosniaque leurs droits sur leurs biens meubles et immeubles. Dans certains cas, des civils musulmans bosniaques et croates bosniaques qui avaient quitté leurs collectivités ont été

IT-95-5-I 330

RADOVAN KARADŽIĆ and **RATKO MLADIĆ**. These deportations and others were not conducted as evacuations for safety, military necessity or for any other lawful purpose and have, in conjunction with other actions directed against Bosnian Muslim and Bosnian Croat civilians, resulted in a significant reduction or elimination of Bosnian Muslims and Bosnian Croats in certain occupied regions.

SHELLING OF CIVILIAN GATHERINGS

26. Beginning in July 1992 and continuing through to July 1995, Bosnian Serb military forces, under the direction and control of **RADOVAN KARADŽIĆ** and **RATKO MLADIĆ**, unlawfully fired on civilian gatherings that were of no military significance in order to kill, terrorise and demoralise the Bosnian Muslim and Bosnian Croat civilian population. These incidents include, but are not limited to the following:

Location/Type of Civilian Gathering	Municipality	Date	Casualties
Sarajevo (picnic)	Sarajevo	03/07/92	10
Sarajevo (airport)	Sarajevo	11/02/93	4
Srebrenica (playground)	Srebrenica	12/4/93	15
Dobrinja (soccer game)	Sarajevo	01/06/93	146
Dobrinja (water line)	Sarajevo	12/07/93	27
Sarajevo (residential street)	Sarajevo	28/11/93	11
Ciglane Market (fruit market)	Sarajevo	06/12/93	20
Alipašino Polje (children playing)	Sarajevo	22/01/94	10
Cetinjska St (children playing)	Sarajevo	26/10/94	7
Sarajevo (Livanjska Street)	Sarajevo	08/11/94	7
Sarajevo (flea market)	Sarajevo	22/12/94	9
Tuzla (plaza)	Tuzla	24/05/95	195

APPROPRIATION AND PLUNDER OF PROPERTY

27. Shortly after armed hostilities broke out in the Republic of Bosnia and Herzegovina, Bosnian Serb forces quickly suppressed armed resistance in most villages and cities. During and after the course of consolidating their gains, Bosnian Serb military and police personnel, and other agents of the Bosnian Serb administration, under the direction and control of **RADOVAN KARADŽIĆ** and **RATKO MLADIĆ**,

IT-95-5-I 11/337bis

autorisés à emmener des montants limités de biens personnels et d'argent, mais même ces biens ont été volés aux postes de contrôle serbes bosniaques ou en d'autres endroits.

E. Dans de nombreux cas durant et après la prise militaire de villes et villages par les forces serbes bosniaques, le personnel militaire et policier serbe bosniaque et leurs agents sont entrés dans les maisons de civils musulmans bosniaques et croates bosniaques et ont pillé leurs biens personnels.

DESTRUCTION DE BIENS

29. La persécution dans l'ensemble du territoire occupé par les forces militaires et policières serbes bosniaques et leurs agents, ou par des tiers avec leur consentement, a comporté la destruction systématique des maisons et établissements industriels ou commerciaux musulmans bosniaques et croates bosniaques. Ces maisons et établissements industriels ou commerciaux ont été sélectionnés et systématiquement détruits dans des zones où les hostilités avaient cessé ou qui avaient été épargnées par les hostilités. Le but de cette destruction illégale était de s'assurer que les habitants ne pourraient pas rentrer et ne rentreraient pas dans leurs domiciles et collectivités. Les villes et villages, ou les quartiers musulmans bosniaques et croates bosniaques de ceux-ci, marqués par la destruction sur une grande échelle des biens immeubles musulmans bosniaques et croates bosniaques comprennent, sans y être limités :

Ville/village	Municipalité	Dates approximatives de destruction
Grebnice	Bosanski Šamac	19-22 avril 1992
Hrvatska Tisina	Bosanski Šamac	19-22 avril 1992
Hasići	Bosanski Šamac	19-22 avril 1992
Derventa	Derventa	4 avril 1992
Vijaka	Derventa	4 avril 1992
Bosanski Brod	Bosanski Brod	3 mars 1992
Odžak	Odžak	juillet 1992
Modriča	Modriča	fin avril 1992
Vidovice	Orašje	29 avril et 4 mai 1992
Gradačac	Gradačac	milieu de 1992
Piskavice	Vlasenica	22 avril 1992
Gobelje	Vlasenica	28 avril 1992
Turalići	Vlasenica	28 avril 1992
Djile	Vlasenica	1-3 mai 1992
Pomol	Vlasenica	1er mai 1992
Gaj	Vlasenica	1er mai 1992
Bešići	Vlasenica	1er mai 1992
Nurići	Vlasenica	1er mai 1992
Vrsinje	Vlasenica	1er mai 1992
Džamdžići	Vlasenica	8 mai 1992
Pivici	Vlasenica	11 mai 1992
Hambarine	Prijedor	23 mai 1992
Ljubija	Prijedor	23 mai 1992
Kozarac	Prijedor	24 mai 1992

systematically and wantonly appropriated and looted the real and personal property of Bosnian Muslim and Bosnian Croat civilians. The appropriation of property was extensive and not justified by military necessity. It occurred from April 1992 to January 1993 in the municipalities of Prijedor, Vlasenica, and Bosanski Šamac, among others.

28. The appropriation and looting of said property was accomplished in the following manner and by the following means, among others:

A. Thousands of Bosnian Muslim and Bosnian Croat civilians were forced into detention facilities where they remained for protracted periods of time. Upon entering these internment facilities, the personnel who ran the internment facilities systematically stole the personal property of the detainees, including jewellery, watches, money and other valuables. The detainees were rarely provided receipts for the property taken from them or given their property back upon their release.

B. Civilians interned in these camps witnessed and/or were subjected to physical and psychological abuse. After witnessing or experiencing serious abuse, thousands of internees were forcibly transferred from these camps to locations inside and outside the Republic of Bosnia and Herzegovina. Before being forcibly transferred, many detainees were compelled to sign official Bosnian Serb documents wherein they "voluntarily" relinquished to the Bosnian Serb administration title to and possession of their real and personal property.

C. In many instances, Bosnian Muslim and Bosnian Croat civilian detainees were taken from internment camps to their homes and businesses and forced to turn over to their escorts money and other valuables. In other instances, they were used as labourers to load property from Bosnian Muslim and Bosnian Croat homes and businesses onto trucks for transportation to parts unknown. This occurred with the consent and approval of those in control of the detention facilities.

D. Many Bosnian Muslim and Bosnian Croat civilians who were not interned in camps were forced to stay in their communities where they were subjected to physical and psychological abuse from Bosnian Serb military and police and their agents, paramilitary forces and lawless elements of the Bosnian Serb community. Conditions for many became intolerable and they left. Before leaving, many civilians were compelled to sign official Bosnian Serb documents wherein they "voluntarily" relinquished to the Bosnian Serb administration their rights to their real and personal property. In some cases, Bosnian Muslim and Bosnian

IT-95-5-I 10/337bis

Biščani	Prijedor	20 juillet 1992
Carakovo	Prijedor	20 juillet 1992
Rizvanovići	Prijedor	20 juillet 1992
Sredice	Prijedor	20 juillet 1992
Žikovi	Prijedor	20 juillet 1992

DESTRUCTION D'EDIFICES DU CULTE

30. Les édifices musulmans et catholiques consacrés au culte ont été systématiquement endommagés et/ou détruits par les forces militaires serbes bosniaques et autres. Dans de nombreux cas, ces édifices du culte ont également été endommagés et/ou détruits en l'absence d'action militaire ou après que celle-ci ait cessé. Ces édifices du culte comprennent, sans y être limités, ceux mentionnés au paragraphe 37 du présent acte d'accusation. Les forces militaires et policières serbes bosniaques n'ont pas pris les mesures raisonnables et nécessaires pour assurer la protection de ces édifices du culte.

31. Les évènements décrits ci-dessus étaient dirigés contre des civils musulmans bosniaques et croates bosniaques. Individuellement et collectivement, ces actions réalisées par l'administration serbe bosniaque ou pour son compte ont eu lieu sur une si grande échelle et de façon tellement systématique qu'elles ont détruit, traumatisé ou déshumanisé la plupart des aspects de la vie des collectivités musulmanes bosniaques et croates bosniaques dans les régions tombées sous le contrôle de l'administration des Serbes de Bosnie.

32. **RADOVAN KARADŽIĆ** et **RATKO MLADIĆ** savaient ou avaient des raisons de savoir que des subordonnés, dans les camps d'internement, s'apprêtaient à tuer ou à infliger des atteintes physiques ou mentales graves à des Musulmans bosniaques et Croates bosniaques dans l'intention de les détruire, en tout ou en partie, en tant que groupe national, ethnique ou religieux, ou l'avaient fait, et n'ont pas pris les mesures nécessaires et raisonnables pour empêcher lesdits actes ou pour en punir les auteurs.

33. **RADOVAN KARADŽIĆ** et **RATKO MLADIĆ** ont, individuellement et de concert avec d'autres, planifié, incité à commettre, ordonné ou de toute autre manière aidé et encouragé à planifier, préparer ou exécuter des persécutions pour des raisons politiques et religieuses, ou savaient ou avaient des raisons de savoir que des subordonnés s'apprêtaient à commettre ces persécutions, ou l'avaient fait, et n'ont pas pris les mesures nécessaires et raisonnables pour empêcher que ces actes ne soient commis ou en punir leurs auteurs.

Par ces actes et omissions, RADOVAN KARADŽIĆ et RATKO MLADIĆ ont commis :

Chef d'accusation 1 : un GENOCIDE, sanctionné par les articles 4 (2) (a) (b) (c) et 7 (3) du Statut du Tribunal.

Chef d'accusation 2 : un CRIME CONTRE L'HUMANITE, sanctionné par les articles 5(h), 7(1) et 7(3) du Statut du Tribunal.

IT-95-5-I 328

Croat civilians who left their communities were permitted to take with them limited amounts of personal property and money, but even that property was stolen from them at Bosnian Serb checkpoints or at other locations.

E. In many instances during and after the Bosnian Serb military take-over of towns and villages, Bosnian Serb military, police and their agents, entered the homes of non-Serb civilians and plundered the personal property of non-Serb civilians.

DESTRUCTION OF PROPERTY

29. Persecution throughout the occupied territory by Bosnian Serb military, police and their agents, or third parties with their acquiescence, involved the systematic destruction of Bosnian Muslim and Bosnian Croat homes and businesses. These homes and businesses were singled out and systematically destroyed in areas where hostilities had ceased or had not taken place. The purpose of this unlawful destruction was to ensure that the inhabitants could not and would not return to their homes and communities. The cities, villages and towns, or Bosnian Muslim and Bosnian Croat portions thereof, where extensive destruction of property occurred include, but are not limited to the following:

Town/Village	Municipality	Approximate dates of destruction
Grebnice	Bosanski Šamac	19-22 April 1992
Hrvatska Tisina	Bosanski Šamac	19-22 April 1992
Hasići	Bosanski Šamac	19-22 April 1992
Derventa	Derventa	4 April 1992
Vijaka	Derventa	4 April 1992
Bosanski Brod	Bosanski Brod	3 March 1992
Odžak	Odžak	July 1992
Modriča	Modriča	Late April 1992
Vidovice	Orašje	29 April and 4 May 1992
Gradačac	Gradačac	mid-1992
Piskavice	Vlasenica	22 April 1992
Gobelje	Vlasenica	28 April 1992
Turalići	Vlasenica	28 April 1992
Djile	Vlasenica	1-3 May 1992
Pomol	Vlasenica	1 May 1992

IT-95-5-I 9/337 bis

CHEFS D'ACCUSATION 3 ET 4
(INTERNEMENT ILLÉGAL DE CIVILS)

34. Dès l'ouverture des hostilités en République de Bosnie-Herzégovine, des milliers de civils musulmans bosniaques et croates bosniaques ont été illégalement détenus dans des camps d'internement. Bon nombre de ces camps ont été établis et administrés par les forces militaires et policières serbes bosniaques et leurs agents, sous la direction et le contrôle de **RADOVAN KARADŽIĆ** et **RATKO MLADIĆ**. Les conditions de vie dans ces camps étaient inhumaines, ainsi qu'il est décrit aux paragraphes 18 et 20 à 22 du présent acte d'accusation, ici intégralement incorporé. Des civils sans nombre ont fait l'objet de violences ou ont péri dans ces camps d'internement.

35. RADOVAN KARADŽIĆ et RATKO MLADIĆ ont, individuellement et de concert avec d'autres, planifié, ordonné, incité à commettre ou de toute autre manière aidé et encouragé à planifier, préparer ou exécuter la détention illégale de civils, ou savaient ou avaient des raisons de savoir que des subordonnés détenaient illégalement des civils, et ils n'ont pas pris les mesures nécessaires et raisonnables pour empêcher que de tels actes ne soient commis ou pour en punir les auteurs.

Par ces actes et omissions, RADOVAN KARADŽIĆ et RATKO MLADIĆ ont commis :

Chef d'accusation 3 : une INFRACTION GRAVE, sanctionnée par les articles 2(g) (détention illégale de civils), 7(1) et 7(3) du Statut du Tribunal.

Chef d'accusation 4 : une VIOLATION DES LOIS OU COUTUMES DE LA GUERRE, (atteintes à la dignité des personnes), sanctionnée par les articles 3, 7(1) et 7(3) du Statut du Tribunal.

CHEF D'ACCUSATION 5
(PILLONNAGE DE RASSEMBLEMENTS CIVILS)

36. Les forces militaires serbes bosniaques ont tiré sur des rassemblements civils ne présentant aucun intérêt militaire, blessant et tuant ainsi des centaines de civils, ainsi qu'il est décrit au paragraphe 24 du présent acte d'accusation, ici intégralement incorporé. **RADOVAN** KARADŽIĆ et RATKO MLADIĆ ont, individuellement et de concert avec d'autres, planifié, incité à commettre, ordonné ou de toute autre manière aidé et encouragé à planifier, préparer ou exécuter des attaques illégales contre la population civile et des civils au moyen d'armes de zone comme les mortiers, roquettes et tirs d'artillerie, ou savaient ou avaient des raisons de savoir que les forces militaires serbes bosniaques s'apprêtaient à attaquer illégalement la population civile ou des civils, ou l'avaient déjà fait, et n'ont pas pris les mesures nécessaires et raisonnables pour empêcher ce pillonnage ou pour en punir les auteurs.

Par ces actes et omissions, RADOVAN KARADŽIĆ et RATKO MLADIĆ ont commis :

Ched d'accusation 5 : une VIOLATION DES LOIS OU COUTUMES DE LA GUERRE, (attaques délibérées contre la population civile et contre des civils), sanctionnée par les articles 3, 7(1) et 7(3) du Statut du Tribunal.

IT-95-5-I 327

Gaj	Vlasenica	1 May 1992
Bešići	Vlasenica	1 May 1992
Nurići	Vlasenica	1 May 1992
Vrsinje	Vlasenica	1 May 1992
Džamdžići	Vlasenica	8 May 1992
Pivići	Vlasenica	11 May 1992
Hambarine	Prijedor	23 May 1992
Ljubija	Prijedor	23 May 1992
Kozarac	Prijedor	24 May 1992
Bišćani	Prijedor	20 July 1992
Carakovo	Prijedor	20 July 1992
Rizvanovići	Prijedor	20 July 1992
Sredice	Prijedor	20 July 1992
Žikovi	Prijedor	20 July 1992

DESTRUCTION OF SACRED SITES

30. Muslim and Catholic places of worship were systematically damaged and/or destroyed by Bosnian Serb military forces and others. In many instances, where no military action had taken place or had ceased, these sacred sites were also damaged and/or destroyed. These places of worship include, but are not limited to those mentioned in paragraph 37 of this indictment. Bosnian Serb military and police forces failed to take reasonable and necessary measures to ensure that these religious sites would be protected.

31. The events described above were directed against Bosnian Muslim and Bosnian Croat civilians. Individually and collectively, these actions taken by or on behalf of the Bosnian Serb administration, have been on such a large scale and implemented in such a systematic way that they have destroyed, traumatised or dehumanised most aspects of Bosnian Muslim and Bosnian Croat life in those areas where the Bosnian Serb administration has taken control.

32. **RADOVAN KARADŽIĆ** and **RATKO MLADIĆ** knew or had reason to know that subordinates in detention facilities were about to kill or cause serious physical or mental harm to Bosnian Muslims and Bosnian Croats with the intent to destroy them, in whole or in part, as national, ethnic or religious groups or had done so and failed to take necessary and reasonable measures to prevent such acts or to punish the perpetrators thereof.

IT-95-5-I 8/337 bis

CHEF D'ACCUSATION 6
(DESTRUCTION D'ÉDIFICES DU CULTE)

37. D'avril 1992 à la fin mai 1995, les édifices des cultes musulman et catholique romain ont fait l'objet de dommages et de destruction généralisés et systématiques sur le territoire de la République de Bosnie-Herzégovine contrôlé par les forces militaires et policières serbes bosniaques, y compris des zones épargnées par le conflit militaire. Ces édifices du culte ont été pratiquement rasés dans des régions comme celle de Banja Luka. Les édifices du culte dans cette dernière région comprennent :

EDIFICES DU CULTE MUSULMAN

Nom de la mosquée	Lieu	Date de la destruction ou des dommages
Sefer Beg	Banja Luka	09/04/93
Ferhadija	Banja Luka	07/05/93
Arnaudija	Banja Luka	07/05/93
Mosquée de Vrbanje	Banja Luka	11/05/93
Zulfikarova	Banja Luka	15/05/93
Behram-Efendija	Banja Luka	26/05/93
Mehidibeg	Banja Luka	04/06/03
Sufi Mehmed Pasa	Banja Luka	04/06/93
Hadji Begzade	Banja Luka	04/06/93
Gazanferija	Banja Luka	04/06/93
Hadji Sebenova	Banja Luka	14/06/93
Hadji Kurt	Banja Luka	14/06/93
Hadji Pervis	Banja Luka	06/09/93
Hadji Osmanija	Banja Luka	08/09/93
Hadji Omer	Banja Luka	09/09/93
Hadji Salihija	Banja Luka	09/09/93

EDIFICES DU CULTE CATHOLIQUE ROMAIN

Nom de l'église	Ville	Date de la destruction ou des dommages
St Joseph à Trno	Banja Luka	24/10/91
Eglise de paroisse	Banja Luka	00/12/91
Cath. St.Bonaventure	Banja Luka	31/12/91
Monastère St Vincent	Banja Luka	00/12/92
Eglise de village	Vujnovicii	05/05/95
Eglise de paroisse	Petricevac	06/05/95
St Antoine de Padoue et monastère franciscain	Banja Luka	07/05/95
Eglise de paroisse	Sergovac	07/05/95

IT-95-5-I 326

33. **RADOVAN KARADŽIĆ** and **RATKO MLADIĆ** individually and in concert with others planned, instigated, ordered or otherwise aided and abetted in the planning, preparation or execution of persecutions on political and religious grounds or knew or had reason to know that subordinates were about to do the same or had done so and failed to take necessary and reasonable measures to prevent such acts or to punish the perpetrators thereof.

By these acts and omissions, **RADOVAN KARADŽIĆ** and **RATKO MLADIĆ** committed:

Count 1: GENOCIDE as recognised by Articles 4(2)(a),(b),(c) and 7(3) of the Statute of the Tribunal.

Count 2: a **CRIME AGAINST HUMANITY** as recognised by Articles 5(h) and 7(1) and 7(3) of the Statute of the Tribunal.

COUNTS 3-4
(UNLAWFUL CONFINEMENT OF CIVILIANS)

34. From the outset of hostilities in the Republic of Bosnia and Herzegovina, thousands of Bosnian Muslim and Bosnian Croat civilians were unlawfully interned in detention facilities. Many of these facilities were established and operated by the Bosnian Serb military, police and their agents under the direction and control of **RADOVAN KARADŽIĆ** and **RATKO MLADIĆ**. As described in paragraphs 18 and 20-22 of this indictment and incorporated in full herein, the conditions in these facilities were inhumane. Countless civilians were abused and many perished in these internment facilities.

35. **RADOVAN KARADŽIĆ** and **RATKO MLADIĆ** individually and in concert with others planned, ordered, instigated or otherwise aided and abetted in the planning and preparation or execution of the unlawful detention of civilians or knew or had reason to know that subordinates were unlawfully detaining civilians and failed to take necessary and reasonable measures to prevent such acts or to punish the perpetrators thereof.

IT-95-5-I 7/337bis

Eglise de village	Majdan	08/05/95
Eglise de paroisse	Presnace	12/05/95

38. Dans d'autres régions, l'endommagement et la destruction d'édifices du culte ont été généralisés. Ces édifices comprennent, sans y être limités : la mosquée d'Aladža (Foča); la mosquée du sultant Selim (Doboj); l'église St Pierre et St Paul, la chapelle Obri et la mosquée de Sevri-Hadji (Mostar); l'église de paroisse (Novi Seher) et la mosquée de Čaršijska (Konjic). Les forces militaires et policières serbes bosniaques ont négligé de prendre les mesures raisonnables et nécessaires pour assurer la protection de ces édifices religieux.

39. **RADOVAN KARADŽIĆ** et **RATKO MLADIĆ** ont, individuellement et de concert avec d'autres, planifié, incité à commettre, ordonné ou de toute autre manière aidé et encouragé à planifier, préparer ou exécuter la destruction d'édifices du culte, ou savaient ou avaient des raisons de savoir que des subordonnés s'apprêtaient à endommager ou à détruire ces édifices ou l'avaient déjà fait, et n'ont pas pris les mesures nécessaires et raisonnables pour empêcher que lesdits actes ne soient commis ou pour en punir les auteurs.

Par ces actes et omissions, **RADOVAN KARADŽIĆ** et **RATKO MLADIĆ** ont commis :

Chef d'accusation 6 : une **VIOLATION DES LOIS OU COUTUMES DE LA GUERRE** sanctionnée par les articles 3 (d) (destruction ou endommagement délibéré d'édifices consacrés à la religion), 7(1) et 7(3) du Statut du Tribunal.

CHEF D'ACCUSATION 7
(DESTRUCTION CONSIDERABLE DE BIENS)

40. Après la prise de Foča (8 avril 1992), Bosanski Šamac (17 avril 1992), Vlasenica (21 avril 1992), Prijedor (30 avril 1992), Brčko (30 avril 1992) et d'autres municipalités en République de Bosnie-Herzégovine, les forces militaires et policières serbes bosniaques et d'autres éléments qu'elles contrôlaient, sous la direction et le contrôle de **RADOVAN KARADŽIĆ** et **RATKO MLADIĆ**, ont systématiquement détruit, ou permis à d'autres de détruire, sans que le justifient les exigences militaires, des établissements industriels ou commerciaux et des résidences musulmans bosniaques et croates bosniaques dans les villes et villages occupés. Les régions touchées par ces destructions considérables comprennent celles décrites au paragraphe 29 du présent acte d'accusation, ici intégralement incorporé.

41. **RADOVAN KARADŽIĆ** et **RATKO MLADIĆ**, individuellement et de concert avec d'autres, ont planifié, incité à commettre, ordonné ou de toute autre manière aidé et encouragé à planifier, préparer ou exécuter la destruction sur une grande échelle, de façon illicite et arbitraire des biens de Musulmans bosniaques ou de Croates bosniaques, non justifiée par des nécessités militaires, ou savaient ou avaient des raisons de savoir que des subordonnés s'apprêtaient à commettre ou autorisaient d'autres à commettre la destruction de biens de civils musulmans bosniaques et croates bosniaques, ou l'avaient fait, et n'ont pas pris les mesures nécessaires et raisonnables pour empêcher que ces destructions ne soient commises ou en punir les auteurs.

IT-95-5-I 325

By these acts and omissions, **RADOVAN KARADŽIĆ** and **RATKO MLADIĆ** committed:

Count 3: a **GRAVE BREACH** as recognised by Articles 2(g) (unlawful confinement of civilians), 7(1) and 7(3) of the Statute of the Tribunal.

Count 4: a **VIOLATION OF THE LAWS OR CUSTOMS OF WAR** (outrages upon personal dignity) as recognised by Articles 3, 7(1) and 7(3) of the Statute of the Tribunal.

COUNT 5
(SHELLING OF CIVILIAN GATHERINGS)

36. As described in paragraph 26 of this indictment, which is incorporated in full herein, Bosnian Serb military forces fired upon civilian gatherings that were of no military significance, thereby causing injury and death to hundreds of civilians. **RADOVAN KARADŽIĆ** and **RATKO MLADIĆ**, individually and in concert with others planned, instigated, ordered or otherwise aided and abetted in the planning, preparation or execution of unlawful attacks against the civilian population and individual civilians with area fire weapons such as mortars, rockets and artillery or knew or had reason to know that the Bosnian Serb military forces were about to unlawfully attack the civilian population and individual civilians, or had already done so, and failed to take the necessary and reasonable steps to prevent such shelling or to punish the perpetrators thereof.

By these acts and omissions, **RADOVAN KARADŽIĆ** and **RATKO MLADIĆ** committed:

Count 5: a **VIOLATION OF THE LAWS OR CUSTOMS OF WAR** (deliberate attack on the civilian population and individual civilians) as recognised by Articles 3, 7(1) and 7(3) of the Statute of the Tribunal.

COUNT 6
(DESTRUCTION OF SACRED SITES)

37. Since April 1992 to the end of May 1995, in territory of the Republic of Bosnia and Herzegovina controlled by the Bosnian Serb military and

IT-95-5-I 6/337bis

Par ces actes et omissions, **RADOVAN KARADŽIĆ** et **RATKO MLADIĆ** ont commis :

Chef d'accusation 7 : une **INFRACTION GRAVE**, sanctionnée par les articles 2(d) (destruction de biens), 7(1) et 7(3) du Statut du Tribunal.

CHEFS D'ACCUSATION 8 ET 9
(APPROPRIATION ET PILLAGE DE BIENS)

42. Ainsi qu'il est décrit aux paragraphes 25 et 26 du présent acte d'accusation, ici intégralement incorporé, le personnel militaire et policier serbe bosniaque et d'autres agents de l'administration serbe bosniaque, sous la direction et le contrôle de **RADOVAN KARADŽIĆ** et **RATKO MALADIC**, se sont appropriés et ont pillé systématiquement les biens meubles et immeubles de civils musulmans bosniaques et croates bosniaques.

43. **RADOVAN KARADŽIĆ** et **RATKO MLADIĆ** ont, individuellement et de concert avec d'autres, planifié, incité à commettre, ordonné, ou de toute autre manière aidé et encouragé à planifier, préparer ou exécuter l'appropriation sur une grande échelle, illicite et arbitraire de biens meubles et immeubles appartenant à des civils musulmans bosniaques ou croates bosniaques, ou savaient ou avaient des raisons de savoir que des subordonnés s'apprêtaient à s'approprier les biens meubles et immeubles de civils musulmans bosniaques et croates bosniaques, ou l'avaient fait, et n'ont pas pris les mesures nécessaires et raisonnables pour empêcher cette appropriation ou en punir les auteurs.

Par ces actes et omissions, **RADOVAN KARADŽIĆ** et **RATKO MLADIĆ** ont commis :

Chef d'accusation 8 : une **INFRACTION GRAVE**, sanctionnée par les articles 2(d) (appropriation de biens), 7(1) et 7(3) du Statut du Tribunal.

Chef d'accusation 9 : une **VIOLATION DES LOIS OU COUTUMES DE LA GUERRE**, sanctionnée par les articles 3(e) (pillage de biens publics ou privés), 7(1) et 7(3) du Statut du Tribunal.

PARTIE II

CHEFS D'ACCUSATION 10 à 12
(TIRS ISOLES SUR SARAJEVO)

44. La ville de Sarajevo est assiégée depuis le 5 avril 1992 par des forces de l'armée serbe bosniaque. Durant toute la durée de ce siège, on a observé une campagne systématique de ciblage délibéré de civils par des tireurs isolés des forces militaires serbes bosniaques ou de leurs agents. La campagne de tirs isolés a terrorisé la population de Sarajevo et s'est traduite par un nombre considérable de victimes civiles, tuées ou blessées, y compris des femmes, enfants et personnes âgées. Entre le 5 mai 1992 et le 31 mai 1995, des tireurs isolés ont systématiquement, illégalement et délibéremment tué et blessé des civils dans la région de Sarajevo, y compris, sans y être limité, les personnes suivantes :

IT-95-5-I 324

police, including areas where no military conflict was ongoing, there has been widespread and systematic damage to and destruction of Muslim and Roman Catholic sacred sites. In areas such as Banja Luka, the near total obliteration of these religious sites has occurred. The sites in the Banja Luka area include the following:

MUSLIM SACRED SITES

Name of Mosque	Location	Date of Destruction or Damage
Sefer-Beg Mosque	Banja Luka	09.04.93
Ferhadija Mosque	Banja Luka	07.05.93
Arnaudija Mosque	Banja Luka	07.05.93
Mosque in Vrbanje	Banja Luka	11.05.93
Zulfikarova Mosque	Banja Luka	15.05.93
Behram-Efendija Mosque	Banja Luka	26.05.93
Mehidibeg Mosque	Banja Luka	04.06.93
Sufi Mehmed-Paša Mosque	Banja Luka	04.06.93
Hadži-Begzade Mosque	Banja Luka	04.06.93
Gazanferija Mosque	Banja Luka	04.06.93
Hadži-Sebenova Mosque	Banja Luka	14.06.93
Hadži-Kurt Mosque	Banja Luka	14.06.93
Hadži-Pervis Mosque	Banja Luka	06.09.93
Hadži-Osmanija Mosque	Banja Luka	08.09.93
Hadži-Omer Mosque	Banja Luka	09.09.93
Hadži-Salihija Mosque	Banja Luka	09.09.93

ROMAN CATHOLIC SACRED SITES

Name of Church	City	Date of Destruction or Damage
Church of St. Joseph at Trno	Banja Luka	24.10.91
Parish Church	Banja Luka	00.12.91
St. Bonaventura Cathedral	Banja Luka	31.12.91
St. Vincent Monastery	Banja Luka	00.12.92
Village Church	Vujnovići	05.05.95

IT-95-5-I 5/337 bis

TUES

Enfants

Elma Jakupović, 2 ans, Jukićeva Street, No. 17, 20 juillet 1993
Elvedina Čolić, 4 ans, Kobilja Glava, 8 août 1993
Adnan Kasapović, 16 ans, D.A. Kuna Street, 24 octobre 1994
Nermina Omerović, 11 ans, Djure Daničića Street, 8 novembre 1994

Femmes

Almasa Konjhodžić, 56 ans, croisement de Kranjčevića et Brodska Streets, 27 juin 1993
Sevda Kustura, 50 ans, Špicasta Stijena, 5 août 1993
Sada Pohara, 19 ans, Žarka Zgonjanina Street, No. 13, 30 août 1993
Saliha Čomaga, 38 ans, Mujkića Brdo, Ugorsko, 8 septembre 1993
Edina Trto, 25 ans, Ivana Krndelja Street, 26 septembre 1993
Hatema Mukanović, 38 ans, Obala 27 July 89 Street, 11 janvier 1994
Radmila Plainović, 51 ans, Vojvode Putnika Street, 7 février 1994
Lejla Bajramović, 24 ans, B Boris Kidrič Street, No. 3, 8 décembre 1994

Personnes âgées

Hajrija Dizdarević, 66 ans, Ivo Kranjčević Street, 17 juillet 1993
Marko Stupar, 64 ans, Zmaja od Bosne No. 64 Street, 12 janvier 1994
Fadil Zuko, 63 ans, Stara Cesta Street, bb, 2 février 1994
Dragomir Ćulibrk, 61 ans, Prvomajska BB, 16 juin 1994

Hommes

Adnan Mesihović, 34 ans, Hasana Brkića Street, 3 septembre 1993
Junuz Čampara, 59 ans, Milutin Durasković Street, 6 septembre 1993
Augustin Vučić, 57 ans, Ante Babića Street, 13 mars 1994
Jasmin Podžo, 23 ans, Mala Berkuša Street 10, 14 mars 1995

BLESSES

Enfants

Garçon, 2 ans, Stara Cesta Street, 26 juin 1993
Garçon, 12 ans, piscine de Kupališta, 5 août 1993
Fille, 9 ans, Kobilja Glava, 8 août 1993
Garçon, 14 ans, Džemal Bijedić Street, 3 septembre 1993
Fille, 8 ans, Ivana Krndelja Street, 3 septembre 1993
Garçon, 15 ans, à X transversale Street bb, 4 octobre 1993
Garçon, 13 ans, Donji Hotonj II Street, 10 novembre 1993
Garçon, 12 ans, Petra Drapšina Street, 28 novembre 1993

IT-95-5-I 323

Name of Church	City	Date of Destruction or Damage
Parish Church	Petričevac	06.05.95
St. Anthony of Padua Church and Franciscan Monastery	Banja Luka	07.05.95
Parish Church	Sergovac	07.05.95
Village Church	Majdan	08.05.95
Parish Church	Presnace	12.05.95

38. In other areas, damage and destruction to places of worship has been widespread These sites include, but are not limited to the Aladža Mosque (Foča); the Sultan Selim Mosque (Doboj); the Church of St. Peter and St. Paul, the Obri Chapel and the Sevri-Hadži Mosque (Mostar); the parish church (Novi Šeher) and the Čaršijska Mosque (Konjic). Bosnian Serb military and police forces failed to take reasonable and necessary measures to ensure that these religious sites were protected.

39. **RADOVAN KARADŽIĆ** and **RATKO MLADIĆ**, individually and in concert with others planned, instigated, ordered or otherwise aided and abetted in the planning, preparation or execution of the destruction of sacred sites or knew or had reason to know that subordinates were about to damage or destroy these sites or had done so and failed to take necessary and reasonable measures to prevent them from doing so or to punish the perpetrators thereof.

By these acts and omissions, **RADOVAN KARADŽIĆ** and **RATKO MLADIĆ** committed:

Count 6: a **VIOLATION OF THE LAWS OR CUSTOMS OF WAR** (destruction or wilful damage to institutions dedicated to religion) as recognised by Articles 3(d), 7(1) and 7(3) of the Statute of the Tribunal.

IT-95-5-I 4/337bis

Garçon, 17 ans, Džemala Bijedića Street, 10 janvier 1994
Garçon, 5 ans, Zmaja od Bosne Street, 19 juin 1994
Fille, 16 ans, Senada Mandića-Dende Street, 26 juin 1994
Garçon, 13 ans, Miljenka Cvitkovića Street, 22 juillet 1994
Garçon, 7 ans, Zmaja od Bosne Street, 18 novembre 1994
Fille, 13 ans, croisement de Rogina et Sedrenik Streets, 22 novembre 1994
Garçon, 14 ans, Sedrenik Street, 6 mars 1995

Femmes

Femme, 20 ans, Hotonj, 5 août 1993
Femme, 52 ans, Franca Rozmana Street, 6 août 1993
Femme, 66 ans, Ivo Kranjcevic Street, 17 juillet 1993
Femme, 55 ans, Španskih Boraca Street, 30 août 1993
Femme, 35 ans, Ivana Krndelja Street, 3 septembre 1993
Femme, 32 ans, Nikola Demonja/Grada Bakua Street, 6 janvier 1994
Femme, 46 ans, Olimpijska Street, No. 15, 18 janvier 1994
Femme, 42 ans, 21 Maj Street, 9 mai 1994
Femme, 50 ans et femme, 62 ans, Nikole Demonje Street, 25 mai 1994
Femme, 45 ans, Mojmilo-Dobrinja Road, 13 juin 1994
Femme, 46 ans, Zaim Imamović Street, No. 15, 20 juillet 1994
Femme, 54 ans, Baruthana Street, 8 novembre 1994
Femme, 28 ans, Zmaja od Bosne Street, 9 novembre 1994
Femme, 28 ans, Zmaja od Bosne Street, 18 novembre 1994
Femme, 24 ans, Franca Lehara Street, No. 3, 8 décembre 1994
Femme, 49 ans, Sedrenik Street, 10 décembre 1994

Personnes âgées

Femme, 71 ans, marché "Ciglane", 17 septembre 1993
Femme, 72 ans, Nikole Demonje Street, 2 octobre 1993
Femme, 60 ans, Lovćenska Street, 7 décembre 1993
Homme, 63 ans, St Anto Babić, 13 mars 1994
Homme, 62 ans, Omladinskih Rradnih Brigada Street, 16 juin 1994
Homme, 61 ans, Prvomajska BB, 16 juin 1994
Homme, 67 ans, Senad Mandić Denda Street, 17 juillet 1994
Homme, 63 ans, Sedrenik Street, 11 décembre 1994
Homme, 62 ans, Sedrenik Street, 13 décembre 1994
Femme, 73 ans, croisement de Zmaja od Bosne et Muzejska Streets, 18 décembre 1994

Hommes

Homme, 36 ans, Trg of Zavnobih, 1er février 1993
Homme, 52 ans, Kobilja Glava, 25 juin 1993
Homme, 29 ans, Stara Cesta Street, 7 octobre 1993
Homme, 50 ans, et homme, 56 ans, Braće Ribara Street, 2 novembre 1993
Homme, 36 ans, Stara Cesta Street, 14 décembre 1993

IT-95-5-I 322

COUNT 7
(EXTENSIVE DESTRUCTION OF PROPERTY)

40. After the take-over of Foča (8 April 1992), Bosanski Šamac (17 April 1992), Vlasenica (21 April 1992), Prijedor (30 April 1992), Brčko (30 April 1992) and other municipalities in the Republic of Bosnia and Herzegovina, Bosnian Serb military and police forces and other elements over whom they had control, under the direction and control of **RADOVAN KARADŽIĆ** and **RATKO MLADIĆ**, systematically destroyed, or permitted others to destroy, for no justifiable military reasons, Bosnian Muslim and Bosnian Croat businesses and residences in occupied cities and villages. The areas where extensive destruction occurred include those areas described in paragraph 29 of this indictment, which is incorporated in full herein.

41. **RADOVAN KARADŽIĆ** and **RATKO MLADIĆ**, individually and in concert with others planned, instigated, ordered or otherwise aided and abetted in the planning, preparation or execution of the extensive, wanton and unlawful destruction of Bosnian Muslim and Bosnian Croat property, not justified by military necessity or knew or had reason to know that subordinates were about to destroy or permit others to destroy the property of Bosnian Muslim or Bosnian Croat civilians or had done so and failed to take necessary and reasonable measures to prevent this destruction or to punish the perpetrators thereof.

By these acts and omissions, **RADOVAN KARADŽIĆ** and **RATKO MLADIĆ** committed:

Count 7: a **GRAVE BREACH** as recognised by Articles 2(d) (destruction of property), 7(1) and 7(3) of the Statute of the Tribunal.

COUNTS 8-9
(APPROPRIATION AND PLUNDER OF PROPERTY)

42. As described in paragraphs 27-28 of this indictment, which are incorporated in full herein, Bosnian Serb military and police personnel and other agents of the Bosnian Serb administration, under the direction and control of **RADOVAN KARADŽIĆ** and **RATKO MLADIĆ**, systematically appropriated and looted the real and personal property of Bosnian Muslim and Bosnian Croat civilians.

IT-95-5-I 3/337bis

Homme, 27 ans, Zmaja od Bosne Street, 19 juin 1994
Homme, 20 ans, homme, 27 ans, homme, 39 ans et homme, 34 ans à Zmaja od Bosne Street, 9 novembre 1994
Homme, 29 ans, Sedrenik Street, 8 décembre 1994
Homme, 46 ans et homme, 33 ans, croisement de Franje Račkog et Maršala Tita Streets, 3 mars 1995
Homme, 52 ans, Sedrenik Street, 6 mars 1995

45. **RADOVAN KARADŽIĆ** et **RATKO MLADIĆ** ont, individuellement et de concert avec d'autres, planifié, incité à commettre, ordonné ou de toute autre manière aidé et encouragé à planifier, préparer ou exécuter des tirs isolés contre des civils, ou savaient ou avaient des raisons de savoir que des subordonnés tiraient sur des civils, et n'ont pas pris les mesures nécessaires et raisonnables pour empêcher ces tirs isolés ou en punir les auteurs.

S'agissant des attaques délibérées par tirs isolés contre la population civile et contre des civils, qui ont entraîné la mort et les blessures desdits civils, ainsi que des actes et omissions qui s'y rapportent, **RADOVAN KARADŽIĆ** et **RATKO MLADIĆ** ont commis :

Chef d'accusation 10 : une **VIOLATION DES LOIS OU COUTUMES DE LA GUERRE**, (attaque délibérée contre la population civile et contre des civils), sanctionnée par les articles 3, 7(1) et 7(3) du Statut du Tribunal.

S'agissant du meurtre par tirs isolés de ces civils, notamment, et des actes et omissions qui s'y rapportent, **RADOVAN KARADŽIĆ** et **RATKO MLADIĆ** ont commis :

Chef d'accusation 11 : un **CRIME CONTRE L'HUMANITE** sanctionné par les articles 5(a) (meurtre), 7(1) et 7(3) du Statut du Tribunal.

S'agissant des blessures infligées à ces civils par des tirs isolés, notamment, et des actes et omissions qui s'y rapportent, **RADOVAN KARADŽIĆ** et **RATKO MLADIĆ** ont commis :

Chef d'accusation 12 : un **CRIME CONTRE L'HUMANITE** sanctionné par les articles 5(i) (actes inhumains), 7(1) et 7(3) du Statut du Tribunal.

PARTIE III

CHEFS D'ACCUSATION 13 À 16
(OTAGES/BOUCLIERS HUMAINS)

46. Entre le 26 mai et le 2 juin 1995, du personnel militaire serbe bosniaque, sous la direction et le contrôle de **RADOVAN KARADŽIĆ** et **RATKO MLADIĆ**, a saisi 284 membres des forces de maintien de la paix des Nations Unies à Pale, Sarajevo, Gorazde et autres endroits et les ont pris en otages en vue d'éviter de nouvelles interventions aériennes par les forces de l'Organisation du Traité de l'Atlantique Nord (OTAN). Le personnel militaire serbe bosniaque a détenu les membres des forces de maintien de la paix des Nations Unies durant toute leur captivité en recourant à la force ou en menaçant d'y recourir. Dans certains cas, des violences ont été infligées à ces otages. Durant et à l'issue de négociations prolongées avec les dirigeants

43. **RADOVAN KARADŽIĆ** and **RATKO MLADIĆ**, individually and in concert with others planned, instigated, ordered or otherwise aided and abetted in the planning, preparation or execution of the extensive, wanton and unlawful appropriation of real and personal property owned by Bosnian Muslim and Bosnian Croat civilians or knew or had reason to know that subordinates were about to appropriate real and personal property of Bosnian Muslim and Bosnian Croat civilians or had done so and failed to take necessary and reasonable measures to prevent this appropriation or to punish the perpetrators thereof.

By these acts and omissions, **RADOVAN KARADŽIĆ** and **RATKO MLADIĆ** committed:

Count 8: a **GRAVE BREACH** as recognised by Articles 2(d) (appropriation of property), 7(1) and 7(3) of the Statute of the Tribunal.

Count 9: a **VIOLATION OF THE LAWS OR CUSTOMS OF WAR** (plunder of public or private property) as recognised by Articles 3(e), 7(1) and 7(3) of the Statute of the Tribunal.

PART II

COUNTS 10-12
(SARAJEVO SNIPING)

44. Since 5 April 1992, the City of Sarajevo has been besieged by forces of the Bosnian Serb army. Throughout this siege, there has been a systematic campaign of deliberate targeting of civilians by snipers of the Bosnian Serb military and their agents. The sniping campaign has terrorised the civilian population of Sarajevo and has resulted in a substantial number of civilian casualties, killed and wounded, including women, children and elderly. Between 5 May 1992 and 31 May 1995, snipers have systematically, unlawfully and wilfully killed and wounded civilians in the area of Sarajevo, including but not limited to the following individuals:

serbes bosniaques, les otages des Nations Unies ont été relâchés par étapes entre le 3 et le 19 juin 1995.

47. Après avoir saisi des membres des forces de maintien de la paix des Nations Unies dans la région de Pale, le personnel militaire serbe bosniaque, sous la direction et le contrôle de **RADOVAN KARADŽIĆ** et **RATKO MLADIĆ**, a immédiatement sélectionné un certain nombre d'otages pour servir de "boucliers humains" y compris, sans y être limités, Capt. Patrick A. Rechner (Canada), Capt. Oldrich Zidlik (République tchéque), Capt. Teversky (russie), Maj. Abdul Razak Bello (Nigéria), Capt. Ahmad Manzoor (Pakistan) et Maj. Gunnar Westlund (Suède). Vers le 26 mai 1995 jusqu'au 27 mai 1995, le personnel militaire serbe bosniaque a physiquement attaché ou autrement détenu les membres des forces de maintien de la paix des Nations Unies contre leur volonté à des cibles potentielles des interventions aériennes de l'OTAN, y compris le dépôt de munitions de Jahorinski Potok, le site de radars de Jahorina et un centre de communications voisin, afin de protéger ces sites contre de nouvelles interventions aériennes de l'OTAN. Des délégations militaires et politiques serbes bosniaques de haut niveau ont inspecté et photographié les otages des Nations Unies qui étaient attachés par des menottes aux dépôts de munition de Jahorinski Potok.

48. **RADOVAN KARADŽIĆ** et **RATKO MLADIĆ**, individuellement et de concert avec d'autres, ont planifié, incité à commettre, ordonné ou de toute autre manière aidé et encouragé à planifier, préparer ou exécuter la prise de civils, c'est-à-dire les membres des forces de maintien de la paix des Nations Unies, en tant qu'otages et, en outre, leur utilisation comme "boucliers humains", et savaient ou avaient des raisons de savoir que des subordonnés s'apprêtaient à prendre des membres des forces de maintien de la paix des Nations Unies en otages et à s'en servir comme "boucliers humains", ou l'avaient fait, et n'ont pas pris les mesures nécessaires et raisonnables pour les en empêcher ou pour en punir les auteurs.

S'agissant des membres des forces de maintien de la paix des Nations Unies pris et détenus comme otages entre le 26 mai et le 19 juin 1995, **RADOVAN KARADŽIĆ** et **RATKO MLADIĆ**, par leurs actes et omissions, ont commis :

Chef d'accusation 13 : une **INFRACTION GRAVE** sanctionnée par les articles 2(h) (prise de civils en otages), 7(1) et 7(3) du Statut du Tribunal.

Chef d'accusation 14 : une **VIOLATION DES LOIS OU COUTUMES DE LA GUERRE** (prises d'otages), sanctionnée par les articles 3, 7(1) et 7(3) du Statut du Tribunal.

S'agissant de l'utilisation des membres des forces de maintien de la paix des Nations Unies en tant que "boucliers humains" les 26 et 27 mai 1995, **RADOVAN KARADŽIĆ** et **RATKO MLADIĆ**, par leurs actes et omissions, ont commis :

Chef d'accusation 15 : une **INFRACTION GRAVE** sanctionnée par les articles 2(b) (traitements inhumains), 7(1) et 7(3) du Statut du Tribunal.

KILLED

Children

Elma Jakupović, age 2, at Jukićeva Street, No 17, on 20 July 1993
Elvedina Čolić, age 4, at Kobilja Glava on 8 August 1993
Adnan Kasapović, age 16, at Dj.A.Kuna Street on 24 October 1994
Nermina Omerović, age 11, at Djure Daničića Street on 8 November 1994

Women

Almasa Konjhodžić, age 56, at the intersection of Kranjčevića and Brodska Streets on 27 June 1993
Sevda Kustura, age 50, at Špicasta Stijena on 5 August 1993
Sada Pohara, age 19, at Žarka Zgonjanina Street, No 13, on 30 August 1993
Saliha Čomaga, age 38, at Mujkića Brdo, Ugorsko, on 8 September 1993
Edina Trto, age 25, at Ivana Krndelja Street on 26 September 1993
Hatema Mukanović, age 38, at Obala 27 July 89 Street on 11 January 1994
Radmila Plainović, age 51, at Vojvode Putnika Street on 7 February 1994
Lejla Bajramović, age 24, at B. Boris Kidrič Street, No 3, on 8 December 1994

Elderly

Hajrija Dizdarević, age 66, at Ivo Kranjčević Street 11 on 17 July 1993
Marko Stupar, age 64, at Zmaja od Bosne No 64 Street on 12 January 1994
Fadil Zuko, age 63, at Stara Cesta Street, bb on 2 February 1994
Dragomir Ćulibrk, aged 61, at Prvomajska BB on 16 June 1994

Men

Adnan Mesihović, age 34, at Hasana Brkića Street on 3 September 1993
Junuz Čampara, age 59, at Milutin Djurašković Street on 6 September 1993
Augustin Vučić, age 57, at Ante Babića Street on 13th March 1994
Jasmin Podžo, age 23, at Mala Berkuša Street 10 on 4 March 1995

IT-95-5-I 1/337bis

Chef d'accusation 16 : une **VIOLATION DES LOIS OU COUTUMES DE LA GUERRE** (traitement cruel) sanctionnée par les articles 3, 7(1) et 7(3) du Statut du Tribunal.

juillet 1995

Richard J. Goldstone
Procureur

IT-95-5-I 319

WOUNDED

Children

Boy, age 2, at Stara Cesta Street on 26 June 1993
Boy, age 12, at Kupališta swimming pool on 5 August 1993
Girl, age 9, at Kobilja Glava on 8 August 1993
Boy, age 14, at Džemal Bijedić Street on 3 September 1993
Girl, age 8, at Ivana Krndelja Street on 3 September 1993
Boy, age 15, at X transverzale Street bb on 4 October 1993
Boy, age 13, at Donji Hotonj II Street on 10 November 1993
Boy, age 12, at Petra Drapšina Street on 28 November 1993
Boy, age 17, at Džemala Bijedića Street on 10 January 1994
Boy, age 5, at Zmaja od Bosne Street on 19 June 1994
Girl, age 16, at Senada Mandića-Dende Street on 26 June 1994
Boy, age 13, at Miljenka Cvitkovića Street on 22 July 1994
Boy, age 7, at Zmaja od Bosne Street on 18 November 1994
Girl, age 13, at the cross-roads of Rogina and Sedrenik Streets on 22 November 1994
Boy, age 14, at Sedrenik Street on 6 March 1995

Women

Female, age 20, at Hotonj on 5 August 1993
Female, age 52, at Franca Rozmana Street on 6 August 1993
Female, age 55, at Španskih Boraca Street on 30 August 1993
Female, age 35, at Ivana Krndelja Street on 3 September 1993
Female, age 32, at Nikola Demonja/ Grada Bakua Street area on 6 January 1994
Female, age 46, at Olimpijska Street, No 15, on 18 January 1994
Female, age 42, at 21 Maj Street on 9 May 1994
Female, age 50, and female, age 62, at Nikole Demonje Street on 25 May 1994
Female, age 45, at Mojmilo- Dobrinja Road on 13 June 1994
Female, age 46, at Zaim Imamović Street, No 15 on 20 July 1994
Female, age 54, at Baruthana Street on 8 November 1994
Female, age 28, at Zmaja od Bosne Street on 9 November 1994
Female, age 28, at Zmaja od Bosne Street on 18 November 1994
Female, age 24, at Franca Lehara Street, No 3 on 8 December 1994
Female, age 49, at Sedrenik Street on 10 December 1994

IT-95-5-I 318

Elderly

Female, age 71, at "Ciglane" Market on 17 September 1993
Female, age 72, at Nikole Demonje Street on 2 October 1993
Female, age 60, at Lovćenska Street on 7 December 1993
Male, age 63, at St Anto Babić on 13 March 1994
Male, age 62, at Omladinskih Radnih Brigada Street on 16 June 1994
Male, age 61, at Prvomajska BB on 16 June 1994
Male, age 67, at Senad Mandić Denda Street, on 17 July 1994
Male, age 63, at Sedrenik Street on 11 December 1994
Male, age 62, at Sedrenik Street on 13 December 1994
Female, age 73, at the intersection of Zmaja od Bosne and Muzejska Streets on 18 December 1994

Men

Male, age 36, at Trg of Zavnobih on 1 February 1993
Male, age 52, at Kobilja Glava on 25 June 1993
Male, age 29, at Stara Cesta Street on 7 October 1993
Male, age 50, and male, age 56, at Braće Ribara Street on 2 November 1993
Male, age 36, at Stara Cesta Street on 14 December 1993
Male, age 27, at Zmaja od Bosne Street on 19 June 1994
Male, age 20, male, age 27, male, age 39, and male, age 34, at Zmaja od Bosne Street on 9 November 1994
Male, age 29, at Sedrenik Street on 8 December 1994
Male, age 46, and male, age 33, at intersection of Franje Račkog and Maršala Tita Streets on 3 March 1995
Male, age 52, at Sedrenik Street on 6 March 1995

45. **RADOVAN KARADŽIĆ** and **RATKO MLADIĆ** individually and in concert with others planned, ordered, instigated or otherwise aided and abetted in the planning, preparation or execution of the sniping of civilians or knew or had reason to know that subordinates were sniping civilians and failed to take necessary and reasonable measures to prevent such acts or to punish the perpetrators thereof.

As to the deliberate attacks by sniper fire against the civilian population and individual civilians, which resulted in death and injury to said civilians, and acts and omissions related thereto, **RADOVAN KARADŽIĆ** and **RATKO MLADIĆ** committed:

IT-95-5-I 317

Count 10: a **VIOLATION OF THE LAWS OR CUSTOMS OF WAR** (deliberate attack on the civilian population and individual civilians) as recognised by Articles 3, 7(1) and 7(3) of the Statute of the Tribunal.

As to the killing by sniper fire of these civilians, among others, and acts and omissions related thereto, **RADOVAN KARADŽIĆ** and **RATKO MLADIĆ** committed:

Count 11: a **CRIME AGAINST HUMANITY** as recognised by Articles 5(a) (murder), 7(1) and 7(3) of the Statute of the Tribunal.

As to the wounding by sniper fire of these civilians, among others, and acts and omissions related thereto, **RADOVAN KARADŽIĆ** and **RATKO MLADIĆ** committed:

Count 12: a **CRIME AGAINST HUMANITY** as recognised by Articles 5(i) (inhumane acts), 7(1) and 7(3) of the Statute of the Tribunal.

PART III

COUNTS 13-16 (HOSTAGES/HUMAN SHIELDS)

46. Between 26 May 1995 and 2 June 1995, Bosnian Serb military personnel, under the direction and control of **RADOVAN KARADŽIĆ** and **RATKO MLADIĆ**, seized 284 UN peacekeepers in Pale, Sarajevo, Goražde and other locations and held them hostage in order to prevent further North Atlantic Treaty Organisation (NATO) airstrikes. Bosnian Serb military personnel held the UN peacekeepers throughout their captivity by force or by the threat of force. In some instances, the UN hostages were assaulted. During and after protracted negotiations with Bosnian Serb leaders, the UN hostages were released in stages between 3 June 1995 and 19 June 1995.

47. After seizing UN peacekeepers in the Pale area, Bosnian Serb military personnel, under the direction and control of **RADOVAN**

KARADŽIĆ and **RATKO MLADIĆ**, immediately selected certain UN hostages to use as "human shields," including but not limited to Capt. Patrick A. Rechner (Canada), Capt. Oldrich Zidlik (Czech Republic) Captain Teterevsky (Russia), Maj. Abdul Razak Bello (Nigeria), Capt. Ahmad Manzoor (Pakistan) and Maj. Gunnar Westlund (Sweden). From on or about 26 May 1995 through 27 May 1995, Bosnian Serb military personnel physically secured or otherwise held the UN peacekeepers against their will at potential NATO air targets, including the ammunition bunkers at Jahorinski Potok, the Jahorina radar site and a nearby communications centre in order to render these locations immune from further NATO airstrikes. High level Bosnian Serb political and military delegations inspected and photographed the UN hostages who were handcuffed at the ammunition bunkers at Jahorinski Potok.

48. **RADOVAN KARADŽIĆ** and **RATKO MLADIĆ**, individually and in concert with others planned, instigated, ordered or otherwise aided and abetted in the planning, preparation or execution of the taking of civilians, that is UN peacekeepers, as hostages and, additionally, using them as "human shields" and knew or had reason to know that subordinates were about to take and hold UN peacekeepers as hostages and about to use them as "human shields" or had done so and failed to take necessary and reasonable measures to prevent them from doing so or to punish the perpetrators thereof.

In regard to UN peacekeepers seized and held hostage between 26 May 1995 and 19 June 1995, **RADOVAN KARADŽIĆ** and **RATKO MLADIĆ**, by their acts and omissions, committed:

Count 13: a **GRAVE BREACH** as recognised by Articles 2(h) (taking civilians as hostage), 7(1) and 7(3) of the Statute of the Tribunal.

Count 14: a **VIOLATION OF THE LAWS OR CUSTOMS OF WAR** (taking of hostages) as recognised by Articles 3, 7(1) and 7(3) of the Statute of the Tribunal.

In regard to the UN peacekeepers used as "human shields" on 26 and 27 May 1995, **RADOVAN KARADŽIĆ** and **RATKO MLADIĆ**, by their acts and omissions, committed:

Count 15: a **GRAVE BREACH** as recognised by Articles 2(b) (inhuman treatment), 7(1) and 7(3) of the Statute of the Tribunal.

IT-95-5-I 315

Count 16: a **VIOLATION OF THE LAWS OR CUSTOMS OF WAR** (cruel treatment) as recognised by Articles 3, 7(1) and 7(3) of the Statute of the Tribunal.

24 July 1995

Richard J. Goldstone
Prosecutor

UNITED NATIONS NATIONS UNIES

INTERNATIONAL CRIMINAL TRIBUNAL FOR THE FORMER YUGOSLAVIA
CHURCHILLPLEIN, 1. P.O. Box 13888
2501 EW THE HAGUE, NETHERLANDS
TELEPHONE: 31 70 416-5343
FAX: 31 70 416-5355
PRESS AND INFORMATION OFFICE

TRIBUNAL PÉNAL INTERNATIONAL POUR L'EX-YOUGOSLAVIE
CHURCHILLPLEIN, 1. B.P. 13888
2501 EW LA HAYE, PAYS-BAS
TÉLÉPHONE: 31 70 416-5343
FAX: 31 70 416-5355
BUREAU DE PRESSE ET D'INFORMATION

INDICTMENT
ACTE D'ACCUSATION

Karadzic & Mladic
("Srebrenica")

(16 November 1995)
(16 novembre 1995)

PRESS AND INFORMATION OFFICE
BUREAU DE PRESSE ET D'INFORMATION

TEL.: (31) 70 - 416 5343
FAX : (31) 70 - 416 5355

ICTY, The Hague,
16 November 1995

THIS PRESS FOLDER CONTAINS:

- **Press Release of 16 November 1995 - English version**
- **The Indictment / Acte d'Accusation**
- **Review of Indictment / Examen de l'Acte d'Accusation.**

*****

United Nations
Nations Unies

International
Criminal Tribunal
for the Former Yugoslavia

Tribunal
Pénal International
pour l'ex-Yougoslavie

Press Release . Communiqué de presse

(Exclusively for the use of media. Not an official record)

CC/PIO/026-E
The Hague, 16 November 1995

RADOVAN KARADZIC AND RATKO MLADIC ACCUSED OF GENOCIDE FOLLOWING THE TAKE-OVER OF SREBRENICA

Today, Thursday 16 November 1995, the International Criminal Tribunal for the former Yugoslavia indicts again:

- Radovan KARADZIC, President of the Bosnian Serb Administration in Pale, and

- Ratko MLADIC, Commander of the army of the Bosnian Serb Administration.

Both accused are alleged to be directly responsible for the atrocities committed in July 1995 against the Bosnian Muslim population of the UN designated safe area of Srebrenica (Eastern Bosnia-and-Herzegovina).

As a result of an attack on the "safe area" which was launched on 6 July 1995 and of other actions which were completed by 23 July 1995, the "*Muslim population of the enclave of Srebrenica was virtually eliminated by Bosnia Serb Military personnel (...) under the command and control of Radovan KARADZIC and Ratko MLADIC*".

After review of the evidence submitted by the Prosecutor, Judge Riad confirmed the indictment stating that:

"After Srebrenica fell to besieging Serbian forces in July, 1995, a truly terrible massacre of the Muslim population appears to have taken place. The evidence tendered by the Prosecutor describes scenes of unimaginable savagery: thousands of men executed and buried in mass graves, hundreds of men buried alive, men and women mutilated and slaughtered, children killed before their mothers' eyes, a grandfather forced to eat the liver of his own grandson. These are truly scenes from hell, written on the darkest pages of human history".

Churchillplein 1, 2517 JW The Hague . P.O. Box 13888, 2501 EW The Hague . Netherlands
Churchillplein 1, 2517 JW La Haye . B.P. 13888, 2501 EW La Haye . Pays-Bas

Press and Information Office / Bureau de presse et d'information:
Press 31 70 416-5343 Documentation 31 70 416-5285
Public information 31 70 416-5232 Fax 31 70 416-5355

THE FACTS ALLEGED IN THE INDICTMENT

Bosnian Serb military forces, under the command and control of Radovan KARADZIC and of Ratko MLADIC, attacked the UN designated safe area of Srebrenica in July of 1995. As a result of these attacks, the Bosnian Muslim inhabitants of Srebrenica sought refuge near the UN compound in Potocari or fled in a large column in the direction of Tuzla.

Between 12 and 13 July 1995, many Muslims around the UN compound in Potocari were summarily executed by Bosnian Serb military personnel and the remaining refugees, numbering in the thousands, were placed on busses by Bosnian Serb soldiers and removed from Srebrenica. Before boarding these busses, Bosnian Serb soldiers separated Muslim men from women and children and placed them on different busses for removal from the enclave.

The Bosnian Muslims who fled Srebrenica in a huge column during the night of 11 July 1995 were attacked by Bosnian Serb forces and thousands of them surrendered or were captured in the days following their flight. Hundreds of them were summarily executed by Bosnian Serb soldiers at the locations of their capture or surrender and others were transported to two locations near Karakaj.

On 14 July 1995, at the two locations near Karakaj, thousands of Bosnian Muslim men who had been separated from the refugees in Potocari or who had surrendered or been captured after fleeing Srebrenica, were transported to two large fields and summarily executed.

The killings of Muslims by Bosnian Serb soldiers, under the command and control of Radovan KARADZIC and Ratko MLADIC, in Potocari, at surrender or capture locations, and at mass execution sites near Karakaj resulted in the deaths of thousands of persons. These killings form the basis of the charges genocide, crimes against humanity and violations of the laws or customs of war against Radovan KARADZIC and Ratko MLADIC that are contained in this indictment.

THE INVESTIGATION

Today's indictment is the result of an investigation by the Office of the Prosecutor which commenced as soon as in July 1995, and which is still ongoing in respect to other suspects.

THE CRIMES AND THE CHARGES

Radovan KARADZIC and Ratko MLADIC are alleged to be individually responsible for the planning, instigation, ordering or otherwise aiding and abetting in the planning, preparation or execution of the crimes referred to in the indictment.

They are also alleged to be criminally responsible for the acts of their subordinates.

They are charged with: **Genocide, Crimes against humanity and Violations of the laws or customs of war**, for:

the summary executions of Bosnian Muslim men and women in and around the UN-Military compound of Potocari (12 and 13 July 1995),

the summary executions of Bosnian Muslim men who where *hors-de-combat* because of injuries, surrender or capture after fleeing into the woods towards Tuzla (between 13 July and 22 July 1995),

the summary executions of Bosnian Muslim men which occurred at mass execution sites in and around Karakaj (on or about 14 July 1995).

THE INDICTMENT AND THE PROCEDURE

The Prosecutor filed this indictment with the Registry on Tuesday 14 November 1995.

The indictment was reviewed by Judge Fouad Riad who confirmed it on Thursday 16 November 1995, considering "*prima facie, that the facts of the case disclose, above all, the commission of genocide*" Judge Riad signed warrants for the arrest of the accused.

The indictments and the warrants will be forwarded to the relevant authorities in Sarajevo, Pale and Belgrade.

*****

15 November 1995
IT-95-18-I 338
D338 - D325

INDICTMENT

THE INTERNATIONAL CRIMINAL TRIBUNAL
FOR THE FORMER YUGOSLAVIA

THE PROSECUTOR
OF THE TRIBUNAL

AGAINST

RADOVAN KARADŽIĆ
RATKO MLADIĆ

INDICTMENT

Richard J. Goldstone, Prosecutor of the International Criminal Tribunal for the former Yugoslavia, pursuant to his authority under Article 18 of the Statute of the International Criminal Tribunal for the former Yugoslavia ("The Statute of the Tribunal"), charges

RATKO MLADIĆ and **RADOVAN KARADŽIĆ**

with **GENOCIDE, CRIMES AGAINST HUMANITY** and **VIOLATIONS OF THE LAWS OR CUSTOMS OF WAR**, as set forth below:

"Safe Area" of Srebrenica

1. After war erupted in the Republic of Bosnia and Herzegovina, Bosnian Serb military forces occupied Bosnian Muslim villages in the eastern part of the country, resulting in an exodus of Bosnian Muslims to enclaves in Goražde, Žepa, Tuzla, and Srebrenica. All of the events referred to in this indictment took place in the Republic of Bosnia and Herzegovina.

IT-95-18-I
D 11/346 BIS - D 1/346 BIS
15 NOVEMBER 1995

11/346 BIS

TRIBUNAL PENAL INTERNATIONAL
POUR L'EX-YOUGOSLAVIE

LE PROCUREUR DU TRIBUNAL

CONTRE

RADOVAN KARADŽIĆ
RATKO MLADIĆ

ACTE D'ACCUSATION

Richard J. Goldstone, Procureur du Tribunal pénal international pour l'ex-Yougoslavie, en vertu des pouvoirs que lui confère l'article 18 du Statut du Tribunal pénal international pour l'ex-Yougoslavie ("le Statut du Tribunal"), accuse :

RATKO MLADIĆ et RADOVAN KARADŽIĆ

de **GENOCIDE, CRIMES CONTRE L'HUMANITE** et **VIOLATIONS DES LOIS OU COUTUMES DE LA GUERRE**, de la manière décrite ci-après :

"Zone de sécurité" de Srebrenica

1. Après que la guerre eut éclaté en République de Bosnie-Herzégovine, des soldats serbes bosniaques ont occupé des villages musulmans bosniaques dans la partie orientale du pays, provoquant ainsi l'exode de Musulmans bosniaques vers les enclaves de Goražde, Žepa, Tuzla et Srebrenica. Tous les événements décrits dans le présent acte d'accusation se sont produits en République de Bosnie-Herzégovine.

2. Le 16 avril 1993, le Conseil de sécurité des Nations Unies, agissant en vertu du Chapitre VII de la Charte, a adopté la résolution 819 exigeant que toutes les parties au conflit en République de Bosnie-Herzégovine considèrent Srebrenica et ses environs comme une zone de sécurité ne devant pas être la cible d'offensives armées ou de tout autre acte hostile. Le texte de la résolution 819 a été réaffirmé dans les résolutions 824 du 6 mai 1993 et 836 du 4 juin 1993.

3. Avant l'offensive des forces serbes bosniaques, telle que décrite dans le présent acte d'accusation, la population musulmane bosniaque dans la zone de sécurité de Srebrenica était estimée à 60.000 individus environ.

2. On 16 April 1993, the Security Council of the United Nations, acting pursuant to Chapter VII of its Charter, adopted resolution 819, in which it demanded that all parties to the conflict in the Republic of Bosnia and Herzegovina treat Srebrenica and its surroundings as a safe area which should be free from any armed attack or any other hostile act. Resolution 819 was reaffirmed by Resolution 824 on 6 May 1993 and by Resolution 836 on 4 June 1993.

3. Before the attack by Bosnian Serb forces, as described in this indictment, the estimated Bosnian Muslim population in the safe area of Srebrenica, was approximately 60,000.

Attack on the Safe Area of Srebrenica

4. On or about 6 July 1995, the Bosnian Serb army shelled Srebrenica and attacked United Nations observation posts that were manned by Dutch soldiers and located in the safe area. The attack on the Srebrenica safe area by the Bosnian Serb army continued through 11 July 1995, when the first units of the attacking Bosnian Serb forces entered Srebrenica.

5. The Bosnian Muslim men, women and children who remained in Srebrenica after the beginning of the Bosnian Serb attack took two courses of action. Several thousand women, children and some mostly elderly men fled to the UN compound in Potočari, located within the safe area of Srebrenica, where they sought the protection of the Dutch battalion responsible for the compound. They remained at the compound from 11 July 1995 until 13 July 1995, when they were all evacuated by buses and trucks under the control of and operated by Bosnian Serb military personnel.

6. A second group of approximately 15,000 Bosnian Muslim men, with some women and children, gathered at Susnjari during the evening hours of 11 July 1995 and fled, in a huge column, through the woods towards Tuzla. Approximately one-third of this group consisted of armed Bosnian military personnel and armed civilians. The rest were unarmed civilians.

Events in Potočari

7. On 11 July 1995 and 12 July 1995, **RATKO MLADIĆ** and members of his staff met in Bratunac with Dutch military officers and

IT-95-18-I 10/346 BIS

Offensives contre la zone de sécurité de Srebrenica

4. Vers le 6 juillet 1995, l'armée serbe bosniaque a pilonné Srebrenica et attaqué des postes d'observation de l'ONU situés dans la zone de sécurité, où étaient stationnés des soldats néerlandais. L'offensive dirigée par l'armée serbe bosniaque contre la zone de sécurité de Srebrenica s'est poursuivie jusqu'au 11 juillet 1995, date à laquelle les premières unités de forces serbes bosniaques assaillantes sont entrées dans Srebrenica.

5. Les hommes, femmes et enfants musulmans bosniaques qui sont demeurés à Srebrenica après le début de l'offensive des Serbes bosniaques ont adopté deux lignes de conduite différentes. Plusieurs milliers de femmes, d'enfants et d'hommes, ces derniers étant âgés pour la plupart, ont fui vers la base de l'ONU à Potočari, dans la zone de sécurité de Srebrenica, où ils ont demandé la protection du bataillon néerlandais responsable de la base. Ils sont demeurés à la base du 11 au 13 juillet 1995, date à laquelle ils ont tous été évacués, sous la surveillance des soldats serbes bosniaques, dans des bus et des camions conduits par ces derniers.

6. Un second groupe d'environ 15.000 hommes musulmans bosniaques, accompagnés de quelques femmes et enfants, s'est formé à Šušnjari dans la soirée du 11 juillet 1995 et a fui, en une immense colonne, à travers les bois en direction de Tuzla. Un tiers de ce groupe environ se composait de soldats bosniaques armés et de civils armés. Les autres étaient des civils non armés.

Evénements à Potočari

7. Les 11 et 12 juillet 1995, **RATKO MLADIĆ** et des membres de son état-major ont rencontré à Bratunac des officiers militaires néerlandais et des représentants des réfugiés musulmans de Potočari. Lors de ces réunions, **RATKO MLADIĆ** a notamment informé ses interlocuteurs que les soldats musulmans bosniaques qui rendaient leurs armes seraient traités comme des prisonniers de guerre aux termes des Conventions de Genève et qu'il ne serait fait aucun mal aux réfugiés évacués de Potočari.

8. Vers le 12 juillet 1995, des soldats serbes bosniaques ont incendié et pillé des maisons appartenant à des Musulmans bosniaques, à Potočari et dans les environs.

9. Vers le 12 juillet 1995, dans la matinée, des soldats serbes bosniaques sont arrivés à la base de l'ONU à Potočari et dans les environs.

10. Vers le 12 juillet 1995, **RATKO MLADIĆ** est arrivé à Potočari, accompagné de ses officiers et d'une équipe de télévision. Il a à maintes reprises menti aux Musulmans bosniaques à Potočari et dans les environs, en leur certifiant qu'il ne leur serait fait aucun mal et qu'ils seraient transportés en toute sécurité hors de Srebrenica.

representatives of the Muslim refugees from Potočari. At these meetings, **RATKO MLADIĆ** informed them, among other things, that Bosnian Muslim soldiers who surrendered their weapons would be treated as prisoners of war according to the Geneva Conventions and that refugees evacuated from Potočari would not be hurt.

8. On or about 12 July 1995, Bosnian Serb military forces burned and looted Bosnian Muslim houses in and around Potočari.

9. On or about 12 July 1995, in the morning hours, Bosnian Serb military forces arrived at the UN military compound in Potočari and its environs.

10. On or about 12 July 1995, **RATKO MLADIĆ** arrived in Potočari, accompanied by his military aides and a television crew. He falsely and repeatedly told Bosnian Muslims in and around Potočari that they would not be harmed and that they would be safely transported out of Srebrenica.

11. On or about 12 July 1995, at the direction and in the presence of **RATKO MLADIĆ**, approximately 50-60 buses and trucks arrived near the UN military compound in Potočari. Shortly after the arrival of these vehicles, the evacuation process of Bosnian Muslim refugees started. As Muslim women, children and men started to board the buses and trucks, Bosnian Serb military personnel separated the men from the women and children. This selection and separation of Muslim men took place in the presence of and at the direction of **RATKO MLADIĆ.**

12. The Bosnian Muslim men who had been separated from other refugees were taken to divers locations in and around Potočari. On or about 12 July 1995, **RATKO MLADIĆ** and Bosnian Serb military personnel under his command, informed some of these Muslim men that they would be evacuated and exchanged for Bosnian Serbs being held in Tuzla.

13. Most of the Muslim men who had been separated from the other refugees in Potočari were transported to Bratunac and then to the area of Karakaj, where they were massacred by Bosnian Serb military personnel.

14. Between 12 July 1995 and 13 July 1995, Bosnian Serb military personnel summarily executed Bosnian Muslim men and women at divers locations around the UN compound where they had taken refuge. The bodies of those summarily executed were left in fields and buildings in the immediate vicinity of the compound. These arbitrary killings

11. Vers le 12 juillet 1995, sur les ordres et en présence de **RATKO MLADIĆ**, environ 50 à 60 bus et camions sont arrivés près de la base militaire de l'ONU à Potočari. Peu après l'arrivée de ces véhicules, l'évacuation des réfugiés musulmans bosniaques a débuté. Alors que les femmes, enfants et hommes musulmans commençaient à monter dans les bus et les camions, les soldats serbes bosniaques ont séparé les hommes des femmes et des enfants. Ce processus de sélection et de séparation des hommes musulmans s'est déroulé en présence et sur les instructions de **RATKO MLADIĆ**.

12. Les hommes musulmans bosniaques qui avaient été séparés des autres réfugiés ont été emmenés en divers endroits à Potočari et dans les environs. Vers le 12 juillet 1995, **RATKO MLADIĆ** et des soldats serbes bosniaques sous son commandement ont informé certains de ces hommes musulmans qu'ils seraient évacués et échangés contre des prisonniers serbes bosniaques de Tuzla.

13. La plupart des hommes musulmans qui avaient été séparés des autres réfugiés à Potočari ont été transportés à Bratunac et ensuite dans la région de Karakaj, où ils ont été massacrés par des soldats serbes bosniaques.

14. Entre le 12 et le 13 juillet 1995, des soldats serbes bosniaques ont sommairement exécuté des hommes et des femmes musulmans bosniaques en divers endroits autour de la base de l'ONU où ils s'étaient réfugiés. Les corps des victimes sommairement exécutées ont été abandonnés sur des terrains et dans des bâtiments à proximité de la base. Ces massacres arbitraires ont suscité une terreur et une panique telles parmi les Musulmans qui étaient restés sur place que certains se sont suicidés et que tous les autres ont accepté de quitter l'enclave.

15. L'évacuation de tous les réfugiés musulmans valides a pris fin le 13 juillet 1995. Suite à l'offensive des Serbes bosniaques contre la zone de sécurité et à d'autres actes, la population musulmane de l'enclave de Srebrenica a pratiquement été éliminée par les soldats serbes bosniaques.

Redditions et exécutions

16. Entre la soirée du 11 juillet 1995 et la matinée du 12 juillet 1995, l'immense colonne de Musulmans qui s'était formée à Šušnjari a fui Srebrenica à travers les bois vers Tuzla.

17. Des soldats serbes bosniaques en possession de véhicules blindés de transport de troupes, de chars d'assaut, de missiles antiaériens et d'artillerie, se sont placés le long de la route Bratunac-Milići pour tenter de bloquer la colonne de Musulmans bosniaques en fuite vers Tuzla.

18. Dès que la colonne a pénétré dans les zones contrôlées par les Serbes bosniaques dans les environs de Buljim, elle a été attaquée par des soldats serbes bosniaques. Suite à cette offensive et à d'autres lancées par l'armée serbe bosniaque, un grand nombre de Musulmans ont été tués et blessés, et la colonne s'est divisée en plusieurs sections plus petites qui ont continué à fuir vers Tuzla. Environ un tiers de la colonne, essentiellement composée de soldats, a traversé la route Bratunac-Milići près de Nova Kasaba et a atteint Tuzla saine et sauve. Les autres ont été pris au piège derrière les lignes serbes bosniaques.

IT-95-18-I 335

instilled such terror and panic amongst the Muslims remaining there that some of them committed suicide and all the others agreed to leave the enclave.

15. The evacuation of all able-bodied Muslim refugees concluded on 13 July 1995. As a result of the Bosnian Serb attack on the safe area and other actions, the Muslim population of the enclave of Srebrenica was virtually eliminated by Bosnian Serb military personnel.

Surrender and Executions

16. Between the evening of 11 July 1995 and the morning of 12 July 1995, the huge column of Muslims which had gathered in Šušnjari fled Srebrenica through the woods towards Tuzla.

17. Bosnian Serb military personnel, supported by armoured personnel carriers, tanks, anti-aircraft guns and artillery, positioned themselves along the Bratunac - Milići road in an effort to interdict the column of Bosnian Muslims fleeing towards Tuzla.

18. As soon as the column reached Bosnian Serb held territory in the vicinity of Buljim, Bosnian Serb military forces attacked it. As a result of this and other attacks by Bosnian Serb military forces, many Muslims were killed and wounded and the column divided into several smaller parts which continued towards Tuzla. Approximately one-third of the column, mostly composed of military personnel, crossed the Bratunac-Milići road near Nova Kasaba and reached safety in Tuzla. The remaining Muslims were trapped behind the Bosnian Serb lines.

19. Thousands of Muslims were captured by or surrendered to Bosnian Serb military forces under the command and control of **RATKO MLADIĆ** and **RADOVAN KARADŽIĆ**. Many of the Muslims who surrendered did so because they were assured that they would be safe if they surrendered. In many instances, assurances of safety were provided to the Muslims by Bosnian Serb military personnel who were with other Bosnian Serb soldiers wearing stolen UN uniforms, and by Muslims who had been captured and ordered to summon their fellow Muslims from the woods.

20. Many of the Bosnian Muslims who were captured by or surrendered to Bosnian Serb military personnel were summarily executed by Bosnian Serb military personnel at the locations of their surrender or capture, or at

19. Des milliers de Musulmans ont été fait prisonniers ou se sont rendus aux soldats serbes bosniaques sous le commandement et le contrôle de **RATKO MLADIĆ** et de **RADOVAN KARADŽIĆ**. Parmi les Musulmans qui se sont rendus, beaucoup ont agi ainsi parce qu'on leur avait certifié qu'il ne leur serait fait aucun mal en cas de reddition. Dans de nombreux cas, des garanties de sécurité ont été données aux Musulmans par des soldats serbes bosniaques accompagnés d'autres soldats serbes bosniaques portant des uniformes volés aux "casques bleus" et par des prisonniers musulmans qui avaient reçu l'ordre de sommer les Musulmans en fuite à travers les bois de se rendre.

20. Un grand nombre de Musulmans bosniaques qui ont été fait prisonniers ou qui se sont rendus aux soldats serbes bosniaques ont été sommairement exécutés par ceux-ci soit à l'endroit même de leur reddition ou de leur capture, soit en d'autres endroits peu de temps après. Les cas d'exécutions sommaires comprennent notamment, sans y être limités :

20.1 Vers le 13 juillet 1995, près de Nezuk, en République de Bosnie-Herzégovine, un groupe de 10 hommes musulmans bosniaques a été fait prisonnier. Des soldats serbes bosniaques ont sommairement exécuté certains de ces hommes, et notamment Mirsad Alispahić et Hajrudin Mešanović.

20.2 Vers le 13 juillet 1995, au bord de la rivière Jadar, entre Konjević Polje et Drinjača, des soldats serbes bosniaques ont sommairement exécuté 15 hommes musulmans bosniaques qui s'étaient rendus ou avaient été fait prisonniers. Parmi les victimes se trouvaient Hamed Omerović, Azem Mujić et Ismet Ahmetović.

20.3 Vers le 13 juillet 1995, près de Konjević Polje, des soldats serbes bosniaques ont sommairement exécuté des centaines de Musulmans, y compris des femmes et des enfants.

20.4 Vers le 17 ou le 18 juillet 1995, dans les environs de Konjević Polje, des soldats serbes bosniaques ont fait prisonniers 150 à 200 Musulmans bosniaques et ont sommairement exécuté la moitié d'entre-eux environ.

20.5 Vers le 18 ou le 19 juillet 1995, près de Nezuk, environ 20 groupes comptant chacun 5 à 10 hommes musulmans bosniaques se sont rendus aux soldats serbes bosniaques. Après leur reddition, des soldats serbes bosniaques leur ont donné l'ordre de s'aligner et les ont sommairement exécutés.

20.6 Vers le 20 ou le 21 juillet 1995, près du village de Meces, des soldats serbes bosniaques utilisant des mégaphones ont exhorté les hommes musulmans bosniaques qui avaient fui Srebrenica à se rendre et leur ont certifié qu'il ne leur serait fait aucun mal. Environ 350 hommes musulmans bosniaques ont répondu à ces prières et se sont rendus. Des soldats serbes bosniaques en ont emmené 150 environ, leur ont donné l'ordre de creuser leur propre tombe et les ont sommairement exécutés.

IT-95-18-I D 346
15 NOVEMBER 1995

other locations shortly thereafter. Incidents of such summary executions include, but are not limited to:

20.1 On or about 13 July 1995, near Nezuk in the Republic of Bosnia and Herzegovina, a group of 10 Bosnian Muslim men were captured. Bosnian Serb soldiers summarily executed some of these men, including Mirsad Alispahić and Hajrudin Mešanović.

20.2 On or about 13 July 1995, on the banks of the Jadar River between Konjević Polje and Drinjača, Bosnian Serb soldiers summarily executed 15 Bosnian Muslim men who had surrendered or been captured. Amongst those killed were Hamed Omerović, Azem Mujić and Ismet Ahmetović.

20.3 On or about 13 July 1995, in the vicinity of Konjević Polje, Bosnian Serb soldiers summarily executed hundreds of Muslims, including women and children.

20.4 On or about 17 July 1995 or 18 July 1995, in the vicinity of Konjević Polje, Bosnian Serb soldiers captured about 150-200 Bosnian Muslims and summarily executed about one-half of them.

20.5 On or about 18 July 1995 or 19 July 1995, in the vicinity of Nezuk, about 20 groups, each containing between 5-10 Bosnian Muslim men, surrendered to Bosnian Serb military forces. After the men surrendered, Bosnian Serb soldiers ordered them to line up and summarily executed them.

20.6 On or about 20 July 1995 or 21 July 1995, near the village of Meces, Bosnian Serb military personnel, using megaphones, urged Bosnian Muslim men who had fled Srebrenica to surrender and assured them that they would be safe. Approximately 350 Bosnian Muslim men responded to these entreaties and surrendered. Bosnian Serb soldiers then took approximately 150 of them, instructed them to dig their own graves and then summarily executed them.

20.7 On or about 21 July 1995 or 22 July 1995, near the village of Meces, an excavator dug a large pit and Bosnian Serb soldiers ordered approximately 260 Bosnian Muslim men who had been captured to stand around the hole. The Muslim men were then surrounded by armed Bosnian Serb soldiers and ordered not to move or they would be shot. Some of the men moved and were

IT-95-18-I 7/346 BIS

20.7 Vers le 21 ou 22 juillet 1995, près du village de Meces, une excavatrice a creusé une grande fosse et des soldats serbes bosniaques ont donné l'ordre à environ 260 hommes musulmans bosniaques qui avaient été fait prisonniers de se placer tout autour de la fosse. Ces Musulmans ont ensuite été encerclés par des soldats serbes bosniaques en armes et ont reçu l'ordre de ne pas bouger, faute de quoi ils seraient exécutés. Certains ont bougé et ont été tués. Ceux qui restaient ont été poussés dans la fosse et enterrés vivants.

21. Un grand nombre de Musulmans qui se sont rendus aux soldats serbes bosniaques n'ont pas été tués à l'endroit même de leur reddition, mais ont été transportés vers des points centraux de rassemblement où des soldats serbes bosniaques les ont gardés sous surveillance armée. Ces points de rassemblement comprenaient notamment un hangar à Bratunac; des terrains de football à Kasaba, Konjević Polje, Kravica et Vlasenica; une prairie derrière la gare routière de Sandići et d'autres terrains et prairies le long de la route Bratunac-Milići.

22. Entre le 12 et le 14 juillet 1995, en plusieurs de ces points de rassemblement, y compris le hangar de Bratunac et le terrain de football de Kasaba, **RATKO MLADIĆ** s'est adressé aux détenus musulmans bosniaques. Il leur a à maintes reprises menti en leur certifiant qu'il ne leur serait fait aucun mal et qu'ils seraient échangés contre des Serbes bosniaques prisonniers de l'armée gouvernementale bosniaque.

23. Entre le 12 et le 14 juillet 1995, des soldats serbes bosniaques ont procédé à une sélection arbitraire de détenus musulmans bosniaques, qu'ils ont sommairement exécutés.

Exécutions en masse près de Karakaj

24. Vers le 14 juillet 1995, des soldats serbes bosniaques ont transporté des milliers de détenus musulmans de Bratunac, Kravica et ailleurs vers un point de rassemblement, à savoir un centre scolaire près de Karakaj. A cet endroit, des soldats serbes bosniaques ont donné l'ordre aux détenus musulmans de retirer leurs vestes, manteaux et autres vêtements et de les déposer devant la salle de sports. Les détenus ont ensuite été regroupés dans l'école et dans la salle de sports adjacente, où ils ont été gardés sous surveillance armée.

25. Vers le 14 juillet 1995, dans ce centre scolaire près de Karakaj, **RATKO MLADIĆ** s'est entretenu avec ses subordonnés militaires et s'est adressé à certains des Musulmans détenus à cet endroit.

26. A plusieurs reprises le 14 juillet 1995, des soldats serbes bosniaques ont tué des détenus musulmans bosniaques dans ce centre scolaire.

27. Pendant toute la journée du 14 juillet 1995, des soldats serbes bosniaques ont emmené tous les détenus musulmans, répartis en petits groupes, hors de l'école et de la salle de sports et les ont fait monter dans des camions conduits et surveillés par des soldats serbes bosniaques. Avant de faire monter les détenus dans les camions, ils leur ont souvent ligoté les mains derrière le dos ou bandé les yeux. Les détenus ont ensuite été conduits en deux endroits au moins près de Karakaj.

shot. The remaining men were pushed into the hole and buried alive.

21. Many of the Muslims who surrendered to Bosnian Serb military personnel were not killed at the locations of their surrender, but instead were transported to central assembly points where Bosnian Serb soldiers held them under armed guard. These assembly points included, among others, a hangar in Bratunac; soccer fields in Kasaba, Konjević Polje, Kravica, and Vlasenica; a meadow behind the bus station in Sandići and other fields and meadows along the Bratunac - Milići road.

22. Between 12 July 1995 and 14 July 1995, at various of these assembly points, including the hangar in Bratunac and the soccer stadium in Kasaba, **RATKO MLADIĆ** addressed the Bosnian Muslim detainees. He falsely and repeatedly assured them that they would be safe and that they would be exchanged for Bosnian Serb prisoners held by Bosnian government forces.

23. Between 12 July 1995 and 14 July 1995, Bosnian Serb military personnel arbitrarily selected Bosnian Muslim detainees and summarily executed them.

Mass Executions Near Karakaj

24. On or about 14 July 1995, Bosnian Serb military personnel transported thousands of Muslim detainees from Bratunac, Kravica and other locations to an assembly point in a school complex near Karakaj. At this assembly point, Bosnian Serb military personnel ordered the Muslim detainees to take off their jackets, coats and other garments and place them in front of the sports hall. They were then crowded into the school building and adjacent sports hall and held under armed guard.

25. On or about 14 July 1995, at this school complex near Karakaj, **RATKO MLADIĆ** conferred with his military subordinates and addressed some of the Muslims detained there.

26. At various times during 14 July 1995, Bosnian Serb military personnel killed Bosnian Muslim detainees at this school complex.

27. Throughout 14 July 1995, Bosnian Serb military personnel removed all the Muslim detainees, in small groups, from the school building and sports hall and loaded them onto trucks guarded and driven by Bosnian Serb soldiers. Before boarding the trucks, many of the detainees had

28. Après l'arrivée des camions à ces endroits, les soldats serbes bosniaques ont donné l'ordre aux détenus musulmans qui avaient les yeux bandés ou les mains ligotées de descendre des camions et ils les ont sommairement exécutés. Les exécutions sommaires ont eu lieu de midi à minuit environ le 14 juillet 1995.

29. Des soldats serbes bosniaques ont enterré les hommes musulmans bosniaques ainsi exécutés dans des fosses communes à proximité des lieux d'exécution.

30. Vers le 14 juillet 1995, **RATKO MLADIĆ** était présent sur l'un des lieux d'exécutions en masse lorsque des soldats serbes bosniaques ont sommairement exécuté des hommes musulmans bosniaques.

31. Les exécutions sommaires d'hommes musulmans bosniaques, perpétrées le 14 juillet 1995 près de Karakaj, ont entraîné la perte de milliers de vies.

LES ACCUSES

32. **RADOVAN KARADŽIĆ**, né le 19 juin 1945 dans la municipalité de Šavnik, République du Monténégro. Il est le président de l'administration des Serbes de Bosnie à Pale depuis le 13 mai 1992 environ.

33. **RATKO MLADIĆ**, né le 12 mars 1943 dans la municipalité de Kalinovik, en République de Bosnie-Herzégovine. Il est officer de carrière dans l'armée des Serbes de Bosnie avec le rang de Général. Il occupe les fonctions de Commandant de l'armée de l'administration des Serbes de Bosnie depuis le 14 mai 1992 environ.

RESPONSABILITE DES SUPERIEURS HIERARCHIQUES

RADOVAN KARADŽIĆ

34. **RADOVAN KARADŽIĆ** est l'un des membres fondateurs et le président du parti démocratique serbe (SDS) de ce qui était alors la République socialiste de Bosnie-Herzégovine. Le SDS était le principal parti politique des Serbes en Bosnie-Herzégovine. En sa qualité de président du SDS, Karadžić était et reste le plus puissant dirigeant officiel du parti. Ses fonctions de président comprennent la représentation du parti, la coordination des activités de ses différents organes et l'exécution de ses tâches et objectifs programmatiques. Il continue d'occuper ce poste.

35. **RADOVAN KARADŽIĆ** est devenu le premier président de l'administration des Serbes de Bosnie à Pale vers le 13 mai 1992. A l'époque à laquelle il est entré en fonction, ses pouvoirs *de jure*, décrits dans la constitution de l'administration des Serbes de Bosnie, comprenaient, sans y être limités, le commandement de l'armée de ladite administration en temps de guerre et de paix et le pouvoir de nommer, promouvoir et limoger les officiers de ladite armée.

36. En plus de ses pouvoirs constitutionnels, les pouvoirs de **RADOVAN KARADŽIĆ** en qualité de président de l'administration des Serbes de Bosnie sont renforcés par les dispositions de l'article 6 de la Loi serbe bosniaque sur la défense populaire, qui l'habilite notamment à superviser la Défense du territoire en temps de paix et de guerre et à donner des ordres pour l'utilisation des forces de police en cas

their hands tied behind their backs or were blindfolded. They were then driven to at least two locations in the vicinity of Karakaj.

28. Once the trucks arrived at these locations, Bosnian Serb military personnel ordered the bound or blindfolded Muslim detainees off the trucks and summarily executed them. The summary executions took place from approximately noon to midnight on 14 July 1995.

29. Bosnian Serb military personnel buried the executed Bosnian Muslim men in mass graves near the execution sites.

30. On or about 14 July 1995, **RATKO MLADIĆ** was present at one of the mass execution sites when Bosnian Serb military personnel summarily executed Bosnian Muslim men.

31. The summary executions of Bosnian Muslim males, which occurred on 14 July 1995 in the vicinity of Karakaj, resulted in the loss of thousands of lives.

THE ACCUSED

32. **RADOVAN KARADŽIĆ** was born on 19 June 1945 in the municipality of Šavnik of the Republic of Montenegro. From on or about 13 May 1992 to the present, he has been president of the Bosnian Serb administration in Pale.

33. **RATKO MLADIĆ** was born on 12 March 1943 in Kalinovik municipality of the Republic of Bosnia and Herzegovina. He is a career military officer and holds the rank of general in the Bosnian Serb armed forces. From on or about 14 May 1992 to the present, he has been the commander of the army of the Bosnian Serb administration.

SUPERIOR AUTHORITY

RADOVAN KARADŽIĆ

34. **RADOVAN KARADŽIĆ** was a founding member and president of the Serbian Democratic Party (SDS) of what was then the Socialist Republic of Bosnia and Herzegovina. The SDS was the main political party among the Serbs in Bosnia and Herzegovina. As president of the SDS, he was and is the most powerful official in the party. His duties as president include representing the party, co-ordinating the work of party

de guerre, de menace immédiate ou de toute autre urgence. L'article 39 de la même Loi l'habilite, en cas de menaces imminentes de guerre ou autres urgences, à déployer des unités de Défense du territoire en vue de maintenir l'ordre.

37. Les pouvoirs de **RADOVAN KARADŽIĆ** sont encore renforcés par l'article 33 de la Loi serbe bosniaque sur les affaires intérieures, qui l'autorise à mobiliser les forces de réserve de la police en cas d'urgence.

38. **RADOVAN KARADŽIĆ** exerce les pouvoirs décrits ci-avant, agit et est traité à l'échelon international comme le président de l'administration des Serbes de Bosnie à Pale. En cette capacité, il a, *inter alia*, participé à des négociations internationales et conclu personnellement des accords sur des questions comme des cessez-le-feu et l'aide humanitaire, lesquels accords ont été appliqués.

RATKO MLADIĆ

39. **RATKO MLADIĆ** a été nommé Commandant du 9e corps de l'armée populaire yougoslave (JNA) à Knin, en République de Croatie, en 1991. En mai 1992, il a pris le commandement des forces du Deuxième district militaire de la JNA, qui est alors devenue effectivement l'armée des Serbes de Bosnie. Il a le rang de Général et est, depuis le 14 mai 1992 environ, le Commandant de l'armée de l'administration des Serbes de Bosnie.

40. **RATKO MLADIĆ** a démontré sa maîtrise des questions militaires en négociant, *inter alia*, des accords de cessez-le-feu et d'échanges de prisonniers; des accords relatifs à l'ouverture de l'aéroport de Sarajevo; des accords relatifs à l'accès des convois d'aide humanitaire; et des accords contre le recours à des tireurs isolés. Tous les accords précités ont été appliqués.

ALLEGATIONS GENERALES

41. A toutes les époques concernées dans le présent acte d'accusation, le territoire de la République de Bosnie-Herzégovine, en ex-Yougoslavie, était le théatre d'un conflit armé et se trouvait sous occupation partielle.

42. Dans chacun des paragraphes relatifs au chef d'accusation de génocide, lequel est sanctionné par l'article 4 du Statut du Tribunal, les actes ou omissions présumés ont été commis dans l'intention de détruire en tout ou en partie un groupe national, ethnique ou religieux, comme tel.

43. Dans chacun des paragraphes relatifs au chef d'accusation de crimes contre l'humanité, lequels sont sanctionnés par l'article 5 du Statut du Tribunal, les actes ou omissions présumés faisaient partie d'une offensive généralisée, à grande échelle ou systématique, dirigée contre une population civile.

44. **RATKO MLADIĆ** et **RADOVAN KARADŽIĆ** sont individuellement responsables des crimes qui leur sont reprochés dans le présent acte d'accusation conformément à l'article 7(1) du Statut du Tribunal. La responsabilité pénale individuelle d'un individu est notamment engagée lorsque celui-ci a commis, planifié, incité à commettre, ordonné ou de toute autre manière aidé et encouragé

organs and ensuring the realisation of the programmatic tasks and goals of the party. He continues to hold this post.

35. **RADOVAN KARADŽIĆ** became the first president of the Bosnian Serb administration in Pale on or about 13 May 1992. At the time he assumed this position, his *de jure* powers, as described in the constitution of the Bosnian Serb administration, included, but were not limited to, commanding the army of the Bosnian Serb administration in times of war and peace and having the authority to appoint, promote and discharge officers of the army. As president, he was and is a position of superior authority to **RATKO MLADIC** and every member of the Bosnian Serb army and all units and personnel assigned or attached to the Bosnian Serb army.

36. In addition to his powers described in the constitution, **RADOVAN KARADŽIĆ's** powers as president of the Bosnian Serb administration are augmented by Article 6 of the Bosnian Serb Act on People's Defence. This Act vested in him, among other powers, the authority to supervise the Territorial Defence both in peace and war and the authority to issue orders for the utilisation of the police in case of war, immediate threat and other emergencies. Article 39 of the same Act empowered him, in cases of imminent threat of war and other emergencies, to deploy Territorial Defence units for the maintenance of law and order.

37. **RADOVAN KARADŽIĆ's** powers are further augmented by Article 33 of the Bosnian Serb Act on Internal Affairs, which authorised him to activate reserve police in emergency situations.

38. **RADOVAN KARADŽIĆ** has exercised the powers described above and has acted and been dealt with internationally as the president of the Bosnian Serb administration in Pale. In that capacity, he has, *inter alia*, participated in international negotiations and has personally made agreements on such matters as cease-fires and humanitarian relief, and these agreements have been implemented.

RATKO MLADIĆ

39. **RATKO MLADIĆ** was, in 1991, appointed commander of the 9th Corps of the Yugoslav People's Army (JNA) in Knin in the Republic of Croatia. In May 1992, he assumed command of the forces of the Second Military District of the JNA which then effectively became the Bosnian Serb army. He holds the rank of general and from about 14 May 1992 to the present, has been the commander of the army of the Bosnian Serb

à planifier, préparer ou exécuter l'un des crimes sanctionnés par les articles 2 à 5 du Statut du Tribunal.

45. **RATKO MLADIĆ** et **RADOVAN KARADŽIĆ** sont également, ou à défaut, pénalement responsables en leur qualité de supérieurs hiérarchiques pour les actes commis par leurs subordonnés conformément à l'article 7 (3) du Statut du Tribunal. Le supérieur hiérarchique est pénalement responsable des actes de son subordonné s'il savait ou avait des raisons de savoir que le subordonné s'apprêtait à commettre cet acte ou l'avait fait et s'il n'a pas pris les mesures nécessaires et raisonnables pour empêcher que ledit acte ne soit commis ou pour en punir les auteurs.

46. Les allégations générales contenues aux paragraphes 41 à 45 sont réaffirmées et incorporées dans chacun des chefs d'accusation décrits ci-après.

CHEFS D'ACCUSATION

CHEFS D'ACCUSATION 1 - 2
(GENOCIDE)
(CRIME CONTRE L'HUMANITE)

47. Entre le 12 et le 13 juillet 1995 environ, des soldats serbes bosniaques, sous le commandement et le contrôle de **RATKO MLADIĆ** et **RADOVAN KARADŽIĆ**, sont arrivés à Potočari, où des milliers de Musulmans - hommes, femmes et enfants - s'étaient réfugiés à l'intérieur et autour de la base militaire de l'ONU. Des soldats serbes bosniaques, sous le commandement et le contrôle de **RATKO MLADIĆ** et de **RADOVAN KARADŽIĆ**, ont sommairement exécuté nombre de réfugiés musulmans bosniaques qui étaient restés à Potočari.

48. Entre le 13 et le 22 juillet 1995 environ, des soldats serbes bosniaques, sous le commandement et le contrôle de **RATKO MLADIĆ** et **RADOVAN KARADŽIĆ**, ont sommairement exécuté de nombreux Musulmans bosniaques qui s'étaient enfuis à travers les bois et qui ont ensuite été fait prisonniers ou qui se sont rendus.

49. Des milliers d'hommes musulmans bosniaques, qui avaient fui Srebrenica et qui s'étaient rendus ou avaient été fait prisonniers, ont été transportés depuis divers points de rassemblement dans et autour de Srebrenica vers un point central de rassemblement dans un centre scolaire près de Karakaj.

50. Vers le 14 juillet 1995, des militaires serbes bosniaques, sous le commandement et le contrôle de **RATKO MLADIĆ** et **RADOVAN KARADŽIĆ**, ont transporté des milliers d'hommes musulmans depuis ce centre scolaire vers deux endroits situés à courte distance. A ces endroits, des soldats serbes bosniaques ont sommairement exécuté ces détenus musulmans bosniaques et les ont ensevelis dans des fosses communes. **RATKO MLADIĆ** avait connaissance de ces faits.

51. Entre le 6 et le 22 juillet 1995 environ, **RATKO MLADIĆ** et **RADOVAN KARADŽIĆ** ont, individuellement et de concert avec d'autres, planifié, incité à commettre, ordonné ou de toute autre manière aidé et encouragé à planifier, préparer ou exécuter les crimes suivants :

administration. In that capacity, he was and is in a position of superior authority to every member of the Bosnian Serb army and all units and personnel assigned or attached to that army.

40. **RATKO MLADIĆ** has demonstrated his control in military matters by negotiating, *inter alia*, cease-fire and prisoner exchange agreements; agreements relating to the opening of Sarajevo airport; agreements relating to access for humanitarian aid convoys; and anti-sniping agreements, all of which have been implemented.

GENERAL ALLEGATIONS

41. At all times relevant to this indictment, a state of armed conflict and partial occupation existed in the Republic of Bosnia and Herzegovina in the territory of the former Yugoslavia.

42. In each paragraph charging genocide, a crime recognised by Article 4 of the Statute of the Tribunal, the alleged acts or omissions were committed with the intent to destroy, in whole or in part, a national, ethnical, or religious group, as such.

43. In each paragraph charging crimes against humanity, crimes recognised by Article 5 of the Statute of the Tribunal, the alleged acts or omissions were part of a widespread or systematic or large-scale attack directed against a civilian population.

44. **RATKO MLADIĆ** and **RADOVAN KARADŽIĆ** are individually responsible for the crimes alleged against them in this indictment pursuant to Article 7(1) of the Tribunal Statute. Individual criminal responsibility includes committing, planning, instigating, ordering or otherwise aiding and abetting in the planning, preparation or execution of any crimes referred to in Articles 2 to 5 of the Tribunal Statute.

45. **RATKO MLADIĆ** and **RADOVAN KARADŽIĆ** are also, or alternatively, criminally responsible as commanders for the acts of their subordinates pursuant to Article 7(3) of the Tribunal Statute. Command criminal responsibility is the responsibility of a superior officer for the acts of his subordinate if he knew or had reason to know that his subordinate was about to commit such acts or had done so and the superior failed to take the necessary and reasonable measures to prevent such acts or to punish the perpetrators thereof.

IT-95-18-I 3/346 BIS

a) exécutions sommaires d'hommes et de femmes musulmans bosniaques dans et autour de Potočari les 12 et 13 juillet 1995;

b) exécutions sommaires, perpétrées entre le 13 et le 22 juillet 1995, de Musulmans bosniaques qui étaient hors combat pour cause de blessure, de reddition ou de capture après leur fuite à travers les bois vers Tuzla;

c) exécutions sommaires d'hommes musulmans bosniaques, perpétrées vers le 14 juillet 1995 sur des lieux d'exécutions en masse dans et autour de Karakaj.

Par leurs actes et omissions en rapport avec les événements décrits aux paragraphes 13, 14, 20.1-20.7, 23, 26 et 28, **RATKO MLADIĆ** et **RADOVAN KARADŽIĆ** ont commis :

Chef d'accusation 1 : le **GENOCIDE**, tel que sanctionné par l'article 4(2)(a) (meurtre de membres du groupe) du Statut du Tribunal;

Chef d'accusation 2 : un **CRIME CONTRE L'HUMANITE**, tel que sanctionné par l'article 5(b) (extermination) du Statut du Tribunal.

CHEFS D'ACCUSATION 3 - 4
(CRIME CONTRE L'HUMANITE)
(VIOLATION DES LOIS OU DES COUTUMES DE LA GUERRE)

52. Par leurs actes et omissions en rapport avec l'exécution sommaire d'hommes et de femmes musulmans bosniaques, perpétrée dans et autour de Potočari entre le 12 et le 13 juillet 1995, de la manière décrite au paragraphe 13 ci-avant, **RATKO MLADIĆ** et **RADOVAN KARADŽIĆ** ont commis :

Chef d'accusation 3 : un **CRIME CONTRE L'HUMANITE**, tel que sanctionné par l'article 5(a) (meurtre) du Statut du Tribunal.

Chef d'accusation 4 : une **VIOLATION DES LOIS OU COUTUMES DE LA GUERRE**, telle que sanctionnée par l'article 3 (meurtre) du Statut du Tribunal.

CHEFS D'ACCUSATION 5 - 18
(CRIME CONTRE L'HUMANITE)
(VIOLATION DES LOIS OU COUTUMES DE LA GUERRE)

53. Par leurs actes et omissions en rapport avec l'exécution sommaire de Musulmans bosniaques qui avaient fui Srebrenica à travers les bois entre le 13 et le 22 juillet 1995, de la manière décrite aux paragraphes 20.1 à 20.7 ci-avant, **RATKO MLADIĆ** et **RADOVAN KARADŽIĆ** ont commis :

Chef d'accusation 5 : un **CRIME CONTRE L'HUMANITE** (en rapport avec le paragraphe 20.1), tel que sanctionné par l'article 5(a) (meurtre) du Statut du Tribunal.

Chef d'accusation 6 : une **VIOLATION DES LOIS OU COUTUMES DE LA GUERRE** (en rapport avec le paragraphe 20.1), telle que sanctionnée par l'article 3 (meurtre) du Statut du Tribunal.

46. The general allegations contained in paragraphs 41 through 45 are realleged and incorporated into each of the charges set forth below.

CHARGES

COUNTS 1-2
(GENOCIDE)
(CRIME AGAINST HUMANITY)

47. Between about 12 July 1995 and 13 July 1995, Bosnian Serb military personnel, under the command and control of **RATKO MLADIĆ** and **RADOVAN KARADŽIĆ**, arrived in Potočari where thousands of Muslim men, women and children had sought refuge in and around the UN military compound. Bosnian Serb military personnel, under the command and control of **RATKO MLADIĆ** and **RADOVAN KARADŽIĆ,** summarily executed many Bosnian Muslim refugees who remained in Potočari.

48. Between about 13 July 1995 and 22 July 1995, Bosnian Serb military personnel, under the command and control of **RATKO MLADIĆ** and **RADOVAN KARADŽIĆ,** summarily executed many Bosnian Muslim men who fled to the woods and were later captured or surrendered.

49. Thousands of Bosnian Muslim men, who fled Srebrenica and who surrendered or had been captured, were transported from various assembly locations in and around Srebrenica to a main assembly point at a school complex near Karakaj.

50. On or about 14 July 1995, Bosnian Serb military personnel, under the command and control of **RATKO MLADIĆ** and **RADOVAN KARADŽIĆ**, transported thousands of Muslim men from this school complex to two locations a short distance away. At these locations, Bosnian Serb soldiers, with the knowledge of **RATKO MLADIĆ,** summarily executed these Bosnian Muslim detainees and buried them in mass graves.

IT-95-18-I 2/346 BIS

Chef d'accusation 7 : un **CRIME CONTRE L'HUMANITE** (en rapport avec le paragraphe 20.2), tel que sanctionné par l'article 5(a) (meurtre) du Statut du Tribunal.

Chef d'accusation 8 : une **VIOLATION DES LOIS OU COUTUMES DE LA GUERRE** (en rapport avec le paragraphe 20.2), telle que sanctionnée par l'article 3 (meurtre) du Statut du Tribunal.

Chef d'accusation 9 : un **CRIME CONTRE L'HUMANITE** (en rapport avec le paragraphe 20.3), tel que sanctionné par l'article 5(a) (meurtre) du Statut du Tribunal.

Chef d'accusation 10 : une **VIOLATION DES LOIS OU COUTUMES DE LA GUERRE** (en rapport avec le paragraphe 20.3), telle que sanctionnée par l'article 3 (meurtre) du Statut du Tribunal.

Chef d'accusation 11 : un **CRIME CONTRE L'HUMANITE** (en rapport avec le paragraphe 20.4), tel que sanctionné par l'article 5(a) (meurtre) du Statut du Tribunal.

Chef d'accusation 12 : une **VIOLATION DES LOIS OU COUTUMES DE LA GUERRE** (en rapport avec le paragraphe 20.4), telle que sanctionnée par l'article 3 (meurtre) du Statut du Tribunal.

Chef d'accusation 13 : un **CRIME CONTRE L'HUMANITE** (en rapport avec le paragraphe 20.5), tel que sanctionné par l'article 5(a) (meurtre) du Statut du Tribunal.

Chef d'accusation 14 : une **VIOLATION DES LOIS OU COUTUMES DE LA GUERRE** (en rapport avec le paragraphe 20.5), telle que sanctionnée par l'article 3 (meurtre) du Statut du Tribunal.

Chef d'accusation 15 : un **CRIME CONTRE L'HUMANITE** (en rapport avec le paragraphe 20.6), tel que sanctionné par l'article 5(a) (meurtre) du Statut du Tribunal.

Chef d'accusation 16 : une **VIOLATION DES LOIS OU COUTUMES DE LA GUERRE** (en rapport avec le paragraphe 20.6), telle que sanctionnée par l'article 3 (meurtre) du Statut du Tribunal.

Chef d'accusation 17 : un **CRIME CONTRE L'HUMANITE** (en rapport avec le paragraphe 20.7), tel que sanctionné par l'article 5(a) (meurtre) du Statut du Tribunal.

Chef d'accusation 18 : une **VIOLATION DES LOIS OU COUTUMES DE LA GUERRE** (en rapport avec le paragraphe 20.7), telle que sanctionnée par l'article 3 (meurtre) du Statut du Tribunal.

CHEFS D'ACCUSATION 19 - 20
(CRIME CONTRE L'HUMANITE)
(VIOLATION DES LOIS OU COUTUMES DE LA GUERRE)

54. Par leurs actes et omissions en rapport avec l'exécution sommaire d'hommes musulmans bosniaques sur des lieux d'exécutions en masse dans et autour de Karakaj, vers le 14 juillet 1995, de la manière décrite au paragraphe 28, **RATKO MLADIĆ** et **RADOVAN KARADŽIĆ** ont commis :

IT-95-18-I D 345
15 NOVEMBER 1995

51. **RATKO MLADIĆ** and **RADOVAN KARADŽIĆ**, between about 6 July 1995 and 22 July 1995, individually and in concert with others, planned, instigated, ordered or otherwise aided and abetted in the planning, preparation or execution of the following crimes:

a) summary executions of Bosnian Muslim men and women in and around Potočari on 12 July 1995 and 13 July 1995,

b) summary executions, which occurred between 13 July 1995 and 22 July 1995, of Bosnian Muslims who were *hors de combat* because of injury, surrender or capture after fleeing into the woods towards Tuzla,

c) summary executions of Bosnian Muslim men, which occurred on or about 14 July 1995 at mass execution sites in and around Karakaj.

By their acts and omissions in relation to the events described in paragraphs 13, 14, 20.1-20.7, 23, 26 and 28, **RATKO MLADIĆ** and **RADOVAN KARADŽIĆ** committed:

Count 1: **GENOCIDE** as recognised by Article 4(2)(a) (killing members of the group) of the Statute of the Tribunal.

Count 2: A **CRIME AGAINST HUMANITY** as recognised by Article 5(b) (extermination) of the Statute of the Tribunal.

COUNTS 3-4
(CRIME AGAINST HUMANITY)
(VIOLATION OF THE LAWS OR CUSTOMS OF WAR)

52. By their acts and omissions in relation to the summary executions of Bosnian Muslim men and women that occurred in and around Potočari between 12 July 1995 and 13 July 1995, described heretofore in paragraph 13, **RATKO MLADIĆ** and **RADOVAN KARADŽIĆ** committed:

Count 3: A **CRIME AGAINST HUMANITY** as recognised by Article 5(a) (murder) of the Statute of the Tribunal.

IT-95-18-I 1/346 BIS

Chef d'accusation 19 : un **CRIME CONTRE L'HUMANITE**, tel que sanctionné par l'article 5(a) (meurtre) du Statut du Tribunal.

Chef d'accusation 20 : une **VIOLATION DES LOIS OU COUTUMES DE LA GUERRE**, telle que sanctionnée par l'article 3 (meurtre) du Statut du Tribunal.

La Haye, Pays-Bas
Le 14 novembre 1995

Richard J. Goldstone
Procureur

IT-95-18-I D 344
15 NOVEMBER 1995

Count 4: A **VIOLATION OF THE LAWS OR CUSTOMS OF WAR** as recognised by Article 3 (murder) of the Statute of the Tribunal.

COUNTS 5-18
(CRIMES AGAINST HUMANITY)
(VIOLATION OF THE LAWS OR CUSTOMS OF WAR)

53. By their acts and omissions in relation the summary executions of Bosnian Muslims who fled Srebrenica into the woods between 13 July 1995 and 22 July 1995 as described heretofore in paragraphs 20.1 to 20.7, **RATKO MLADIĆ** and **RADOVAN KARADŽIĆ** committed:

Count 5: A CRIME AGAINST HUMANITY (in relation to paragraph 20.1) as recognised by Article 5(a) (murder) of the Statute of the Tribunal.

Counts 6: A VIOLATION OF THE LAWS OR CUSTOMS OF WAR (in relation to paragraph 20.1) as recognised by Article 3 (murder) of the Statute of the Tribunal.

Count 7: A CRIME AGAINST HUMANITY (in relation to paragraph 20.2) as recognised by Article 5(a) (murder) of the Statute of the Tribunal.

Counts 8: A VIOLATION OF THE LAWS OR CUSTOMS OF WAR (in relation to paragraph 20.2) as recognised by Article 3 (murder) of the Statute of the Tribunal.

Count 9: A CRIME AGAINST HUMANITY (in relation to paragraph 20.3) as recognised by Article 5(a) (murder) of the Statute of the Tribunal.

Counts 10: A VIOLATION OF THE LAWS OR CUSTOMS OF WAR (in relation to paragraph 20.3) as recognised by Article 3 (murder) of the Statute of the Tribunal.

Count 11: A CRIME AGAINST HUMANITY (in relation to paragraph 20.4) as recognised by Article 5(a) (murder) of the Statute of the Tribunal.

Counts 12: A VIOLATION OF THE LAWS OR CUSTOMS OF WAR (in relation to paragraph 20.4) as recognised by Article 3 (murder) of the Statute of the Tribunal.

Count 13: A CRIME AGAINST HUMANITY (in relation to paragraph 20.5) as recognised by Article 5(a) (murder) of the Statute of the Tribunal.

Counts 14: A VIOLATION OF THE LAWS OR CUSTOMS OF WAR (in relation to paragraph 20.5) as recognised by Article 3 (murder) of the Statute of the Tribunal.

Count 15: A CRIME AGAINST HUMANITY (in relation to paragraph 20.6) as recognised by Article 5(a) (murder) of the Statute of the Tribunal.

Counts 16: A VIOLATION OF THE LAWS OR CUSTOMS OF WAR (in relation to paragraph 20.6) as recognised by Article 3 (murder) of the Statute of the Tribunal.

Count 17: A CRIME AGAINST HUMANITY (in relation to paragraph 20.7) as recognised by Article 5(a) (murder) of the Statute of the Tribunal.

Counts 18: A VIOLATION OF THE LAWS OR CUSTOMS OF WAR (in relation to paragraph 20.7) as recognised by Article 3 (murder) of the Statute of the Tribunal.

COUNTS 19-20
(CRIME AGAINST HUMANITY)
(VIOLATION OF THE LAWS OR CUSTOMS OF WAR)

IT-95-18-I 325

54. By their acts and omissions in relation to the summary executions of Bosnian Muslim men at mass execution sites in and around Karakaj, on or about 14 July 1995, as described in paragraph 28, **RATKO MLADIĆ** and **RADOVAN KARADŽIĆ** committed:

Count 19: A CRIME AGAINST HUMANITY as recognised by Article 5(a) (murder) of the Statute of the Tribunal.

Count 20: A **VIOLATION OF THE LAWS OR CUSTOMS OF WAR** as recognised by Article 3 (murder) of the Statute of the Tribunal.

The Hague, The Netherlands

Richard J. Goldstone
Prosecutor

14 November 1995

352

D 352 - D 347

THE INTERNATIONAL CRIMINAL TRIBUNAL FOR THE FORMER YUGOSLAVIA **Case no. IT-95-18-I**

BEFORE A JUDGE OF THE TRIAL CHAMBER

Before : Judge Fouad Riad

Registrar : Mrs. Dorothee de Sampayo Garrido-Nijgh

Decision of 16 November 1995

THE PROSECUTOR

V.

RADOVAN KARADZIC
RATKO MLADIC

REVIEW OF THE INDICTMENT

The Prosecutor : by
Eric Ostberg
Mark Harmon
John Ralston

D 6/352 BIS - D 1/352 BIS 6/352 BIS

TRIBUNAL PENAL INTERNATIONAL
POUR L'EX-YOUGOSLAVIE

Affaire n° IT-95-18-I

DEVANT UN JUGE DE LA CHAMBRE DE PREMIERE INSTANCE

Devant : le Juge Fouad Riad

Assisté de : Madame Dorothee de Sampayo Garrido-Nijgh, Greffier

Décision du 16 novembre 1995

LE PROCUREUR

contre

RADOVAN KARADŽIĆ
RATKO MLADIĆ

EXAMEN DE L'ACTE D'ACCUSATION

Le Bureau du Procureur :

M. Eric Ostberg
M. Mark Harmon
M. John Ralston

IT-95-18-I 351

I, Judge Riad, Judge of the International Criminal Tribunal for the former Yugoslavia,

UPON RECEIVING an indictment from the Prosecutor, pursuant to Articles 18 and 19 of the Statute, and Rule 47 of the Rules of Procedure and Evidence,

AND UPON HEARING the Prosecutor, pursuant to Rule 47(D) of the Rules of Procedure and Evidence,

HEREBY GIVE MY DECISION, as follows:

After Srebrenica fell to besieging Serbian forces in July, 1995, a truly terrible massacre of the Muslim population appears to have taken place. The evidence tendered by the Prosecutor describes scenes of unimaginable savagery: thousands of men executed and buried in mass graves, hundreds of men buried alive, men and women mutilated and slaughtered, children killed before their mothers' eyes, a grandfather forced to eat the liver of his own grandson. These are truly scenes from hell, written on the darkest pages of human history.

The indictment submitted by the Prosecutor accuses Ratko Mladic and Radovan Karadzic of responsibility for these crimes. They are charged with genocide, crimes against humanity and violations of the laws or customs of war.

The charges in the indictment all relate to the fall of Srebrenica on 11 July 1995.

Srebrenica is located in Eastern Bosnia, close to the border with Serbia. After the war begun in the former Yugoslavia, Bosnian Muslim villages in this region were occupied by Bosnian Serb forces. The refugees fled from the destruction of their villages to Gorazde, Zepa, Tuzla and Srebrenica.

On 16 April 1993, Srebrenica was declared a "safe area" by the United Nations Security Council. Pursuant to this, the Bosnian Muslims inside the enclave were disarmed under the auspices of the United Nations Protection Force. Refugees continued to enter the enclave, with the result that, before its fall, the Bosnian Muslim population was approximately 60,000.

The evidence tendered by the Prosecutor will be summarised under three general headings - the massacre in the woods, mass executions at Karakaj, and summary executions at Potocari, which correspond to the arrangement of the counts of the indictment. The evidence presented by the Prosecutor is as follows.

The Bosnian Serb army, under the command and control of the two suspects, began the attack on Srebrenica on or about 6 July 1995. When Serb forces began to enter Srebrenica, the Muslim men, women and children in the enclave took two courses of action. Several thousand women, children and mostly elderly men fled to the UN compound in Potocari, where the Dutch battalion was stationed, within Srebrenica, to seek protection there. Most of the men, on the other hand, gathered at Susnjari in the evening of 11 July 1995 and fled, in a huge column, some 10 kilometers long, through the woods towards the Bosnian government-held territory of Tuzla. This column,

IT-95-18-I 5/352 315

NOUS, Fouad Riad, Juge du Tribunal pénal international pour l'ex-Yougoslavie;

AYANT RECU un acte d'accusation déposé par le Procureur conformément aux articles 18 et 19 du Statut et à l'article 47 du Règlement de procédure et de preuve;

AYANT ENTENDU le Procureur conformément à l'article 47(D) du Règlement de procédure et de preuve;

RENDONS CI-APRES NOTRE DECISION, libellée en ces termes :

Après la chute de Srebrenica aux mains des forces serbes en juillet 1995, il semblerait que la population musulmane ait été massacrée de manière véritablement atroce. Les éléments de preuve produits par le Procureur font état de scènes d'une cruauté inimaginable : des milliers d'hommes exécutés et enterrés dans des fosses communes, des centaines d'hommes enterrés vivants, des hommes et des femmes mutilés et sauvagement abattus, des enfants tués sous les yeux de leurs mères, un grand-père obligé de manger le foie de son propre petit-fils. Ces scènes de cauchemar comptent parmi les pages les plus noires de l'histoire de l'humanité.

L'acte d'accusation déposé par le Procureur accuse Ratko Mladić et Radovan Karadžić d'être responsables de ces crimes. Ils sont accusés de génocide, crimes contre l'humanité et violations des lois ou coutumes de la guerre.

Les chefs d'accusation figurant dans l'acte d'accusation concernent tous la chute de Srebrenica le 11 juillet 1995.

Srebrenica est située en Bosnie orientale, près de la frontière serbe. Après l'ouverture des hostilités dans l'ex-Yougoslavie, les villages musulmans bosniaques de la région ont été occupés par l'armée des Serbes de Bosnie. Les réfugiés ont fui la destruction de leurs villages en direction de Goražde, Žepa, Tuzla et Srebrenica.

Le 16 avril 1993, Srebrenica a été déclarée "zone de sécurité" par le Conseil de sécurité des Nations Unies. En conséquence, les Musulmans bosniaques à l'intérieur de l'enclave ont été désarmés sous les auspices de la Force de Protection des Nations Unies. Des réfugiés ont continué d'affluer dans l'enclave, portant la population musulmane bosniaque à environ 60.000 personnes avant la chute de Srebrenica.

Les éléments de preuve produits par le Procureur seront résumés sous trois rubriques générales - les massacres dans les bois, les exécutions en masse à Karakaj et les exécutions sommaires à Potočari - correspondant à la classification des chefs d'accusation dans l'acte d'accusation. Les éléments de preuve produits par le Procureur sont les suivants.

L'armée des Serbes de Bosnie, placée sous le commandement et le contrôle des deux suspects, a lancé la première offensive contre Srebrenica vers le 6 juillet 1995. Lorsque les forces serbes sont entrées dans Srebrenica, les hommes, femmes et enfants musulmans de l'enclave ont adopté deux lignes de conduites différentes. Plusieurs milliers de femmes, d'enfants et d'hommes âgés pour la plupart ont fui vers la base de l'ONU à Potočari, où était stationné le bataillon néerlandais, dans Srebrenica, pour s'y réfugier. Par contre, la plupart des hommes se sont rassemblés à Šušnjari dans la soirée

IT-95-18-I 350

consisted of approximately 15,000 Muslims, mostly unarmed, with women and children among their number.

Massacres in the woods

The fate which befell the column of people who set off to reach Tuzla on the night of 11 July 1995 and the morning of 12 July 1995 was an appalling one. The column was ambushed by Bosnian Serb soldiers on the Bratunac-Milici road, attacking with artillery shells, anti-aircraft guns, automatic weapons and the like. These attacks caused enormous loss of life. Hundreds of Muslims were killed, and many more wounded. Many were driven berserk by the assault and eye-witness accounts describe how tens of people were so horrified that they committed suicide to avoid capture. Many who were captured or surrendered, among them the wounded, were summarily executed. One eye-witness describes how more than a hundred captive Muslim men, women and children were slowly slaughtered by a group of Serbian soldiers using knives. Witnesses also saw hundreds of Muslim men buried in mass graves, some after having been shot, some buried alive.

Mass Executions at Karakaj

Thousands of Muslims from the column then surrendered to Serb military forces under the command and control of Ratko Mladic and Radovan Karadzic, having been assured that they would not be harmed. Some of the Serb soldiers giving assurances were wearing stolen United Nations uniforms. The captive men were then taken to large assembly points, including a football stadium where they were addressed by Ratko Mladic, who gave the same assurances, and thence to an assembly point in a school complex, near Karakaj, where Ratko Mladic was again present. Here too, many were summarily executed.

According to the testimony of the few witnesses who survived, the men were the next day, on or about 14 July 1995, taken in trucks to at least two nearby fields. There, they were taken out in small groups, told to find a spot, and then shot where they stood. The survivors say that the men were shot in their thousands, until the fields were full of bodies. After they were shot, Serbian soldiers walked over the bodies, checking that everyone was dead. If someone was heard to make a sound, or if a body was still warm, another bullet was used to despatch them. According to the survivors, the killing went on all day and all night, with truckloads of men arriving every ten to fifteen minutes. The eye-witnesses survived only by playing dead under the corpses until the soldiers had all left. Ratko Mladic is placed at the scene of the killings by more than one survivor. Hoes and excavators began to bury the dead that night.

Summary Executions at Potocari

Most of the Muslim men, women and children who went to Potocari could not gain access to the UN compound and spent the nights between 11 and 13 July 1995 in nearby factories. During this time, and under the direct supervision of General Mladic, men were separated from the women. Many were apparently summarily executed in the fields and rivers surrounding the compound. Children had their throats slit before their mother's eyes. The witness statements describe a frenzy of terror that led many to take their own lives. There is evidence that women were raped and killed.

du 11 juillet 1995 et ont fui à travers les bois, en formant une immense colonne de 10 kilomètres de long environ, en direction de la zone de Tuzla contrôlée par le gouvernement bosniaque. Cette colonne se composait d'environ 15.000 Musulmans non armés pour la plupart, accompagnés de femmes et d'enfants.

Les massacres dans les bois

Pendant la nuit du 11 juillet 1992 et la matinée du 12 juillet 1995, un sort effroyable a été réservé à la colonne de réfugiés qui tentait de rejoindre Tuzla. Des soldats serbes bosniaques ont tendu une embuscade sur la route Bratunac-Milići et ont attaqué la colonne à l'aide de pièces d'artillerie, de missiles antiaériens, d'armes automatiques et autres. Cette offensive a provoqué des pertes considérables en vies humaines. Des centaines de Musulmans ont été tués et un plus grand nombre encore ont été blessés. Beaucoup ont été affolés par l'agression et des témoins oculaires expliquent que des dizaines de réfugiés étaient à ce point horrifiés qu'ils se sont suicidés pour éviter d'être capturés. Beaucoup de ceux qui ont été fait prisonniers ou qui se sont rendus, et parmi eux les blessés, ont été sommairement exécutés. Un témoin oculaire explique que plus d'une centaine d'hommes, de femmes et d'enfants musulmans prisonniers ont été lentement massacrés par un groupe de soldats serbes utilisant des armes blanches. Les témoins ont également assisté à l'ensevelissement de centaines d'hommes musulmans dans des fosses communes, certains après avoir été exécutés, d'autres enterrés vivants.

Exécutions en masse à Karakaj

Des milliers de musulmans de la colonne se sont ensuite rendus aux soldats serbes sous le commandement et le contrôle de Ratko Mladić et de Radovan Karadžić, après avoir reçu l'assurance qu'ils ne seraient pas maltraités. Certains des soldats serbes qui leur ont donné ces garanties portaient des uniformes volés aux "casques bleus" de l'ONU. Les captifs ont ensuite été conduits à des points de rassemblement, et notamment à un stade de football où Ratko Mladić s'est adressé à eux en les rassurant à nouveau, et ensuite à un point de rassemblement dans un centre scolaire près de Karakaj, où Ratko Mladić était présent à nouveau. A cet endroit également, beaucoup ont été sommairement exécutés.

Selon le récit des quelques témoins qui ont survécu, le jour suivant, c'est-à-dire le 14 juillet 1995 ou aux alentours de cette date, les hommes ont été conduits en camion sur deux terrains avoisinants. On les y a fait sortir des camions en petits groupes et on leur a dit de trouver un emplacement où on les a abattus sur place. Les survivants expliquent que des milliers d'hommes ont ainsi été massacrés, jusqu'à ce que le sol soit jonché de cadavres. Après le massacre, des soldats serbes ont marché parmi les corps pour vérifier que tous étaient bien morts. Si une victime prononçait un son ou si un corps était encore chaud, une balle supplémentaire était utilisée pour l'achever. Selon les survivants, les massacres se sont poursuivis toute la journée et toute la nuit, des camions entiers d'hommes arrivant toutes les dix à quinze minutes. Les témoins oculaires n'ont survécu qu'en feignant d'être morts en-dessous des cadavres jusqu'à ce que les soldats aient tous disparu. Plus d'un survivant affirme avoir vu Ratko Mladić à l'endroit des massacres. Les corps ont commencé à être enterrés dans la nuit même à l'aide de pelleteuses et d'excavatrices.

Trucks arrived to evacuate the women, who were deported from Srebrenica in their thousands. After an initial policy of allowing some men on the buses, it appears from several statements that when Ratko Mladic arrived, he ordered that no men, nor even boys, be allowed to evacuate.

Most of the men and boys who were left behind were then transported to Bratunac and, from there, to the "killing fields" described above.

As a result of the Bosnian Serb attack on Srebrenica, the Muslim population of the enclave was virtually eliminated.

The two suspects are Ratko Mladic and Radovan Karadzic.

Ratko Mladic

The evidence submitted by the Prosecutor, consisting of more than thirty eye-witness statements, provides reasonable grounds for believing that Ratko Mladic personally supervised the take-over of Srebrenica with great attention to detail. Witnesses describe seeing him in the football stadium where thousands of men were gathered, at the school-complex moments before the men were put in trucks to be taken away for execution, and at one of the execution sites. He was also seen by many in Potocari, where the evidence suggests that, despite assurances of safety, he issued orders that the men should not be evacuated but should be executed instead. He was seen personally separating men from the buses on which their wives and children were being deported.

In addition to the personal aspects of his involvement, Ratko Mladic, was at all relevant times the General of the Bosnian Serb army, with command and control over his troops.

Radovan Karadzic

It appears that the suspect, Radovan Karadzic, also exercised effective military control over the Bosnian Serb forces, as commander and political leader of the Bosnian Serb administration in Pale. He had, apparently, total authority and responsibility for the strategies and actions employed by the Bosnian Serbs in Bosnia-Herzegovina.

In these circumstances, the direct responsibility of the two suspects could arise from planning, instigating, ordering, committing or aiding and abetting the alleged crimes.

It is worth noting that it appears from the witness statements that not only Bosnian Serb soldiers, but also soldiers from the Federal Republic of Yugoslavia (Serbia-Montenegro) were present during the take-over of Srebrenica. These soldiers were easily distinguishable by their clean-cut appearance, distinctive uniforms and use of Serbian dialects. Elements of the Yugoslav People's Army ("JNA"), including the Novi Sad Corps and "Uvicc" Corps, as well as irregulars loyal to "Arkan", were seen by a number of witnesses in and around Srebrenica. Either these additional troops

Exécutions sommaires à Potočari

La plupart des hommes, femmes et enfants musulmans qui se sont rendus à Potočari n'ont pas pu pénétrer dans la base de l'ONU et ont passé les nuits du 11 au 13 juillet 1995 dans des usines voisines. Pendant ce temps, et sous la surveillance du Général Mladić en personne, les hommes ont été séparés des femmes. Il semble que beaucoup aient été sommairement exécutés dans les champs et rivières entourant la base. Les enfants ont eu la gorge tranchée sous les yeux de leurs mères. Dans leurs dépositions, les témoins font état d'une vague de terreur qui a conduit de nombreuses personnes à se suicider. Il est prouvé que des femmes ont été violées et tuées.

Des camions sont arrivés pour évacuer les femmes, qui ont été expulsées de Srebrenica par milliers. Après avoir, dans un premier temps, autorisé quelques hommes à monter dans les bus, il ressort de plusieurs dépositions que, lorsque Ratko Mladić est arrivé, il a interdit que l'on évacue les hommes, et même les garçons.

La plupart des hommes et des garçons qui n'ont pas pu partir ont ensuite été transportés à Bratunac et, de là, sur les "terrains d'exécution" décrits plus haut.

Suite à l'offensive des Serbes de Bosnie contre Srebrenica, la population musulmane de l'enclave a été pratiquement éliminée.

Les deux suspects sont Ratko Mladić et Radovan Karadžić.

Ratko Mladić

Les éléments de preuve produits par le Procureur, qui consistent en plus de trente dépositions de témoins oculaires, permettent de soutenir raisonnablement que Ratko Mladić a personnellement supervisé la prise de Srebrenica jusque dans les moindres détails. Des témoins expliquent qu'il était présent au stade de football où des milliers d'hommes ont été regroupés, au centre scolaire avant que les hommes aient été placés dans les camions qui les emmenaient pour être exécutés, et sur l'un des lieux d'exécution. Beaucoup l'ont également vu à Potočari, où les preuves tendent à montrer qu'en dépit des garanties de sécurité, il a donné l'ordre de ne pas évacuer les hommes, mais de les exécuter. Il a été vu en train d'écarter lui-même des hommes des bus dans lesquels leur femmes et enfants étaient expulsés.

Outre le fait de sa participation personnelle, Ratko Mladić était à toutes les époques pertinentes Général de l'armée des Serbe de Bosnie et détenait le commandement et le contrôle de ses troupes.

Radovan Karadžić

Il semble que le suspect Radovan Karadžić ait également détenu le contrôle effectif de l'armée des Serbes de Bosnie en sa qualité de commandant et de leader politique de l'administration des Serbes de Bosnie à Pale. Il semble qu'il contrôlait et qu'il était responsable des stratégies et des actions mises en oeuvre par les Serbes bosniaques en Bosnie-Herzégovine.

IT-95-18-I 348

were also under the command of the suspects, or they were under the control of a different commander.

Having considered the evidence as presented by the Prosecutor, I now consider the charges of the indictment.

The charges of the indictment are arranged according to three sets of events and one summary. First, the Prosecutor presents the crimes committed at Potocari under counts 3 and 4, and there under two different legal characterisations: crimes against humanity and violations of the laws or customs of war. Second, the crimes committed during the flight of the column through the woods are presented under fourteen separate counts covering seven separate events. Each of these events is again presented under a double legal characterisation: crimes against humanity and violations of the laws or customs of war. Third, the acts committed in Karakaj are covered by counts 19 and 20, both of which are presented, again, as crimes against humanity and violations of the laws or customs of war. Finally, the criminal acts taken as a whole are the subject of counts 1 and 2, the former characterising those acts as genocide, the latter as extermination, a crime against humanity.

Subject to any later determination which may be made by a Trial Chamber of the Tribunal, I consider, *prima facie*, that the facts of the case disclose, above all, the commission of genocide.

The mass executions described in the indictment were evidently systematic, being organised by the military and political hierarchy of the Serbian administration of Pale, apparently with close support from elements of the army of the Federal Republic of Yugoslavia (Serbia-Montenegro). These executions were committed in the context of a broader policy of "ethnic cleansing" which is directed against the Bosnian Muslim population and which also includes massive deportations. This policy aims at creating new borders by violently changing the national or religious composition of the population. As a result of this policy, the Muslim population of Srebrenica was totally banished from the area.

Thus the evidence also discloses, *prima facie*, the commission of crimes against humanity, and violations of the laws or customs of war.

The policy of "ethnic cleansing" referred to above presents, in its ultimate manifestation, genocidal characteristics. Furthermore, in this case, the intent to destroy, in whole or in part, a national, ethnical, racial or religous group, which is specific to genocide, may clearly be inferred from the gravity of the "ethnic cleansing" practiced in Srebrenica and its surrounding areas, i.e. principally, the mass killings of Muslims which occurred after the fall of Srebrenica in July 1995, which were committed in circumstances manifesting an almost unparalleled cruelty.

Thus the charge of genocide is indeed appropriate.

Dans ces conditions, les deux suspects pourraient voir leur responsabilité directement engagée du fait qu'ils ont planifié, incité à commettre, ordonné, commis ou aidé et encouragé les crimes présumés.

Il mérite d'être remarqué que, selon des dépositions de témoins, non seulement des soldats serbes bosniaques mais également des soldats de la République fédérale de Yougoslavie (Serbie-Monténégro) étaient présents durant la prise de Srebrenica. Ces soldats étaient aisément reconnaissables à la netteté de leur apparence, à leurs uniformes distincts et aux dialectes serbes qu'ils utilisaient. Des membres de l'armée populaire yougoslave ("JNA"), et notamment le corps Novi Sad et le corps "Uvice", ainsi que des membres de l'armée irrégulière fidèle à "Arkan" ont été vus par un certain nombre de témoins dans Srebrenica même et autour de la ville. Ces troupes supplémentaires se trouvaient soit sous le commandement des suspects, soit sous le commandement d'un autre.

Après avoir examiné les éléments de preuve présentés par le Procureur, nous en venons maintenant aux différents chefs de l'acte d'accusation.

Les différents chefs figurant dans l'acte d'accusation sont présentés sur la base de trois séries d'évènements et d'une récapitulation. Premièrement, le Procureur présente les crimes commis à Potocari sous les chefs 3 et 4 et sous deux qualifications juridiques différentes : crimes contre l'humanité et violations des lois ou coutumes de la guerre. Deuxièmement, les crimes perpétrés durant la fuite de la colonne à travers les bois sont présentés sous quatorze chefs séparés couvrant sept évènements distincts. Chacun de ces évènements est de nouveau présenté sous une double qualification juridique : crimes contre l'humanité et violations des lois ou coutumes de la guerre. Troisièmement, les actes commis à Karakaj sont couverts par les chefs 19 et 20, qui sont également qualifiés de crimes contre l'humanité et de violations des lois ou coutumes de la guerre. Enfin, les actes criminels pris dans leur ensemble font l'objet des chefs 1 et 2, le premier les qualifiant de génocide et le second d'extermination, un crime contre l'humanité.

Sous réserve de toute décision ultérieure d'une Chambre de première instance du Tribunal, je considère de prime abord que les faits de l'affaire révèlent, avant tout, la commission d'un génocide.

Les exécutions massives décrites dans l'acte d'accusation étaient clairement systématiques, du fait de leur organisation par la hiérarchie militaire et politique de l'Administration des Serbes à Pale, apparemment avec le soutien direct d'éléments de l'armée de la République fédérale de Yougoslavie (Serbie-Monténégro). Ces exécutions ont été commises dans le contexte d'une politique plus générale de "purification ethnique" dirigée contre la population musulmane de Bosnie et qui fait également appel à des expulsions massives. Cette politique vise à établir de nouvelles frontières en modifiant par la violence la composition nationale ou religieuse de la population. Du fait de cette politique, la population musulmane a été entièrement bannie de la région.

Les éléments de preuve révèlent donc aussi , de prime abord, la commission de crimes contre l'humanité et des violations des lois ou coutumes de la guerre.

La politique de "purification ethnique" mentionnée ci-dessus présente, dans sa manifestation ultime, des caractéristiques de génocide. De surcroît, dans la présente

IT-95-18-I 347

Considering all of the above, it appears that the crime of genocide, and at least that of crimes against humanity, charged in counts 1 and 2 of the indictment, to the extent that they cover all of the events described, are the most comprehensive.

FOR THE FOREGOING REASONS

CONSIDER that there this is sufficient evidence to provide reasonable grounds for believing that Ratko Mladic and Radovan Karadzic committed the crimes charged in the indictment, which fall within the jurisdiction of the Tribunal under Articles 3,4, and 5.

PURSUANT TO Articles 18 and 19 of the Statute, and Rules 28 and 47 of the Rules of Procedure and Evidencc,

CONFIRM the indictment submitted by the Prosecutor in respect of each and every count of the indictment

Fouad RIAD
Judge,
Trial Chamber

Dated this 16th day of November, 1995,
At The Hague,
The Netherlands

IT-95-18-I 1/352 BIS

affaire, l'intention de détruire, en tout ou en partie, un groupe national, ethnique, racial ou religieux, qui est spécifique au génocide, peut clairement être déduite de la gravité de la "purification ethnique" pratiquée à Srebrenica et dans la région avoisinante, c'est-à-dire essentiellement les exécutions massives de musulmans commises après la chute de Srebrenica en juillet 1995, dans des circonstances démontrant une cruauté presque sans pareille.

L'accusation de génocide est ainsi tout à fait appropriée.

Considérant tout ce qui précède, il semble que le crime de génocide et, au moins, celui de crimes contre l'humanité figurant aux chefs 1 et 2 de l'acte d'accusation, dans la mesure où ils couvrent l'ensemble des évènements décrits, sont les qualifications les plus exhaustives.

POUR LES RAISONS SUSMENTIONNEES

CONSIDERONS qu'il existe des éléments de preuve suffisants pour soutenir raisonnablement que Ratko Mladić et Radovan Karadžić ont commis les crimes qui leur sont reprochés dans l'acte d'accusation , crimes qui relèvent de la compétence du Tribunal en vertu des articles 3, 4 et 5 du Statut,

VU les articles 18 et 19 du Statut et les articles 28 et 47 du Règlement de procédure et de preuve,

CONFIRMONS l'acte d'accusation présenté par le Procureur eu égard à chacun des chefs de l'acte d'accusation.

Fouad Riad
Juge de la Chambre de première instance

Fait le seize novembre 1995
A La Haye, Pays-Bas.

UNITED NATIONS — NATIONS UNIES

INTERNATIONAL CRIMINAL TRIBUNAL FOR THE FORMER YUGOSLAVIA
CHURCHILLPLEIN, 1. P.O. BOX 13888
2501 EW THE HAGUE, NETHERLANDS
TELEPHONE: 31 70 416-5343
FAX: 31 70 416-5355

PRESS AND INFORMATION OFFICE

TRIBUNAL PÉNAL INTERNATIONAL POUR L'EX-YOUGOSLAVIE
CHURCHILLPLEIN, 1. B.P. 13888
2501 EW LA HAYE, PAYS-BAS
TÉLÉPHONE: 31 70 416-5343
FAX: 31 70 416-5355

BUREAU DE PRESSE ET D'INFORMATION

11 JULY 1996

INTERNATIONAL ARREST WARRANTS AND ORDERS FOR SURRENDER

*****

11 JUILLET 1996

MANDATS D'ARRET INTERNATIONAUX PORTANT ORDRES DE DEFEREMENT

RADOVAN KARADZIC
RATKO MLADIC
CASES NO. IT-95-5-R61 & NO. IT-95-18-R61

UNITED NATIONS

International Tribunal for the Prosecution of Persons Responsible for Serious Violations of International Humanitarian Law Committed in the Territory of Former Yugoslavia since 1991

Case No. IT-95-5-R61
IT-95-18-R61
Date: 11 July 1996

English
Original: French

IN THE TRIAL CHAMBER

Before: **Judge Claude Jorda, Presiding**
Judge Elizabeth Odio Benito
Judge Fouad Riad

Registrar: **Mr. Dominique Marro, Deputy Registrar**

Order of: **11 July 1996**

THE PROSECUTOR

v.

RADOVAN KARADŽIĆ
RATKO MLADIĆ

INTERNATIONAL ARREST WARRANT AND ORDER FOR SURRENDER

To all States and to the Implementation Force (IFOR)

<u>Addressed to:</u> All States and to the Implementation Force (IFOR)

TRIAL CHAMBER I of the International Criminal Tribunal for the former Yugoslavia,

CONSIDERING United Nations Security Council Resolution 827 of 25 May 1993, Article 29 of the Statute, as well as Rules 54 to 61 of the Rules of Procedure and Evidence of the Tribunal,

CONSIDERING the indictments submitted against Radovan KARADŽIĆ by the Prosecutor of the Tribunal, confirmed by the order issued by Judge Jorda on 25 July 1995 and Judge Riad on 16 November 1995 copies of which are annexed to this warrant of arrest,

CONSIDERING the decision of the Trial Chamber on 11 July 1996, reconfirming the indictments issued on 25 July and 16 November 1995 following the failure to execute the initial warrant of arrest against Radovan KARADŽIĆ a copy of which is annexed to this warrant of arrest,

HEREBY DIRECTS the authorities and officers and agents of all States to act promptly with all due diligence to secure the arrest, detention and transfer to the Tribunal of:

> Radovan KARADŽIĆ born on 19 June 1945, in Pretnjica, in the municipality of Šavnik, believed to be residing in Pale, Han Pijesak, or Jahorina;
>
> **ACCUSED** of having committed from April 1992 to July 1995 in the Republic of Bosnia and Herzegovina in the territory of the former Yugoslavia the following crimes:
>
> Grave breaches of the Conventions of Geneva of 12 August 1949
> Violations of the laws or customs of war
> Genocide
> Crimes against humanity
>
> within the competence of the Tribunal by virtue of Articles 2, 3, 4 and 5 of the Statute

AND to advise the said Radovan KARADŽIĆ at the time of his arrest, and in a language he understands, of his rights as set forth in Article 21 of the Statute and, *mutatis mutandis*, in Rules 42 and 43 of the Rules of Procedure and Evidence the text of which is annexed to this warrant of arrest, including his right to remain silent and to be cautioned and that any statements he makes shall be recorded and may be used in evidence. The indictment, review of the indictment (and any documents annexed to the present warrant) must be brought to the attention of the accused in a language he understands;

FURTHER REQUESTS that the authorities of all States and the Implementation Force (IFOR) upon the arrest of the accused Radovan KARADŽIĆ, promptly notify the Registrar of the International Criminal Tribunal for the former Yugoslavia.

Claude Jorda, Presiding Judge, Trial Chamber I
International Criminal Tribunal for the former Yugoslavia

Dated this eleventh day of July 1996
At The Hague
The Netherlands

(Seal of the Tribunal)

UNITED NATIONS

International Tribunal for the Prosecution of Persons Responsible for Serious Violations of International Humanitarian Law Committed in the Territory of Former Yugoslavia since 1991	Case No. IT-95-5-R61 IT-95-18-R61 Date: 11 July 1996 English Original: French

<u>IN THE TRIAL CHAMBER</u>

Before: **Judge Claude Jorda, Presiding**
Judge Elizabeth Odio Benito
Judge Fouad Riad

Registrar: **Mr. Dominique Marro, Deputy Registrar**

Order of: **11 July 1996**

THE PROSECUTOR

v.

RADOVAN KARADŽIĆ
RATKO MLADIĆ

INTERNATIONAL ARREST WARRANT AND ORDER FOR SURRENDER

To all States and to the Implementation Force (IFOR)

Addressed to: All States and to the Implementation Force (IFOR)

TRIAL CHAMBER I of the International Criminal Tribunal for the former Yugoslavia,

CONSIDERING United Nations Security Council Resolution 827 of 25 May 1993, Article 29 of the Statute, as well as Rules 54 to 61 of the Rules of Procedure and Evidence of the Tribunal,

CONSIDERING the indictments submitted against Ratko MLADIĆ by the Prosecutor of the Tribunal, confirmed by the order issued by Judge Jorda on 25 July 1995 and Judge Riad on 16 November 1995 copies of which are annexed to this warrant of arrest,

CONSIDERING the decision of the Trial Chamber on 11 July 1996, reconfirming the indictments issued on 25 July and 16 November 1995 following the failure to execute the initial warrant of arrest against Ratko MLADIĆ a copy of which is annexed to this warrant of arrest,

HEREBY DIRECTS the authorities and officers and agents of all States to act promptly with all due diligence to secure the arrest, detention and transfer to the Tribunal of:

> Ratko MLADIĆ born on 12 March 1943, in the village of Božanović near Kalinovik, in the Republic of Bosnia and Herzegovina, believed to be residing in Pale, Han Pijesak, Belgrade or Banja Luka,
>
> **ACCUSED** of having committed from April 1992 to July 1995 in the Republic of Bosnia and Herzegovina in the territory of the former Yugoslavia the following crimes:
>
> Grave breaches of the Conventions of Geneva of 12 August 1949
> Violations of the laws or customs of war
> Genocide
> Crimes against humanity
>
> within the competence of the Tribunal by virtue of Articles 2, 3, 4 and 5 of the Statute,

AND to advise the said Ratko MLADIĆ at the time of his arrest, and in a language he understands, of his rights as set forth in Article 21 of the Statute and, *mutatis mutandis*, in Rules 42 and 43 of the Rules of Procedure and Evidence the text of which is annexed to this warrant of arrest, including his right to remain silent and to be cautioned and that any statements he makes shall be recorded and may be used in evidence. The indictment, review of the indictment (and any documents annexed to the present warrant) must be brought to the attention of the accused in a language he understands;

FURTHER REQUESTS that the authorities of all States and the Implementation Force (IFOR) upon the arrest of the accused Ratko MLADIĆ, promptly notify the Registrar of the International Criminal Tribunal for the former Yugoslavia.

Claude Jorda, Presiding Judge, Trial Chamber I
International Criminal Tribunal for the former Yugoslavia

Dated this eleventh day of July 1996
At The Hague
The Netherlands

(Seal of the Tribunal)

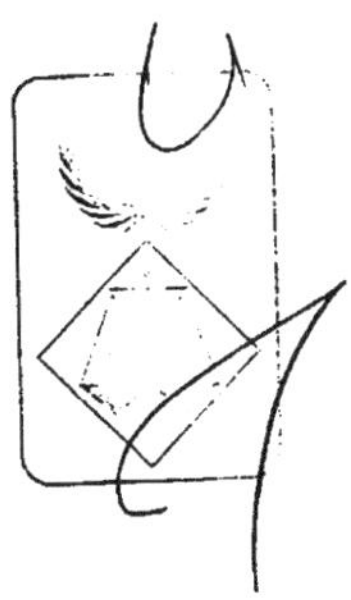

D 1371
D 1371-1:
12 JULY 1996
E.K

NATIONS
UNIES

Tribunal international chargé de poursuivre les personnes présumées responsables de violations graves du droit international humanitaire commises sur le territoire de l'ex-Yougoslavie depuis 1991

Affaires n° IT-95-5-R61
IT-95-18-R61

Date: 11 juillet 1996

Original: Français

LA CHAMBRE DE PREMIERE INSTANCE

Composée comme suit: **M. le Juge Claude Jorda, Président**
Mme le Juge Elizabeth Odio Benito
M. le Juge Fouad Riad

Assistée de: **M. Dominique Marro, Greffier adjoint**

Décision du: **11 juillet 1996**

LE PROCUREUR
c/
RADOVAN KARADŽIĆ
RATKO MLADIĆ

MANDAT D'ARRET INTERNATIONAL PORTANT ORDRE DE DEFEREMENT

Aux autorités de tous les Etats, ainsi qu'à la Force de mise en oeuvre (IFOR)

Adressé à: Tous les Etats ainsi qu'à la Force de mise en oeuvre (IFOR),

LA CHAMBRE DE PREMIÈRE INSTANCE I du Tribunal Pénal International pour l'ex-Yougoslavie

VU la résolution 827 du Conseil de Sécurité du 25 mai 1993, l'article 29 du Statut, ainsi que les articles 54 à 61 du Règlement de procédure et de preuve du Tribunal,

VU les actes d'accusation présentés contre Radovan KARADŽIĆ, par le Procureur du Tribunal, confirmés par ordonnances rendues par le Juge Jorda le 25 juillet 1995 et le Juge Riad le 16 novembre 1995 dont une copie est jointe à ce mandat,

VU la décision de la Chambre de première instance en date du 11 juillet 1996, confirmant de nouveau les actes d'accusation en date des 25 juillet et 16 novembre 1995 et faisant suite à l'inexécution du mandat d'arrêt initial pris contre Radovan KARADŽIĆ, dont une copie est jointe à ce mandat,

MANDE ET ORDONNE aux autorités, aux officiers judiciaires et aux mandataires de tous les Etats de rechercher, arrêter et déférer au Tribunal International, sans délai et avec toute la diligence qui s'impose:

> Radovan KARADŽIĆ, né le 19 juin 1945, à Pretnjica, dans la municipalité de Šavnik, qui résiderait soit à Pale, Han Pijesak, ou Jahorina;

> **ACCUSÉ** d'avoir commis, d'avril 1992 à juillet 1995, dans la République de Bosnie-Herzégovine, sur le territoire de l'ex-Yougoslavie les crimes suivants:
> Infractions graves aux Conventions de Genève du 12 août 1949
> Violations des lois ou coutumes de la guerre
> Génocide
> Crimes contre l'Humanité

> relevant de la compétence du Tribunal en vertu des articles 2, 3, 4 et 5 du Statut,

ET de faire connaître à l'accusé Radovan KARADŽIĆ, lors de son arrestation, dans une langue qu'il comprend, l'ensemble de ses droits définis à l'article 21 du Statut et *mutatis mutandis* aux articles 42 et 43 du Règlement de procédure et de preuve dont le texte est joint en copie au présent mandat, ainsi que son droit de garder le silence et la mise en garde selon laquelle toute déclaration faite par lui est enregistrée et peut être retenue contre lui ainsi que les actes d'accusation et de confirmation, (et tout autre document annexé au présent mandat), dans une langue qu'il comprend;

DEMANDE de surcroît aux autorités de tous les Etats, ainsi qu'à la Force de mise en oeuvre (IFOR), d'informer sans délai le Greffier du Tribunal Pénal International pour l'ex-Yougoslavie de l'arrestation de Radovan KARADŽIĆ.

Claude Jorda, Président de la Chambre de première instance I
Tribunal Pénal International pour l'ex-Yougoslavie

Ainsi ordonné, ce onze juillet 1996
A La Haye,
Pays-Bas

(Sceau du Tribunal)

11 juillet 1996

Affaires No. IT-95-5-R61
IT-95-18-R61

D1374
D1374-1377
12 JULY 1996
E.K.

NATIONS
UNIES

Tribunal international chargé de poursuivre les personnes présumées responsables de violations graves du droit international humanitaire commises sur le territoire de l'ex-Yougoslavie depuis 1991

Affaires n° IT-95-5-R61
IT-95-18-R61

Date: 11 juillet 1996

Original: Français

LA CHAMBRE DE PREMIERE INSTANCE

Composée comme suit: **M. le Juge Claude Jorda, Président**
Mme le Juge Elizabeth Odio Benito
M. le Juge Fouad Riad

Assistée de: **M. Dominique Marro, Greffier adjoint**

Décision du: **11 juillet 1996**

LE PROCUREUR
c/
RADOVAN KARADŽIĆ
RATKO MLADIĆ

MANDAT D'ARRET INTERNATIONAL PORTANT ORDRE DE DEFEREMENT

Aux autorités de tous les Etats, ainsi qu'à la Force de mise en oeuvre (IFOR)

Adressé à: Tous les Etats ainsi qu'à la Force de mise en oeuvre (IFOR),

LA CHAMBRE DE PREMIÈRE INSTANCE I du du Tribunal Pénal International pour l'ex-Yougoslavie

VU la résolution 827 du Conseil de Sécurité du 25 mai 1993, l'article 29 du Statut, ainsi que les articles 54 à 61 du Règlement de procédure et de preuve du Tribunal Pénal pour l'ex-Yougoslavie,

VU les actes d'accusation présentés contre Ratko MLADIĆ, par le Procureur du Tribunal, confirmés par ordonnances rendues par le Juge Jorda le 25 juillet 1995 et par le Juge Riad le 16 novembre 1995, dont une copie est jointe à ce mandat,

VU la décision de la Chambre de première instance en date du 11 juillet 1996, confirmant de nouveau les actes d'accusation en date des 25 juillet et 16 novembre 1995, et faisant suite à l'inexécution du mandat d'arrêt initial pris contre Ratko MLADIĆ, dont une copie est jointe à ce mandat,

MANDE ET ORDONNE aux autorités, aux officiers judiciaires et aux mandataires de tous les Etats de rechercher, arrêter et déférer au Tribunal International, sans délai et avec toute la diligence qui s'impose:

> Ratko MLADIĆ, né le 12 mars 1943, dans le village de Božanović près de Kalinovik, dans la République de Bosnie-Herzégovine, qui résiderait soit à Pale, Han Pijesak, Belgrade ou Banjaluka,
>
> **ACCUSÉ** d'avoir commis d'avril 1992 à juillet 1995, dans la République de Bosnie-Herzégovine, sur le territoire de l'ex-Yougoslavie les crimes suivants:
> Infractions graves aux Conventions de Genève du 12 août 1949
> Violations des lois ou coutumes de la guerre
> Génocide
> Crimes contre l'Humanité
>
> relevant de la compétence du Tribunal en vertu des articles 2, 3, 4 et 5 du Statut,

ET de faire connaître à l'accusé Ratko MLADIĆ, lors de son arrestation, dans une langue qu'il comprend, l'ensemble de ses droits définis à l'article 21 du Statut et *mutatis mutandis* aux articles 42 et 43 du Règlement de procédure et de preuve dont le texte est joint en copie au présent mandat, ainsi que son droit de garder le silence et la mise en garde selon laquelle toute déclaration faite par lui est enregistrée et peut être retenue contre lui ainsi que les actes d'accusation et de confirmation, (et tout autre document annexé au présent mandat), dans une langue qu'il comprend;

DEMANDE de surcroît aux autorités de tous les Etats, ainsi qu'à la Force de mise en oeuvre (IFOR), d'informer sans délai le Greffier du Tribunal Pénal International pour l'ex-Yougoslavie de l'arrestation de Ratko MLADIĆ.

Claude Jorda, Président de la Chambre de première instance I.
Tribunal Pénal International pour l'ex-Yougoslavie

Ainsi ordonné, ce onze juillet 1996
A La Haye,
Pays-Bas

(Sceau du Tribunal)

Affaires No. IT-95-5-R61
IT-95-18-R61

11 juillet 1996

UNITED NATIONS NATIONS UNIES

INTERNATIONAL CRIMINAL TRIBUNAL FOR THE FORMER YUGOSLAVIA
CHURCHILLPLEIN, 1. P.O. BOX 13888
2501 EW THE HAGUE, NETHERLANDS
TELEPHONE: 31 70 416-5343
FAX: 31 70 416-5355

PRESS AND INFORMATION OFFICE

TRIBUNAL PÉNAL INTERNATIONAL POUR L'EX-YOUGOSLAVIE
CHURCHILLPLEIN, 1 B.P. 13888
2501 EW LA HAYE, PAYS-BAS
TELEPHONE 31 70 416-5343
FAX 31 70 416-5355

BUREAU DE PRESSE ET D'INFORMATION

INDICTMENT

Gagovic & others

("Foca")

(26 JUNE 1996)

PRESS AND INFORMATION OFFICE
BUREAU DE PRESSE ET D'INFORMATION

TEL.: (31) 70 - 416 5343
FAX : (31) 70 - 416 5355

United Nations
Nations Unies

International Criminal Tribunal for the former Yugoslavia

Tribunal Pénal International pour l'ex-Yougoslavie

Press Release . Communiqué de presse

(Exclusively for the use of the media. Not an official document)

CC/PIO/093-E
The Hague, 27 June 1996

GANG RAPE, TORTURE AND ENSLAVEMENT OF MUSLIM WOMEN CHARGED IN ICTY'S FIRST INDICTMENT DEALING SPECIFICALLY WITH SEXUAL OFFENCES

Muslim women in Foca (southeastern Bosnia and Herzegovina) were subjected to a brutal regime of gang rape, torture and enslavement by Bosnian Serb soldiers, policemen and members of paramilitary groups after the takeover of the city in April 1992, according to a major indictment issued by the International Tribunal dealing specifically with sexual offences.

The indictment charges **Dragan GAGOVIĆ, Gojko JANKOVIĆ, Janko JANJIĆ, Radomir KOVAĆ, Zoran VUKOVIĆ, Dragan ZELENOVIĆ, Dragoljub KUNARAĆ** and **Radovan STANKOVIĆ** with crimes against humanity, grave breaches of the Geneva Conventions and Violations of the Laws or Customs of War. It was confirmed by Judge VOHRAH on 26 June 1996. Warrants for the accused's arrest were issued on 26 June and were sent to the Federation of Bosnia and Herzegovina and the Republika Srpska.

The indictment is of major legal significance as it is the first time that sexual assaults have been diligently investigated for the purpose of prosecution under the rubric of torture and enslavement as a crime against humanity..

GENERAL ALLEGATIONS

According to the indictment, the municipality of Foca was taken over by the Bosnian Serb Army, assisted by paramilitaries units, including some from Serbia and Montenegro, between April and July 1992. The soldiers separated men and women.

The former were mostly detained in the Foca Kazneno-Popravni Dom (KP Dom Foca), one of the largest prison facilities in the former Socialist Federal Republic of Yugoslavia.

.../...

Churchillplein 1, 2517 JW The Hague . P.O. Box 13888, 2501 EW The Hague . Netherlands
Churchillplein 1, 2517 JW La Haye . B.P. 13888, 2501 EW La Haye . Pays-Bas
Press and Information Office / Bureau de presse et d'information:
Press: +31 (0)70 416-5343/5356 Documentation: +31 (0)70 416-5285
Public Information: +31 (0)70 416-5232 Fax: +31 (0)70 416-5355

The KP Dom Foca is one of several detention facilities mentioned in the Karadzic and Mladic indictment of 25 July 1995 under Counts 1 to 2 (genocide and crimes against humanity).

Muslim women, children and elderly persons were detained in houses, apartments and motels in the town of Foca or surrounding villages, and in short and long-term detention centres, such as Buk Bijela, Foca High School and Partizan Sports Hall. Additionally, several women were held in houses and apartments, which were run in the manner of brothels, by groups of mainly paramilitary soldiers

Many of the detained women, some as young as 12 years of age, endured inhumane conditions of detention and were subjected to *"humiliating and degrading conditions of life, to brutal beatings and to sexual assaults, including rapes (. . .)"*

The detention and other abuses were carried out between April 1992 and February 1993, with the active or passive knowledge of the local Chief of Police, Dragan GAGOVIĆ, and other persons in positions of authority, as sub-commanders of the military police. On at least one occasion, GAGOVIĆ responded to a complaint about the ongoing sexual assaults by later raping the woman who protested.

Among the purposes of the assaults were to extricate information from the women about the whereabouts of their menfolk and the existence of any armed resistance; to punish and intimidate them; and for reasons based upon discrimination.

THE VICTIMS

The indictment charges crimes committed against at least 14 victims, referred to in the indictment by code names and by initials.

These and other women were subjected to almost constant rape and sexual assaults; torture; and other abuses. According to the indictment: *"The physical and psychological health of many female detainees seriously deteriorated as a result of these sexual assaults. Some of the women endured complete exhaustion, vaginal discharges, bladder problems and irregular menstrual bleedings. The detainees lived in constant fear. Some of the sexually abused women became suicidal. Others became indifferent as to what would happen to them and suffered from depression (. . .)"*

"Many women suffered permanent gynaecological harm due to the sexual assaults. All the women who were sexually assaulted suffered psychological and emotional harm; some remain traumatised."

ONE YOUNG GIRL'S ORDEAL: THE STORY OF FWS-87

While all of the women mentioned in the indictment suffered horrendous and unrelenting abuses, the ordeal endured by the young girl referred to in the indictment as FWS-87 exemplifies the pattern of violations experienced by these women.

Only 15-years of age when she was first detained in July 1992, the Prosecutor has alleged that FWS-87 was subjected to at least eight months of routine torture, including gang rape, and enslavement at the hands of accused such as JANKOVIĆ, JANJIĆ, KOVAĆ, VUKOVIĆ, ZELENOVIĆ, KUNARAĆ and STANKOVIĆ and countless other unidentified soldiers.

FWS-87 was first detained at the Buk Bijela complex on the River Drina on or about 3 July 1992. There, she was interrogated by Dragan ZELENOVIĆ and three unidentified soldiers, each of whom raped her in turn. One of the soldiers put a gun to her head as he raped her. FWS-87 suffered severe pain during the attack, followed by heavy vaginal bleeding.

Between 3 and 13 July 1992, FWS-87, together with at least 72 other Muslim inhabitants of Foca, was transferred to Foca High School. FWS-87 was one of several women who, from the second day of their detention, were sexually assaulted, including gang-raped every evening, by groups of soldiers, either in the class-rooms or in nearby apartments. The soldiers consisted of members of the military police and referred to themselves as "Cosa's Guards", after the local commander of the military police, Cosovic. Amongst the perpetrators were the accused JANKOVIĆ, ZELENOVIĆ, JANJIĆ and VUKOVIĆ.

The soldiers threatened to kill the women if they refused to submit. Women who tried to resist were beaten.

On or about 6 or 7 July 1992, FWS-87 was raped by VUKOVIĆ while other detained women were simultaneously raped in the same room.

Between 8 and 13 July, the accused Dragan ZELENOVIĆ led a group of soldiers that sexually abused FWS-87 and another young woman at Foca High School on at least five occasions additional to the one described above.

During this same period, FWS-87 was taken from Foca High School to a nearby apartment owned by ZELENOVIĆ on at least five occasions. There, she was raped by Zoran VUKOVIĆ and Dragan ZELENOVIĆ .

Around 13 July 1992, FWS-87 and the other detainees at Foca High School were transferred to the Partizan Sports Hall. While being held there, until about 2 August 1992, FWS-87 and other female detainees were continuously raped and otherwise sexually assaulted by innumerable soldiers and by the accused Dragan ZELENOVIĆ, Zoran VUKOVIĆ and Dragoljub KUNARAĆ with the actual or constructive knowledge of the accused Dragan GAGOVIĆ. FWS-87 became suicidal as a result of these sexual assaults.

FWS-87, along with other Muslim women, was transferred on 2 August 1992 to a house in Foca which was owned by a Muslim who lived in Germany. Some of these women were as young as 12 years of age. The house was run in the manner of a brothel by the accused Radovan STANKOVIĆ. The women were kept there until 30 October 1992.

FWS-87 and the other women held at the house were not only treated as sexual slaves but were also forced to work for the soldiers, including washing uniforms, cooking and cleaning the house. FWS-87 was also forced to clean and cook for other soldiers in other buildings. FWS-87's suicidal feelings continued throughout this period.

On or about 30 October 1992, FWS-87, together with other Muslim girls and women, was moved back to Foca and shifted different houses. They were raped and otherwise sexually assaulted on numerous occasions by the accused Dragan ZELENOVIĆ, Gojko JANKOVIĆ and Janko JANJIĆ.

Between 31 October 1992 and about 25 February 1993, FWS-87 was enslaved by Radomir KOVAĆ in an apartment block in Foca. She and other detained women were not only frequently sexually assaulted, including by the accused KOVAĆ, but were also forced to perform household chores.

On 25 February 1993, FWS-87 was sold by Radomir KOVAĆ for 500 Deutschmarks to two unidentified Montenegrin soldiers.

THE INVESTIGATION AND THE STRATEGY

The indictment made public today is the result of an investigation which commenced in late 1994.

This indictment fully illustrates the OTP's strategy:

to investigate the operation of detention facilities in connection with the takeover of parts of Bosnia and Herzegovina by the Bosnian Serb forces;

ORDER ON REVIEW

I, Lal C. Vohrah, Judge of the International Criminal Tribunal for the former Yugoslavia,

UPON RECEIVING an indictment from the Prosecutor pursuant to Article 19(1) of the Statute and Rule 47(C) of the Rules of Procedure and Evidence on 20 June 1992,

AND UPON RECEIVING additional material supplied by the Office of the Prosecutor on 24 June 1996,

AND UPON HEARING the Prosecutor pursuant to rule 47(D) of the Rules of Procedure and Evidence on 26 June 1996,

AND UPON BEING SATISFIED that the material which accompanied this indictment establishes a prima facie case against Dragan Gagović, Gojko Janković, Janko Janjić, Radomir Kovać, Zoran Vuković, Dragan Zelenović, Dragoljub Kunarac and Radovan Stanković in respect of the crimes with which they are charged in the indictment,

CONFIRM the indictment pursuant to Article 19(1) of the Statute and Rule 47(D) of the Rules of Procedure and Evidence in respect of each and every count therein.

Lal C. Vohrah
Trial Chamber II

Dated this twenty-sixth day of June 1996
At The Hague
The Netherlands

[Seal of the Tribunal]

Case No. IT-96-23-I

UNITED
NATIONS

International Tribunal for the Prosecution of Persons Responsible for Serious Violations of International Humanitarian Law Committed in the Territory of Former Yugoslavia since 1991	Case No.	IT-96-23-I
	Date:	26 June 1996
	Original:	ENGLISH

Before: Judge Lal C. Vohrah

Registrar: Mrs. Dorothee de Sampayo Garrido-Nijgh

Decision of: 26 June 1996

THE PROSECUTOR

v.

DRAGAN GAGOVIĆ
GOJKO JANKOVIĆ
JANKO JANJIĆ
RADOMIR KOVAČ
ZORAN VUKOVIĆ
DRAGAN ZELENOVIĆ
DRAGOLJUB KUNARAC
RADOVAN STANKOVIĆ

REVIEW OF INDICTMENT PURSUANT TO ARTICLE 19(1) OF THE STATUTE

<u>The Office of the Prosecutor:</u>

Mr. Graham Blewitt
Mrs. Patricia V. Sellers

19 JUNE 1996
D264 - D242
264

THE INTERNATIONAL CRIMINAL TRIBUNAL FOR THE FORMER YUGOSLAVIA

CASE NO.: IT-96-23-I

THE PROSECUTOR
OF THE TRIBUNAL

AGAINST

DRAGAN GAGOVIĆ
GOJKO JANKOVIĆ
JANKO JANJIĆ
RADOMIR KOVAČ
ZORAN VUKOVIĆ
DRAGAN ZELENOVIĆ
DRAGOLJUB KUNARAC
RADOVAN STANKOVIĆ

INDICTMENT

The Prosecutor of the International Criminal Tribunal for the former Yugoslavia, pursuant to his authority under article 18 of the Statute of the Tribunal charges:

DRAGAN GAGOVIĆ
GOJKO JANKOVIĆ
JANKO JANJIĆ
RADOMIR KOVAČ
ZORAN VUKOVIĆ
DRAGAN ZELENOVIĆ
DRAGOLJUB KUNARAC
RADOVAN STANKOVIĆ

with **CRIMES AGAINST HUMANITY, GRAVE BREACHES** OF THE **GENEVA CONVENTIONS (HEREAFTER, GRAVE BREACHES**) and **VIOLATIONS OF THE LAWS OR CUSTOMS OF WAR**, as set forth below:

1

BACKGROUND

1.1 The city and municipality of Foča are located south-east of Sarajevo, in the Republic of Bosnia-Herzegovina and borders Serbia and Montenegro. According to the 1991 census, the population of Foča consisting of 40.513 persons was 51.6 % Muslim, 45.3 % Serbian and 3.1% others. The political and military take-over of the municipality of Foča started with the first military actions in the town of Foča on 7 April 1992. Regular military units from the Bosnian Serb army and irregular military units from Serbia and Montenegro, supported by artillery and heavy weapons, proceeded to take over Foča, section by section. The occupation of Foča town was complete by 16 or 17 April 1992. The surrounding villages continued to be under siege until mid July 1992.

1.2 As soon as the Serb forces had taken over parts of Foča town, military police accompanied by local and non-local soldiers started arresting Muslim and Croat inhabitants. Until mid July 1992 they continued to round up and arrest Muslim villagers from the surrounding villages in the municipality. The Serb forces separated men and women and unlawfully confined thousands of Muslims and Croats in various short and long-term detention facilities or kept them under constructive house arrest. During the arrests many civilians were killed, beaten or subjected to sexual assault.

1.3 During the take-over and the arrest of the non-Serb population, there was a close alliance between the Foča police (hereinafter, SUP) and the Serb forces. The arms and uniforms for the Serb soldiers were distributed from the SUP building. Serb soldiers were constantly going in and out of the SUP building and started their wave of arrests from there.

1.4 The Foča Kazneno-popravni Dom (hereinafter KP Dom), one of the largest prison facilities in the former Republic of Yugoslavia, was the primary detention facility for men. Muslim women, children and the elderly were detained in houses, apartments and motels in the town of Foča or in surrounding villages, or at short and long-term detention centres such as Buk Bijela, Foča High School and Partizan Sports Hall, respectively. Many of the detained women were subjected to humiliating and degrading conditions of life, to brutal beatings and to sexual assaults, including rapes.

1.5 Besides the above mentioned detention places, several women were detained in houses and apartments used as brothels, operated by groups of soldiers, mostly paramilitary. The ICRC and other organisations, unaware of these detention facilities, did not intervene. Therefore those detainees had no possibility of release or exchange.

THE ACCUSED

2.1 **DRAGAN GAGOVIĆ**, son of Milorad, born on 13 June 1960 in Ustikolina, was a permanent resident of Ustikolina in the municipality of Foča. Prior to the war he worked as a department commander of the Foča SUP. He was a member of the Serbian Democratic Party (hereinafter SDS). **DRAGAN GAGOVIĆ**, the former deputy of police, was appointed the Chief of Police in Foča by the SDS after the April 1992 take-over of Foča.

2.2 **GOJKO JANKOVIĆ**, son of Danilo, born on 31 October 1954 in the village of Trbušće in the municipality of Foča, was a permanent resident of Foča at I. G. Kovačića Street. For a period of time he had lived in Herceg Novi, Montenegro. Prior to the take-over of Foča, he worked in the Šipad Maglić Company and owned a cafe in Trnovača. **GOJKO JANKOVIĆ** was a sub-commander of the military police and one of the main paramilitary leaders in Foča.

2.3 **JANKO JANJIĆ** also known as (hereinafter a/k/a/) **"Tuta"**, son of Milorad, born on 17 June 1957 in Miljevina, municipality of Foča, was a permanent resident of Foča at Moše Pijade Street no. 6. He was a car mechanic and unemployed prior to the Bosnian Serb attack on Foča in April 1992 . **JANKO JANJIC** became one of the sub-commanders of the military police and a paramilitary leader in Foča. He was involved in the attack on Foča and its surrounding villages and the arrest of civilians.

2.4 **RADOMIR KOVAĆ, a/k/a "Klanfa,"** son of Milenko, born on 31 March 1961 in Foča, was a permanent resident of Foča at Samoborska Street. **RADOMIR KOVAĆ** was one of the sub-commanders of the military police and a paramilitary leader in Foča. He was involved in the attack on Foča and its surrounding villages and the arrest of civilians.

2.5 **ZORAN VUKOVIĆ**, son of Gojko, born in 1965 in the village of Prijedel, municipality of Foča, was permanent resident of Prijedel. He worked as a waiter and had lived in Herceg Novi, Montenegro. **ZORAN VUKOVIĆ** was involved in the attack on Foča and its surrounding villages and the arrest of civilians. He was one of the sub-commanders of the military police and a paramilitary leader in Foča.

2.6 **DRAGAN ZELENOVIĆ a/k/a "Zelja"** and **"Zeleni"**, son of Bogdan, born on 12 February 1961 in Foča, lives at Nurije Pozderca 21 as of June 1996. He worked as an electrician in Miljevina before the war. **DRAGAN ZELENOVIĆ** was one of the sub-commanders of the military police and a paramilitary leader in Foča. He was involved in the attack on Foča and its surrounding villages and in the arrest of civilians.

2.7 **DRAGOLJUB KUNARAC a/k/a "Zaga"** and **"Dragan"**, son of Aleksa, was born on 15 May 1960 in Foča. He lives at D. Fundića Street No. 3 d as of June 1996. He lived in Tivat, Montenegro prior to the April 1992 attack on Foča. **DRAGOLJUB KUNARAC**, a paramilitary commander, was subordinate to Pero Elez, a paramilitary leader who was killed during the occupation of Foča and the surrounding villages.

2.8 **RADOVAN STANKOVIĆ a/k/a "Raša"**, son of Todor, born on 10 March 1969 in the village of Trebiča, municipality of Foča, was a permanent resident of Miljevina. He belonged to the Serb elite paramilitary unit of Pero Elez. **RADOVAN STANKOVIĆ**, was also a subordinate of Pero Elez. **RADOVAN STANKOVIĆ**, was in charge of Karaman's house in Miljevina, where Muslim women were detained and sexually assaulted, including raped.

SUPERIOR AUTHORITY

3.1 **DRAGAN GAGOVIĆ**, in his capacity as chief of police, was the person in charge of the detention and the release of female Muslim detainees in Foča. He was responsible for the living conditions of the detainees in Partizan Sports Hall, a detention facility that held women, children and elderly men from July 1992 through to August 1992. **DRAGAN GAGOVIĆ** exercised powers and duties indicative of his superior position. He decided that the arrested Muslim women should first be kept in the Foča High School and then transferred to the Partizan Sports Hall. Police staff, subordinate to **DRAGAN GAGOVIĆ**, guarded the detainees in both of these detention facilities. As the person who oversaw female Muslim detainees, **DRAGAN GAGOVIĆ** was responsible for the acts of the police guards and the soldiers who entered the Partizan Sports Hall. He knew or had reason to know that the women who were detained at the Partizan Sports Hall were frequently sexually assaulted. The Partizan Sports Hall was situated very close to the SUP building. Events that happened at the Partizan Hall could be heard and seen from the SUP building. **DRAGAN GAGOVIĆ** was physically present in the Partizan Sports Hall on several occasions. Around 16 July 1992, a group of detainees from the Partizan Sports Hall, went to the SUP building and informed **DRAGAN GAGOVIĆ** about the constant sexual assault of women in the detention facility. On or around 17 July 1992, **DRAGAN GAGOVIĆ** personally raped one of the women who, on the previous day, had complained about the incidences of sexual assaults.

3.2 **GOJKO JANKOVIĆ** was involved in the military attack on Foča town and various surrounding villages and the arrest of civilians in leading positions. **GOJKO JANKOVIĆ**, in his capacity as a sub-commander of the military police in Foča, was in charge of the soldiers who, on 3 July 1992, arrested a group of women and transported them to the military facility at Buk Bijela for interrogation. In his position, **GOJKO JANKOVIĆ** was responsible for the acts of soldiers subordinate to him and knew or had reason to know that his subordinates sexually assaulted Muslim women during or immediately following the interrogations. **GOJKO JANKOVIĆ** personally was involved in the interrogation and rape of women at Buk Bijela.

3.3 **DRAGOLJUB KUNARAC**, the commander of a special volunteer unit of non-local irregular Serb soldiers mainly from Montenegro, had his headquarters in a house in the Aladža neighbourhood in Foča at Ulica Osmana Đikića no. 16. There, he stayed with at least ten Montenegrin soldiers after the take-over of Foča. In his capacity as commander of these soldiers, **DRAGOLJUB KUNARAC** was responsible for the acts of soldiers subordinate to him and knew or had reason to know that his subordinates sexually assaulted Muslim women at his headquarters. He was personally involved in sexual assaults of women at his headquarters.

GENERAL ALLEGATIONS

4.1 At all times relevant to this indictment, a state of international armed conflict and partial occupation existed in the Republic of Bosnia-Herzegovina in the territory of the former Yugoslavia.

4.2 All acts or omissions set forth herein as Grave Breaches of the Geneva Conventions of 1949 and recognised by Article 2 of the Statute of the Tribunal, occurred during that armed conflict and partial occupation.

4.3 At all times relevant to this indictment, the victims, referred to in the charges contained herein were persons protected by the Geneva Conventions of 1949.

IT-96-23-I
26 JUNE 1996

D 281
mg.

4.4 At all times relevant to this indictment, the accused were required to abide by the laws or customs governing the conduct of war.

4.5 Unless otherwise set forth below, all acts and omissions set forth in this indictment took place between April 1992 and February 1993.

4.6 In each count charging torture, the acts were committed by, or at the instigation of, or with the consent or acquiescence of, an official or person acting in an official capacity, and for one or more of the following purposes: to obtain information or a confession from the victim or a third person; to punish the victim for an act the victim or a third person committed or was suspected of having committed; to intimidate or coerce the victim or a third person; and/or for any reason based upon discrimination of any kind.

4.7 In each count charging crimes against humanity, a crime recognised by Article 5 of the Statute of the Tribunal, the acts or omissions were part of a widespread or large-scale or systematic attack against a civilian population, specifically the Muslim population of the municipality of Foča.

4.8 In this indictment, acts of forcible sexual penetration of a person, or forcing a person to sexually penetrate another are alleged. Sexual penetration includes penetration, however slight, of the vagina, anus or oral cavity, by the penis. Sexual penetration of the vulva or anus is not limited to the penis. Such acts can constitute an element of a crime against humanity, (enslavement under Article 5(c), torture under Article 5(f), rape under Article 5(g)), violations of the laws and customs of war, (torture under Article 3 and Article 3(1)(a) of the Geneva Conventions) and a grave breach of the Geneva Conventions,(torture under Article 2 (b)). Where the nature of the sexual assault is unspecified, the Prosecutor is not aware, at the present, of the precise form of penetration or sexual abuse.

4.9 The terms "Serb soldiers" or "Serb forces" used in this indictment refer to persons of Serbian descent under the command of the Bosnian Serb Army or paramilitary forces connected thereto, who were either citizens of Bosnia-Herzegovina or citizens from any other part of the former Yugoslavia.

4.10 Witnesses and victims are identified in this indictment using code names or pseudonyms such as FWS-95 or initials, for example, D.B.

4.11 All accused are individually responsible for the crimes charged against them in this indictment, pursuant to Article 7 (1) of the Statute of the Tribunal. Individual criminal responsibility includes committing, planning, initiating, ordering or aiding and abetting in the planning, preparation or execution of any acts or omissions set forth below.

4.12 **DRAGAN GAGOVIĆ** in respect of counts 29-31, **GOJKO JANKOVIĆ** in respect of counts 1-4 and **DRAGOLJUB KUNARAC** in respect of counts 40-43 are also, or alternatively, criminally responsible as superiors for their subordinates pursuant to Article 7 (3) of the Statute of the Tribunal. Superior criminal responsibility is the responsibility of a superior officer for the acts of his subordinate if the superior knew or had reason to know that his subordinate was about to commit such acts or had done so and the superior failed to take necessary and reasonable measures to prevent such further acts or to punish the subordinates thereof. By failing to take the actions required of a person in superior authority **DRAGAN GAGOVIĆ**,

IT-96-23-I 26 JUNE 1996 D 280

GOJKO JANKOVIĆ and DRAGOLJUB KUNARAC are responsible for all the crimes set out in the respective counts pursuant to Article 7(3) of the Statute of the Tribunal.

THE CHARGES

COUNTS 1-12
Torture and Rape at Buk Bijela

5.1 Buk Bijela refers to a settlement on a hydro-electric dam construction site on the road from Brod to Miljevina by the river Drina which was turned into a local military headquarters and barracks for Bosnian Serb forces and paramilitary soldiers after the April 1992 take-over of Foča and the surrounding villages. The Buk Bijela complex consisted of workers' barracks, where about 200 to 300 soldiers were barracked, and an adjoining motel. Buk Bijela was used as a temporary detention and interrogation facility for civilian women, children and the elderly who were captured in various villages in the municipality of Foča in July 1992.

5.2 On 3 July 1992, soldiers commanded by the accused GOJKO JANKOVIĆ, and among them **JANKO JANJIĆ, DRAGAN ZELENOVIĆ** and **ZORAN VUKOVIĆ**, arrested a group of at least 60 Muslim women, children and a few elderly men from Trosanj and Mjesaja, and took them to Buk Bijela. After the attack on Foča, the villages of Trosanj and Mjesaja had offered armed resistance.

5.3 While detained at Buk Bijela for several hours, all the Muslim civilians were lined up along the river Drina and guarded by armed soldiers. They were threatened with being either killed or raped and were otherwise humiliated. The soldiers approached each detained civilian, and took him or her to the above mentioned accused for questioning. The soldiers separated the women from their children. GOJKO JANKOVIĆ, JANKO JANJIĆ, DRAGAN ZELENOVIĆ and ZORAN VUKOVIĆ interrogated the women. The interrogations focused on the hiding-places of the male villagers and weapons. The accused threatened the women with murder and sexual assault if they lied. JANKO JANJIĆ and DRAGAN ZELENOVIĆ and other soldiers acting under the control of GOJKO JANKOVIĆ gang-raped, several women during or immediately after the interrogation who they suspected of lying. Paragraphs 5.4 to 5.7, hereunder particularise some of those sexual assaults which occurred on or about 3 July 1992.

5.4 A witness code named, FWS-75, was interrogated by GOJKO JANKOVIĆ and DRAGAN ZELENOVIĆ about her village and whether the villagers had weapons. GOJKO JANKOVIĆ warned the witness not to lie, otherwise she would be raped by soldiers and killed afterwards. As FWS-75 did not answer the questions sufficiently, a soldier took her to another room. There, at least ten unidentified soldiers, raped her, in turn. The nature of the rape included vaginal penetration and fellatio. FWS-75 lost consciousness after the tenth soldier sexually assaulted her. The episode of sexual assault lasted between one to two hours.

5.5 Another witness, FWS-87, a 15 year old, was interrogated by **DRAGAN ZELENOVIĆ** and three unidentified soldiers in a room at Buk Bijela. During the interrogation, they accused FWS-87 of not telling the truth. The interrogators removed her clothing and then, each one raped her. The nature of the rape was vaginal penetration. The first soldier also threatened her by putting a gun to her head. FWS-87 experienced severe pain during the assault, followed by heavy vaginal bleeding.

5.6 A further witness, FWS-48, was interrogated by **JANKO JANJIĆ** in a room at Buk Bijela. During the interrogation, **JANKO JANJIĆ** forcibly undressed her. When FWS-48 tried to resist, he slapped and pushed her and threatened to bring in ten soldiers to rape her. **JANKO JANJIĆ** then raped FWS-48 by vaginal penetration.

5.7 A fourth witness, FWS-74, was led by **JANKO JANJIĆ** to a room to be interrogated in the presence of an unidentified soldier. During the interrogation, **JANKO JANJIĆ** instructed FWS-74 to undress. At that moment the other soldier asked **JANKO JANJIĆ** to leave the room. After **JANKO JANJIĆ** had left, the soldier undressed FWS-74. During a period of about twenty minutes, the soldier raped her by vaginal penetration.

5.8 By the foregoing acts and omissions in relation to the victims FWS-75, FWS-87, FWS-48 and FWS-74, described in the paragraphs 5.4, 5.5, 5.6 and 5.7 **GOJKO JANKOVIĆ** committed:

Count 1:
A **CRIME AGAINST HUMANITY** punishable under Article 5 (f) (torture) of the Statute of the Tribunal;

Count 2:
A **CRIME AGAINST HUMANITY** punishable under Article 5 (g) (rape) of the Statute of the Tribunal;

Count 3:
A **GRAVE BREACH** punishable under Article 2 (b) (torture) of the Statute of the Tribunal and;

Count 4:
A **VIOLATION OF THE LAWS OR CUSTOMS OF WAR,** punishable under Article 3 of the Statute of the Tribunal and recognised by Article 3 (1) (a) (torture) of the Geneva Convention.

5.9 By the foregoing acts and omissions in relation to the victims FWS-75 and FWS-87, described in the paragraphs 5.4 and 5.5, **DRAGAN ZELENOVIĆ** committed:

Count 5:
A **CRIME AGAINST HUMANITY** punishable under Article 5 (f) (torture) of the Statute of the Tribunal;

Count 6:

A **CRIME AGAINST HUMANITY** punishable under Article 5 (g) (rape) of the Statute of the Tribunal;

Count 7:
A **GRAVE BREACH** punishable under Article 2 (b) (torture) of the Statute of the Tribunal and;

Count 8:
A **VIOLATION OF THE LAWS OR CUSTOMS OF WAR**, punishable under Article 3 of the Statute of the Tribunal and recognised by Article 3 (1) (a) (torture) of the Geneva Convention.

5.10 By the foregoing acts and omissions in relation to the victims FWS-48 and FWS-74, described in the paragraphs 5.6 and 5.7 **JANKO JANJIĆ** committed:

Count 9:
A **CRIME AGAINST HUMANITY** punishable under Article 5 (f) (torture) of the Statute of the Tribunal;

Count 10:
A **CRIME AGAINST HUMANITY** punishable under Article 5 (g) (rape) of the Statute of the Tribunal;

Count 11:
A **GRAVE BREACH** punishable under Article 2 (b) (torture) of the Statute of the Tribunal and;

Count 12:
A **VIOLATION OF THE LAWS OR CUSTOMS OF WAR**, punishable under Article 3 of the Statute of the Tribunal and recognised by Article 3 (1) (a) (torture) of the Geneva Convention.

COUNTS 13-28
Torture and Rape at Foča High School

6.1 During the occupation that followed the take-over of the town of Foča, the Foča High School, situated in the Aladža area, functioned as a barracks for Serb soldiers, and as a short term detention facility for Muslim women, children and the elderly.

6.2 Between 3 July and about 13 July 1992, at least 72 Muslim inhabitants of the municipality of Foča were detained in two classrooms in the Foča High School, including the women, children and the elderly who had earlier been held at Buk Bijela, mentioned above. On or about 13 July 1992, all detainees were transferred from Foča High School to the Partizan Sports Hall in Foča.

6.3 At the Foča High School, the detainees were surrounded by armed Serb soldiers, who patrolled outside the Foča High School and constantly entered and left the building. There were also two armed police guards from the Foča SUP patrolling the corridor outside of the detention rooms.

6.4 Many of the female detainees were subjected to sexual abuse during their detention at the Foča High School. From the second day of their detention, every evening, groups of Serb soldiers sexually assaulted, including gang-rape, some of the younger women and girls in class-rooms or apartments in neighbouring buildings. Among them were witnesses FWS-50, FWS-75, FWS-87, FWS-95, FWS-74 and FWS-88, as set forth below. The soldiers threatened to kill the women or the women's children if they refused to submit to sexual assaults. Women who dared to resist the sexual assaults were beaten. The above mentioned groups of soldiers consisted of members of the military police. They referred to themselves "Cosa's Guards", named for the local commander of the military police Cosović. The accused **GOJKO JANKOVIĆ, DRAGAN ZELENOVIĆ, JANKO JANJIĆ** and **ZORAN VUKOVIĆ** were among these groups of soldiers.

6.5 The physical and psychological health of many female detainees seriously deteriorated as a result of these sexual assaults. Some of the women endured complete exhaustion, vaginal discharges, bladder problems and irregular menstrual bleedings. The detainees lived in constant fear. Some of the sexually abused women became suicidal. Others became indifferent as to what would happen to them and suffered from depression.

6.6 On or about 6 or 7 July 1992, **DRAGAN ZELENOVIĆ** in concert with **JANKO JANJIĆ** and **ZORAN VUKOVIĆ**, selected FWS-50, FWS-75, FWS-87, FWS-95 out of the group of detainees. The accused led them to another classroom where unidentified soldiers stood waiting. Then **DRAGAN ZELENOVIĆ** decided which woman should go to which man. The women were ordered to remove their clothes. FWS-95 refused to do so and **JANKO JANJIĆ** slapped her and held her at gun point. Then **DRAGAN ZELENOVIĆ** raped FWS-75 (vaginal penetration). **ZORAN VUKOVIĆ** raped FWS-87 (vaginal penetration) and **JANKO JANJIĆ** raped FWS-95 (vaginal penetration) within the same room. One of the other soldiers took FWS-50 to another classroom and raped her (vaginal penetration).

6.7 Between or about 8 July and about 13 July 1992, in addition to the sexual assaults described under paragraph 6.6, on at least five other occasions **DRAGAN ZELENOVIĆ** led a group of soldiers that sexually abused FWS-75 and FWS-87. First the women were taken into another classroom in the Foča High School. There **ZORAN VUKOVIĆ** and **DRAGAN ZELENOVIĆ** raped FWS-75 and FWS-87 (vaginal penetration).

6.8 Between or about 8 July and about 13 July 1992, on three occasions, FWS-75 and FWS-87 were taken from the Foča High School to an apartment building called Brena in the centre of Foča. The building was near the Zelengora hotel, a military headquarters of the Serb forces. The first time, the two women went to an apartment owned by **DRAGAN ZELENOVIĆ**. The accused **JANKO JANJIĆ, DRAGAN ZELENOVIĆ** and two other unidentified soldiers raped FWS-75 (vaginal and anal penetration and fellatio) while **DRAGAN ZELENOVIĆ** raped FWS-87 (vaginal penetration).

6.9 Between about 8 July and about 13 July 1992, on two occasions **DRAGAN ZELENOVIĆ** and several other unidentified soldiers took FWS-75 and FWS-87 to Brena and raped them. On these occasions, the accused raped FWS-75 (vaginal and anal penetration and fellatio) and raped FWS-87 (vaginal penetration).

6.10 Between about 8 July and about 13 July 1992, on another occasion, FWS-75, FWS-87 and Z. G. were taken by **DRAGAN ZELENOVIĆ** to an abandoned house of a Muslim policeman in Gornje Polje. There **DRAGAN ZELENOVIĆ** raped FWS-87 (vaginal penetration). An unidentified soldier raped Z. G.

6.11 Between or about 8 July and about 13 July 1992, in addition to the acts described in paragraph 6.6, FWS-95 was sexually assaulted in different classrooms in the Foča High School. Because she had previously been beaten and threatened when sexually assaulted FWS-95 dared not resist the soldiers again. She was raped on numerous occasions by many perpetrators among them **JANKO JANJIĆ, DRAGAN ZELENOVIĆ** and **GOJKO JANKOVIĆ** (vaginal and anal penetration and fellatio)

6.12 On or about 8 July 1992, **JANKO JANJIĆ** selected FWS-74 and took her to an empty room in Foča High School. On the way to the room, she argued with **JANKO JANJIĆ.** At that moment **DRAGAN ZELENOVIĆ** passed by and threatened to take her to a hundred soldiers on the front line. After this threat, FWS-74 was raped by **JANKO JANJIĆ** (vaginal penetration and fellatio).

6.13 On or about 8 July 1992, **JANKO JANJIĆ** took FWS-88 to an apartment in the Brena block. There, during the whole night, he raped her repeatedly (vaginal and anal penetration and fellatio). As she was a virgin before these acts, FWS-88 experience terrible pain during the rape. Two days later, **JANKO JANJIĆ** took her to the house of a Muslim goldsmith, close to the bus station. There, he again raped her twice (vaginal penetration).

6.14 By the foregoing acts and omissions in relation to the victims FWS-50, FWS-75, FWS-87 and FWS-95, described in the paragraphs 6.6, 6.7, 6.8, 6.9, 6.10 and 6.11 **DRAGAN ZELENOVIĆ** committed:

Count 13:
A **CRIME AGAINST HUMANITY** punishable under Article 5 (f) (torture) of the Statute of the Tribunal;

Count 14:
A **CRIME AGAINST HUMANITY** punishable under Article 5 (g) (rape) of the Statute of the Tribunal;

Count 15:
A **GRAVE BREACH** punishable under Article 2 (b) (torture) of the Statute of the Tribunal and;

Count 16:

IT 96 23 -- I

A **VIOLATION OF THE LAWS OR CUSTOMS OF WAR**, punishable under Article 3 of the Statute of the Tribunal and recognised by Article 3 (1) (a) (torture) of the Geneva Convention.

6.15 By the foregoing acts and omissions in relation to the victims FWS-50, FWS-75, FWS-87, FWS-95, FWS-74 and FWS-88, described in the paragraphs 6.6, 6.8, 6.11, 6.12 and 6.13 **JANKO JANJIĆ** committed:

Count 17:
A **CRIME AGAINST HUMANITY** punishable under Article 5 (f) (torture) of the Statute of the Tribunal;

Count 18:
A **CRIME AGAINST HUMANITY** punishable under Article 5 (g) (rape) of the Statute of the Tribunal;

Count 19:
A **GRAVE BREACH** punishable under Article 2 (b) (torture) of the Statute of the Tribunal and;

Count 20:
A **VIOLATION OF THE LAWS OR CUSTOMS OF WAR**, punishable under Article 3 of the Statute of the Tribunal and recognised by Article 3 (1) (a) (torture) of the Geneva Convention.

6.16 By the foregoing acts and omissions in relation to the victims FWS-50, FWS-95, FWS-75 and FWS-87, described in the paragraphs 6.6 and 6.7, **ZORAN VUKOVIĆ** committed:

Count 21:
A **CRIME AGAINST HUMANITY** punishable under Article 5 (f) (torture) of the Statute of the Tribunal;

Count 22:
A **CRIME AGAINST HUMANITY** punishable under Article 5 (g) (rape) of the Statute of the Tribunal;

Count 23:
A **GRAVE BREACH** punishable under Article 2 (b) (torture) of the Statute of the Tribunal and;

Count 24:
A **VIOLATION OF THE LAWS OR CUSTOMS OF WAR**, punishable under Article 3 of the Statute of the Tribunal and recognised by Article 3 (1) (a) (torture) of the Geneva Convention.

IT 96 23 -- 1'

6.17 By the foregoing acts and omissions in relation to the victim FWS-95, described in paragraph 6.11, **GOJKO JANKOVIĆ** committed:

Count 25:
A **CRIME AGAINST HUMANITY** punishable under Article 5 (f) (torture) of the Statute of the Tribunal;

Count 26:
A **CRIME AGAINST HUMANITY** punishable under Article 5 (g) (rape) of the Statute of the Tribunal;

Count 27:
A **GRAVE BREACH** punishable under Article 2 (b) (torture) of the Statute of the Tribunal and;

Count 28:
A **VIOLATION OF THE LAWS OR CUSTOMS OF WAR**, punishable under Article 3 of the Statute of the Tribunal and recognised by Article 3 (1) (a) (torture) of the Geneva Convention.

COUNTS 29-31

Persecution in Partizan Sports Hall committed by DRAGAN GAGOVIĆ

7.1 Partizan Sports Hall (hereinafter, "Partizan") functioned as a detention centre for women, children and the elderly from at least on or about 13 July 1992, and continued to be so used until at least 13 August 1992. The detainees held at Partizan, during this time period, numbered at least 72. The detainees were all civilian Muslim women, children and a few elderly persons from villages in the municipality of Foča. The accused **DRAGAN GAGOVIĆ**, in his capacity as chief of police in Foča and as the person in charge of the detention and release of the female Muslims, participated in the imprisonment of Muslim inhabitants of the municipality of Foča at Partizan.

7.2 Partizan was a medium sized building situated in the centre of Foča town close to the SUP building. Partizan was separated from the SUP building by about seventy metres. Partizan was on slightly higher ground than the other buildings in the neighbourhood and could therefore be seen clearly from the surrounding areas, including the SUP building. Partizan was also close to the main municipal building, where the Serb authorities had their principle offices. Partizan consisted of two large halls. All detainees were held in one of the halls only. This hall measured roughly 12 metres by 7 metres.

7.3 **DRAGAN GAGOVIĆ**, stationed two policemen, as guards outside the main door of Partizan. The guards, who were subordinate to **DRAGAN GAGOVIĆ**, were armed at all times with automatic weapons. People who entered Partizan had to pass the guards on their way into the halls. Detainees could not leave Partizan because of the armed guards.

7.4 Living conditions in Partizan were brutal. The detention was characterised by inhumane treatment, unhygienic facilities, overcrowding, starvation, physical and psychological torture, including sexual assaults. There were neither blankets nor towels provided for the detainees. Only a few mattresses were provided for sleeping. Food, allotted on an irregular basis, was meagre. Medical care for the detainees, either

IT 96 23 -- I' 252

on a regular or on an emergency basis was not authorised. Some women were beaten and in need of urgent care. Women bled and suffered pain as a result of sexual abuse. Two women died in Partizan due to beatings inflicted upon them by Serb soldiers.

7.5 Immediately after the transfer of women to Partizan, a pattern of sexual assaults commenced that was similar to the sexual abuse experienced at Foča High School. Armed soldiers, mostly in groups of three to five, entered Partizan, usually in the evenings, and removed women. The guards at the entrance, with the exception of one shift, did not attempt to stop these soldiers. When the women resisted or hid, the soldiers beat or threatened the women to force them to obey. The Serb soldiers took the women from Partizan to houses and apartments or to hotels and barracks, such as the Hotel Zelengora or Buk Bijela respectively. Among the women subjected to sexual assaults were witnesses FWS-48, FWS-87, FWS-75, FWS-50 and FWS-95 as set forth below.

7.6 In addition to these specified sexual assaults, unidentified soldiers removed witnesses FWS-31 and FWS-95 from Partizan on numerous occasions and witness FWS-51 from Partizan once, to various places and sexually abused them.

7.7 On one occasions, on or about 12 August 1992, the evening prior to the release of the detainees, two unidentified soldiers took FWS-95 and victim H. B. to the stadium in Foča, which is close to the Zelengora Hotel. There, a large group of soldiers, among them Montenegrins and soldiers from Serbia, stood waiting. That night, countless soldiers gang-raped FWS-95 and H.B. on the benches in the stadium. Groups of soldiers raped FWS-95 and H.B. while other soldiers watched the scene.

7.8 Afterwards, on the same night, several soldiers took FWS-95 and H. B. to Buk Bijela. At Buk Bijela, the soldiers separated the women and raped them (vaginal penetration).

7.9 Two groups of perpetrators operated at Partizan. One group described themselves as "Cosa's Guards", which operated at the Foča High School also operated at Partizan. The other group, under the command of **DRAGOLJUB KUNARAC**, was a volunteer guard detail comprising mostly irregular Serb soldiers from Montenegro. This second group maintained their headquarters in a house in the Aladža neighbourhood in Foča at Ulica Osmana Đikića no. 16.

7.10 On or around 13 August, 1992, most detainees were released from Partizan and were deported to Montenegro. The women who left on the 13 August convoy, received medical care for the first time in Montenegro. Many women suffered permanent gynaecological harm due to the sexual assaults. At least one woman can no longer have children. All the women who were sexually assaulted suffered psychological and emotional harm; some remain traumatised.

7.11 **DRAGAN GAGOVIĆ**, in his capacity as chief of police in Foča and as the person in charge of the detention of the female Muslim population in Foča, was responsible for the detention conditions at Partizan. He was also responsible for the release and issuing of exit permits for the detainees. **DRAGAN GAGOVIĆ** knew about the brutal living conditions at Partizan. He was physically present at Partizan on numerous occasions and saw the conditions in which the women lived. He likewise knew about the sexual abuse of the women at Partizan. On one occasion, the guards at

Partizan allowed some detainees to go to the SUP building to lodge a complaint with **DRAGAN GAGOVIĆ** about the sexual assaults. In his capacity as Chief of Police, responsible for the detention of the female Muslim, **DRAGAN GAGOVIĆ** failed to take the necessary and reasonable measures to improve the detention conditions and to prevent sexual assaults.

7.12 By his participation in these acts and omissions, **DRAGAN GAGOVIĆ** committed:

Count 29:
A **CRIME AGAINST HUMANITY** punishable under Article 5 (h) (persecution on political, racial and/or religious grounds) of the Statute of the Tribunal;

Count 30:
A **GRAVE BREACH** punishable under Article 2 (c) (wilfully causing great suffering) of the Statute of the Tribunal and;

Count 31:
A **VIOLATION OF THE LAWS OR CUSTOMS OF WAR**, punishable under Article 3 of the Statute of the Tribunal and recognised by Article 3 (1) (c) (outrages upon personal dignity) of the Geneva Convention.

COUNTS 32-35
Torture and Rape of FWS-48 at Partizan Sports Hall committed by DRAGAN GAGOVIĆ

8.1 Around 16 July 1992, FWS-48 and FWS-95 went to the SUP building and complained to **DRAGAN GAGOVIĆ** about the sexual assaults. As a result of this complaint, the next day, around 10:30 a.m., **DRAGAN GAGOVIĆ** entered Partizan, and ordered FWS-48 to come with him for interrogation. **DRAGAN GAGOVIĆ** took FWS-95 and FWS-48 to an apartment close to Partizan. On the way to the apartment, FWS-48 told **DRAGAN GAGOVIĆ** about the continuous sexual assaults that were taking place in Partizan. In the apartment, **DRAGAN GAGOVIĆ** took FWS-48 to a room pretending to take a statement, while FWS-95 waited in the kitchen. Instead of taking a statement, **DRAGAN GAGOVIĆ** pushed FWS-48 on a bed and ripped off her clothes. FWS-48 resisted, and **DRAGAN GAGOVIĆ** threatened her with his pistol. To punish or intimidate her for reporting sexual assaults, **DRAGAN GAGOVIĆ** then raped FWS-48 (vaginal and anal penetration and fellatio). During the sexual assault, he pointed his rifle at FWS-48's neck. After the assault, **DRAGAN GAGOVIĆ** threatened, intimidated and coerced FWS-48 saying that he would find her in five different countries if she told anyone that he had raped her.

8.2 By the foregoing acts, **DRAGAN GAGOVIĆ** committed:

Count 32:
A **CRIME AGAINST HUMANITY** punishable under Article 5 (f) (torture) of the Statute of the Tribunal;

Count 33:
A **CRIME AGAINST HUMANITY** punishable under Article 5 (g) (rape) of the Statute of the Tribunal;

Count 34:
A **GRAVE BREACH** punishable under Article 2 (b) (torture) of the Statute of the Tribunal and ;

Count 35:
A **VIOLATION OF THE LAWS OR CUSTOMS OF WAR**, punishable under Article 3 of the Statute of the Tribunal and recognised by Article 3 (1) (a) (torture) of the Geneva Convention.

COUNT 36-55

Torture and Rape of FWS-48, FWS-50, FWS-75, FWS-87, FWS-95 and other women at Partizan Sports Hall

9.1 The witnesses FWS-48, FWS-95 and FWS-50, a 16 year old girl, were detained at Partizan from about 13 July until 13 August 1992. FWS-75 and FWS-87, a 15 year old girl, were detained in Partizan from about 13 July until 2 August 1992. During their detention, Serb soldiers frequently raped FWS-48, FWS-95, FWS-50, FWS-75 and FWS-87 (vaginal and anal penetration and fellatio). Almost every night soldiers took FWS-48, FWS-95, FWS-50, FWS-75 and FWS-87 out of Partizan to houses and apartments and sexually abused them. Often, one group of soldiers removed the women as soon as they had been returned by another group of soldiers.

9.2 On or around 13 July 1992, **JANKO JANJIĆ** took FWS-48 together with two other female detainees to a house across the road from Partizan. There, **JANKO JANJIĆ** raped FWS-48 (vaginal penetration), while two unidentified soldiers raped the other two females in the same room.

9.3 The same night, after **JANKO JANJIĆ** returned the women to Partizan, **DRAGOLJUB KUNARAC** took the same three women to the Hotel Zelengora. FWS-48 refused to go with him and **DRAGOLJUB KUNARAC** kicked her and dragged her out. At Hotel Zelengora, FWS-48 was placed in a separate room and both **DRAGOLJUB KUNARAC** and **ZORAN VUKOVIĆ** raped her (vaginal penetration and fellatio). Both perpetrators told her that she would now give birth to Serb babies.

9.4 On or around 14 July 1992, **JANKO JANJIĆ** again took FWS-48 together with FWS-87 and Z. G. to the Brena apartment block near Hotel Zelengora. When they arrived, **ZORAN VUKOVIĆ** and an unidentified soldier were waiting. Then, **ZORAN VUKOVIĆ**, raped FWS-48 (vaginal penetration) while the unidentified soldier raped FWS-87 (vaginal penetration) and **JANKO JANJIĆ** raped Z. G.

9.5 On or around 14 July 1992, **ZORAN VUKOVIĆ** came to Partizan to remove FWS-50 and FWS-87. As FWS-50 hid, **ZORAN VUKOVIĆ** threatened to kill the other detainees if she did not come out of hiding. FWS-50 then did so. The two girls were taken to an apartment close to Partizan, where an unidentified soldier stood waiting. There **ZORAN VUKOVIĆ** raped FWS-50 (vaginal penetration), while the unidentified soldier raped FWS-87.

9.6 On one occasion in July 1992, **JANKO JANJIĆ** and two other soldiers took FWS-75 together with FWS-87 and drove them to the Brena building. There, **JANKO JANJIĆ** removed FWS-75 from the car and led her to an apartment, while the other soldiers drove away with FWS-87. In the apartment, **JANKO JANJIĆ** raped FWS-75 (vaginal penetration). Afterwards on three occasions, **JANKO JANJIĆ** took FWS-75 to the same place and raped her each time.

9.7 In July 1992, witnesses FWS-87 were frequently taken out, and raped (vaginal and anal penetration and fellatio). On one occasion witness FWS-87 was gang-raped by 4 men including **DRAGAN ZELENOVIĆ** and **ZORAN VUKOVIĆ**.

9.8 On two occasions, **DRAGOLJUB KUNARAC** took FWS-87 to the Montenegrin headquarters in the Aladža area, knowing that she might be sexually assaulted there. On both occasions, two Montenegrin soldiers were present and raped FWS-87.

9.9 Among the men who frequently sexually assaulted FWS-87 at Partizan were **JANKO JANJIĆ, GOJKO JANKOVIĆ** and **DRAGOLJUB KUNARAC.** Due to the frequent sexual assaults, FWS-87 became suicidal, during her detention at Partizan.

9.10 **DRAGOLJUB KUNARAC** took FWS-75 and D. B. at least five times to his headquarters, that housed a group of Montenegrin soldiers in the Aladža neighbourhood at Ulica Osmana Đikica No. 16. **DRAGOLJUB KUNARAC** commanded these soldiers. In mid July 1992, FWS-75 and D. B. were brought to this house for the first time. When they arrived at the headquarters, a group of soldiers were waiting. **DRAGOLJUB KUNARAC** took D. B. to a separate room and sexually assaulted her, while FWS-75 was left behind together with the other Montenegrin soldiers. For about 3 hours, FWS-75 was gang-raped by at least 15 soldiers (vaginal and anal penetration and fellatio). They sexually abused her in all possible ways. The soldiers put their penises into her hands and ejaculated all over her. During the sexual assault, one soldier took out a knife and threatened to cut off her breast, but another soldier prevented him from doing so. This incident was the only gang-rape FWS-75 experienced in the Montenegrin headquarters. At other times in the headquarters, one to three soldiers, in turn, raped her.

9.11 On or around 15 July 1992, **GOJKO JANKOVIĆ** led FWS-48 to an empty Muslim house in the Aladža neighbourhood. When FWS-48 arrived, about 14 Montenegrin soldiers were already present. **DRAGAN ZELENOVIĆ** then arrived with about 8 more soldiers, among them **ZORAN VUKOVIĆ. DRAGAN ZELENOVIĆ** took FWS-48 to a room and threatened to slash her throat if she resisted. Then, **DRAGAN ZELENOVIĆ** raped FWS-48 (vaginal penetration and fellatio) together with at least other 7 soldiers. **ZORAN VUKOVIĆ** was the 6th man.

who raped her. During the sexual assault, **ZORAN VUKOVIĆ** bit her nipples a number of times. Although the witness was bleeding from these bites, the 7th man squeezed and pinched her breasts as he raped her. FWS-48 fainted as a result of the pain.

9.12 On or around 18 July 1992, **GOJKO JANKOVIĆ** took FWS-48, FWS-95 and B. P. to a house near the bus station. From there, FWS-48 **DRAGOLJUB KUNARAC** took her to another house in the Donje Polje neighbourhood where he raped her (vaginal penetration and fellatio).

9.13 On or around 23 July 1992, **DRAGAN ZELENOVIĆ** and some unidentified soldiers took FWS-48 to a house close to Partizan. **DRAGAN ZELENOVIĆ** took her into a separate room and raped her (vaginal penetration). During this incident, he said that she would give birth to good Serbian children. After this sexual assault, an unidentified soldier took her to another room where FWS-48 saw another women being sexually assaulted. At that moment, the soldier who had taken her to that room pushed FWS-48 onto a bed and raped her.

9.14 The same night, after being taken back to Partizan, **JANKO JANJIĆ,** took FWS-48, together with two other women, to the Brena apartment block, where **ZORAN VUKOVIĆ** and a certain Panto were already waiting. Panto raped FWS-48 (vaginal penetration). She heard **ZORAN VUKOVIĆ** and **JANKO JANJIĆ** , at the same time, sexually assaulting the other women in the next room.

9.15 On 2 August 1992, **DRAGOLJUB KUNARAC** took FWS-75, FWS-87, FWS-50 and D. B. to the Montenegrin headquarters. Some women from the Kalinovik women's detention camp were also present. On this occasion, **DRAGOLJUB KUNARAC** and three other soldiers raped FWS-87. Several unidentified perpetrators raped FWS-75 during the whole night. A Montenegrin soldier who raped FWS-50 (vaginal penetration) threatened to cut her arms and legs and to take her to church to baptise her.

9.16 On or around 11 August 1992, **DRAGAN ZELENOVIĆ** and other soldiers took FWS-48 to the Hotel Zelengora. When she arrived, many soldiers were present, eating and drinking. Immediately thereafter, a person identified as Spomenko approached FWS-48, took her to a room upstairs and raped her (vaginal penetration).

9.17 On 12 August 1992, **DRAGAN ZELENOVIĆ** and **GOJKO JANKOVIĆ** took FWS-48 together with FWS-95 and other women to a house in Donje Polje. There **DRAGAN ZELENOVIĆ** raped FWS-48 twice. That night **DRAGAN ZELENOVIĆ** told FWS-48 that everything would end in a few days.

9.18 After midnight, on the same night, **JANKO JANJIĆ** took FWS-48 together with other women to the Brena apartments. While leaving Partizan, a group of soldiers approached the women and tried to pull them away. **JANKO JANJIĆ** told these soldiers that he needed these women for his own people and that they should go into Partizan and find other women. **ZORAN VUKOVIĆ** and Panto joined them at the Brena apartments. That night, **JANKO JANJIĆ** raped FWS-48. During the sexual assault, he mentioned that it would be the last time.

9.19 On 13 August 1992, FWS-48 was deported to Montenegro. Due to the multiple sexual assaults, FWS-48 can no longer give birth to children.

9.20 From July 1992 to 13 August 1992, FWS-95 was removed to different houses and apartments, almost every night by groups of soldiers, commanded by **DRAGOLJUB KUNARAC, JANKO JANJIĆ** and **DRAGAN ZELENOVIĆ**. Sometimes, she was taken alone, sometimes together with other women. On each of these occasions, FWS-95 was raped, (vaginal penetration and fellatio). Sometimes, she was gang-raped. **DRAGOLJUB KUNARAC, JANKO JANJIĆ, GOJKO JANKOVIĆ** and **DRAGAN ZELENOVIĆ** were among the soldiers who frequently assaulted her.

9.21 On or about 2 August 1992, **DRAGOLJUB KUNARAC**, in concert with Pero Elez, a Serb paramilitary leader in a position of regional authority, transferred FWS-75, FWS-87 and two other women from Partizan to Miljevina.

9.22 By the foregoing acts and omissions in relation to the victims FWS-48, FWS-75, FWS-87 and FWS-95, described in the paragraphs 9.2, 9.4, 9.6, 9.9, 9.14, 9.18 and 9.20, **JANKO JANJIĆ** committed:

Count 36:
A **CRIME AGAINST HUMANITY** punishable under Article 5 (f) (torture) of the Statute of the Tribunal;

Count 37:
A **CRIME AGAINST HUMANITY** punishable under Article 5 (g) (rape) of the Statute of the Tribunal;

Count 38:
A **GRAVE BREACH** punishable under Article 2 (b) (torture) of the Statute of the Tribunal and;

Count 39:
A **VIOLATION OF THE LAWS OR CUSTOMS OF WAR**, punishable under Article 3 of the Statute of the Tribunal and recognised by Article 3 (1) (a) (torture) of the Geneva Convention.

9.23 By the foregoing acts and omissions in relation to the victims FWS-48, FWS-50, FWS-75, FWS-87 and FWS-95, described in the paragraphs 9.3, 9.8, 9.9, 9.10, 9.12, 9.15 and 9.21, **DRAGOLJUB KUNARAC** committed:

Count 40:
A **CRIME AGAINST HUMANITY** punishable under Article 5 (f) (torture) of the Statute of the Tribunal;

Count 41:
A **CRIME AGAINST HUMANITY** punishable under Article 5 (g) (rape) of the Statute of the Tribunal;

Count 42:
A **GRAVE BREACH** punishable under Article 2 (b) (torture) of the Statute of the Tribunal and;

Count 43:
A **VIOLATION OF THE LAWS OR CUSTOMS OF WAR**, punishable under Article 3 of the Statute of the Tribunal and recognised by Article 3 (1) (a) (torture) of the Geneva Convention.

9.24 By the foregoing acts and omissions in relation to the victims FWS-48, FWS-50 and FWS-87, described in the paragraphs 9.3, 9.4, 9.5, 9.7, 9.11 and 9.14, **ZORAN VUKOVIĆ** committed:

Count 44:
A **CRIME AGAINST HUMANITY** punishable under Article 5 (f) (torture) of the Statute of the Tribunal;

Count 45:
A **CRIME AGAINST HUMANITY** punishable under Article 5 (g) (rape) of the Statute of the Tribunal;

Count 46:
A **GRAVE BREACH** punishable under Article 2 (b) (torture) of the Statute of the Tribunal;

Count 47:
A **VIOLATION OF THE LAWS OR CUSTOMS OF WAR**, punishable under Article 3 of the Statute of the Tribunal and recognised by Article 3 (1) (a) (torture) of the Geneva Convention.

9.25 By the foregoing acts and omissions in relation to the victims FWS-48, FWS-87 and FWS-95, described in the paragraphs 9.9, 9.11, 9.17 and 9.20, **GOJKO JANKOVIĆ** committed:

Count 48:
A **CRIME AGAINST HUMANITY** punishable under Article 5 (f) (torture) of the Statute of the Tribunal;

Count 49:
A **CRIME AGAINST HUMANITY** punishable under Article 5 (g) (rape) of the Statute of the Tribunal;

Count 50:
A **GRAVE BREACH** punishable under Article 2 (b) (torture) of the Statute of the Tribunal and;

IT-96-23-I D 279
26 JUNE 1996

Count 51:
A VIOLATION OF THE LAWS OR CUSTOMS OF WAR, punishable under Article 3 of the Statute of the Tribunal and recognised by Article 3 (1) (a) (torture) of the Geneva Convention.

9.26 By the foregoing acts and omissions in relation to the victims FWS-48, FWS-87 and FWS-95, described in the paragraphs 9.7, 9.11, 9.13, 9.16, 9.17 and 9.20, **DRAGAN ZELENOVIĆ** committed:

Count 52:
A **CRIME AGAINST HUMANITY** punishable under Article 5 (f) (torture) of the Statute of the Tribunal;

Count 53:
A **CRIME AGAINST HUMANITY** punishable under Article 5 (g) (rape) of the Statute of the Tribunal;

Count 54:
A **GRAVE BREACH** punishable under Article 2 (b) (torture) of the Statute of the Tribunal and;

Count 55:
A **VIOLATION OF THE LAWS OR CUSTOMS OF WAR,** punishable under Article 3 of the Statute of the Tribunal and recognised by Article 3 (1) (a) (torture) of the Geneva Convention.

COUNTS 56-59
Enslavement and Rape of FWS-75, FWS-87 and Seven Other Women in Karaman's House

10.1 Pero Elez, a Serb paramilitary leader in a position of regional authority commanded an elite unit of Vukovar fighters. Pero Elez's headquarters were in the Miljevina Hotel. On 2 August 1992, **DRAGOLJUB KUNARAC,** in concert with Pero Elez, took FWS-75, FWS-87 and D. B. from the Montenegrin headquarters in Foča to the Miljevina Hotel because the women had spoken to journalists the day before about the living conditions in Partizan Sports Hall. Pero Elez ordered the detention of the three women in a house, which was close to the Hotel, and owned by Nusret Karaman, a Muslim who lived in Germany.. Later on, other women and girls were detained at Karaman's house. Some were as young as twelve and fourteen years of age. The number of women and girls detained at Karaman's house between 2 August 1992 and at least until 30 October 1992 totalled nine. **RADOVAN STANKOVIĆ,** a soldier from the elite unit commanded by Pero Elez, was in charge of Karaman's house after the death of Pero Elez. **RADOVAN STANKOVIĆ** ran Karaman's house similar to a brothel.

10.2 In contrast to Partizan Sports Hall, the detainees at Karaman's house had sufficient food. They were not guarded or locked inside the house. The detainees

IT-96-23-I D 278
26 JUNE 1996

even had a key they could use to lock the door and prevent soldiers, not belonging to Pero Elez's group, from entering. The detainees were also given the telephone number of the Miljevina motel, and were told that they should call this number if any soldier without authorisation tried to enter the house. When the women did call this number, either **RADOVAN STANKOVIĆ** or Pero Elez would come to prevent other persons from entering the house. Although the detainees were not guarded, they could not escape. They had nowhere to go as they were surrounded by Serbs, both soldiers and civilians.

10.3 FWS-75 and FWS-87 were detained in Karaman's house between or about 3 August until or about 30 October 1992, together with 7 other women. Pero Elez treated the women as his personal property.

10.4 During the entire period of their detention at Karaman's house, FWS-75, FWS-87 and the other female detainees were subjected to repeated rapes and sexual assaults at night. All the perpetrators were Serb soldiers who belonged to Pero Elez's group. Among the soldiers who frequently raped FWS-75 and FWS-87 (vaginal and anal penetration) was **RADOVAN STANKOVIĆ**.

10.5 The first time both women were raped in Karaman's house was on or about 3 August 1992, shortly after their arrival. An unidentified soldier raped FWS-75 (vaginal penetration) while **RADOVAN STANKOVIĆ** raped FWS-87 that day.

10.6 In addition to the rapes and other sexual assaults, all the female detainees were forced to work for the Serb soldiers, washing uniforms, cooking and cleaning the house. FWS-87 was taken three times from Karaman's house to other buildings in Miljevina. On these occasions, she was forced to clean rooms in the buildings, cook for the soldiers and paint the window-frames. On one of the three occasions, when she was taken out with another woman, two Montenegrin soldiers sexually assaulted both women.

10.7 At Karaman's house, the detainees constantly feared for their lives. If any woman refused to obey orders, she would be beaten. Soldiers often told the women that they would be killed after the soldiers were finished with them because they knew too much. FWS-87 felt suicidal during the entire time of her detention in Karaman's house.

10.8 By the foregoing acts and omissions, **RADOVAN STANKOVIĆ** committed:

Count 56:
A **CRIME AGAINST HUMANITY** punishable under Article 5 (c) (enslavement) of the Statute of the Tribunal;

Count 57:
A **CRIME AGAINST HUMANITY** punishable under Article 5 (g) (rape) of the Statute of the Tribunal;

Count 58:

IT-96-23-I D 277
26 JUNE 1996

A **GRAVE BREACH** punishable by Article 2 (b) (inhuman treatment) of the Statute of the Tribunal and;

Count 59:
A **VIOLATION OF THE LAWS OR CUSTOMS OF WAR**, punishable under Article 3 of the Statute of the Tribunal and recognised by Article 3 (1) (c) (outrages upon personal dignity) of the Geneva Convention.

COUNT 60
Rape of FWS-75 and FWS-87 and Two Other Women

11.1 On or about 30 October 1992, FWS-75, FWS-87 and two other women were taken from Karaman's house to Foča by **DRAGAN ZELENOVIĆ, GOJKO JANKOVIĆ** and **JANKO JANJIĆ**. These women continued to be detained at different houses and apartments, and continued to be subjected to sexual assaults.

11.2 On or about 30 October 1992, the three above-mentioned perpetrators took FWS-75, FWS-87 and the two other women into an apartment near the Fish Restaurant in Foča. There, all four women were raped by **DRAGAN ZELENOVIĆ, GOJKO JANKOVIĆ** and **JANKO JANJIĆ**.

11.3 By the acts, described in paragraph 11.2 , **GOJKO JANKOVIĆ, DRAGAN ZELENOVIĆ** and **JANKO JANJIĆ** committed:

Count 60:
A **CRIME AGAINST HUMANITY** punishable under Article 5 (g) (rape) of the Statute of the Tribunal;

COUNTS 61-62
Enslavement and Rape. of FWS-75 and FWS-87 in the Brena Apartment

12.1 **RADOMIR KOVAĆ** detained, between or about 31 October 1992 until December 1992 witness FWS-75 and until February 1993 witness FWS-87. **RADOMIR KOVAĆ** was in charge of an apartment in the Brena block and had taken over the two witnesses together with two other women he had received from **DRAGAN ZELENOVIĆ, GOJKO JANKOVIĆ** and **JANKO JANJIĆ**. Their situation was similar to what they had experienced in Karaman's house. They had to perform household chores and were frequently sexually assaulted.

12.2 FWS-75 was detained in this apartment from about 31 October until about 20 November 1992. During that time she had to do household chores and sexually please soldiers. **RADOMIR KOVAĆ** and others frequently raped her. Around 20 November 1992, **RADOMIR KOVAĆ** took FWS-75 and victim A. B. from the apartment to a house near the Hotel Zelengora. They were kept there for about twenty days, during which time they were frequently sexually assaulted by a group of Serbian soldiers. Although the two women were no longer in the Brena apartment, **RADOMIR KOVAĆ** still was in charge of them. Around 10 December 1992, FWS-75 and victim A.B. were moved from the house near Hotel Zelengora to a flat in the Pod

IT 96 23 -- I 142

Masala neighbourhood of Foča. There, they stayed for about fifteen days, together with the same soldiers as the weeks before. FWS-75 and A.B. were frequently raped during those fifteen days. On the night when FWS-75 and the other women were brought back to the apartment, **RADOMIR KOVAĆ** sold A. B. to a an unidentified soldier for 200 DM. In December 1992 FWS-75 was handed over to **JANKO JANJIĆ**.

12.3 FWS-87 was detained in **RADOMIR KOVAĆ**'s apartment from on or about 31 October until about 25 February, 1993. During this entire time, she was raped by **RADOMIR KOVAĆ** and another unidentified man.

12.4 On one occasion, during their detention in **RADOMIR KOVAĆ**'s place, FWS-75, FWS-87 and the other women were forced to take all their clothes off and dance naked on a table, while **RADOMIR KOVAĆ** watched.

12.5 On or about 25 February, 1993, FWS-87 and another woman were sold by **RADOMIR KOVAĆ** for 500 DM each to two unidentified Montenegrin soldiers, who took them to Montenegro.

12.6 By the foregoing acts and omissions, **RADOMIR KOVAĆ** committed:

Count 61:
A **CRIME AGAINST HUMANITY** punishable under Article 5 (c) (enslavement) of the Statute of the Tribunal;

Count 62:
A **CRIME AGAINST HUMANITY** punishable under Article 5 (g) (rape) of the Statute of the Tribunal;

Richard J. Goldstone
Prosecutor
13-6-96

Appendix 12

Coalition for International Justice Whereabouts List (Sightings of Indicted War Criminals)

Name (Ethnicity) Where Crimes Committed	Town/Country/ Entity	Whereabouts
1) Mirko Babic (Bosnian Serb) Omarska	Prijedor, Republika Srpska	Lives in Prijedor and works as a metal worker at the Bosna Montaza construction company (Human Rights Watch source, December 1996).
2) Nenad Banovic (Bosnian Serb) Keraterm	Prijedor, Republika Srpska	Frequents "Express" restaurant in Prijedor. Lives at home in Prijedor. Twin brother to Predrag Banovic. One of the Banovic brothers was seen driving a motor scooter in Prijedor in late November 1996 (*Christian Science Monitor*, November 28, 1996).
3) Predrag Banovic (Bosnian Serb) Keraterm	31 Cirkin Polje Street Prijedor Republika Srpska	Frequents "Express" restaurant in Prijedor. Lives in Prijedor. Twin brother to Nenad Banovic. One of the Banovic brothers was seen driving a motor scooter in Prijedor in late November 1996. (*Christian Science Monitor*, November 28, 1996).

Name (Ethnicity) Where Crimes Committed	Town/Country/Entity	Whereabouts
Pedrag Banovic (cont.)		Australian reporter Gordon Weiss saw Banovic at Banovic's home, at 31 Cirkin Polje Street. Local police stated that the Banovics (Predrag and Nenad) both work for reserve police. They share a red motorbike and are often seen riding through town ("In the Land of the War Criminals" by Gordon Weiss, The Associated Press, April 17, 1997).
4) Ranko Cesic (Bosnian Serb) Luka/Brcko	Brcko (currently under Bosnian Serb control)	Lives in Brcko. Spotted in a café in Brcko in late 1996 (Human Rights Watch source, December 1996).
5) Damir Dosen (Bosnian Serb) Keraterm	Omlandinski Put 42–suburb of Prijedor Republika Srpska	Lives at Omlandinski Put 42, in the Prijedor suburbs and occasionally visits his parents who live in the town (SFOR Wanted poster January 21, 1997; *Stern* Magazine, July, 1997).
6) Dragan Fustar (Bosnian Serb) Keraterm	Prijedor, Republika Srpska	Residence address listed on the IFOR Wanted poster was 41 First of May (Prvomajska) Street in Prijedor. A journalist found Fustar's mother and wife living there in late November 1996. The number sign has been pulled from the house. His mother and wife say that they live at 27 First of May Street, even though the building is located between 39 and 43 First of May Street. He is unemployed (*Christian*

NAME (ETHNICITY) WHERE CRIMES COMMITTED	TOWN/COUNTRY/ENTITY	WHEREABOUTS
Dragan Fustar (cont.)		*Science Monitor*, November 28, 1996). Dragan Fustar visits his mother in First of May Street 41 (The Associated Press, May 25, 1997).
7) Dragan Gagovic (Bosnian Serb) Foca/Srbinje	Foca/Srbinje, Republika Srpska	Chief of police in Foca/Srbinje (Sunday *Times* of London, July 28, 1996). In April 1997 Dragan Gagovic was working as a police trainer in a police training school in Trjentiste. The school is run by General Soric. Gagovic owns a bar in Foca/Srbinje and can be seen in town driving a green Rabbit (Thomas Keenan, SUNY, Binghamton). Owns the Krsma bar in Foca, where Janko Janic (also indicted, see below) often drinks. (Harald Doornbas, Rotterdams Nieuwsblad , February 20, 1998).
8) Momcilo Gruban (Bosnian Serb), Omarska	Prijedor, Republika Srpska	Unemployed and living in Prijedor (SFOR Wanted poster, January 21, 1997).
9) Janko Janic (Bosnian Serb), Foca/Srbinje	Mose Pijade Street Foca/Srbinje, Republika Srpska	Lives on Mose Pijad Street in Foca/Srbinje. Spotted by a Greek journalist monitoring elections in September, 1997 and interviewed on film by CBS. Story aired on *Public Eye* (CBS) October 15, 1997. Extensively tattooed (including eyelids) (*Stern* Magazine, July 1997; CBS *Public Eye*, October 15, 1997; CBS *Public Eye*, October 15, 1997;

Name (Ethnicity) Where Crimes Committed	Town/Country/Entity	Whereabouts
Janko Janjic (cont.)		*Wall Street Journal-Europe*, September 24, 1997). Nicknamed "Tuta." Drinks coffee and rakija every morning around 9 o'clock at "Merkur," "Passenger" or "Krsma." Passes the local IPTF headquarters on favorite bars. One tattoo on his his way to his forehead reads "I was dead even before I was born" (Harald Doornbos, Rotterdams Nieuwsblad, February 20, 1998).
10) Nikica Janjic (Bosnian Serb) Omarska and Keraterm	Banja Luka, Republika Srpska	According to friends and his father, he killed himself in September 1995 (*Christian Science Monitor,* November 28, 1996).
11) Gojko Jankovic (Bosnian Serb), Foca/Srbinje	Foca/Srbinje, Republika Srpska	Seen by a journalist at a Foca/Srbinje cafe while "French soldiers from IFOR . . . leant against a nearby wall smoking cigarettes and paying no attention as Jankovic, accompanied by bodyguards, casually ordered a drink" (*Sunday Times of London*, July 28, 1996). Tried to get on the ballot for municipal elections. OSCE spotted it and stopped him. The business partner of Nedzad Njuhovic, a Foca goldsmith who has been Janko Janic's best friend since childhood (statement of partnership by Njuhovic). Owns a local bar and works for the police. Has traveled to

Name (Ethnicity) Where Crimes Committed	Town/Country/Entity	Whereabouts
Gojko Jankovic (cont.)		Serbia at least once in 1998 to close a business deal (statement by Njuhovic) (Harald Doornbos, Roterdams Nieuwsblad, February 20, 1998).
12) Radovan Karadzic (Bosnian Serb) Sarajevo and Srebenica **Indicted for genocide**	Pale, Republika Srpska Banja Luka, Republika Srpska	Pale house—large house on a mountainside—pointed out to Purdue Prof. Charles Ingrao on trip to Pale (*New York Times*, October 28, 1996). Has a friend, Slavko Rogulic, who runs a gas station and hotel for him in Banja Luka. Also buildng a house in Koljani village near Banja Luka. "[M]akes little effort to conceal his daily movements" (The Associated Press, November 9, 1996). Karadzic lives less than a kilometer from SFOR troops. He is described as "a creature of habit." UN sources say that he travels regularly between his home and his office in a black Mercedes limousine ("NATO bid to capture Karadzic" by Chris Stephen in Agence France Presse May 20, 1997. The Office of Carl Bilt has "hard evidence" that Radovan Karadzic holds meetings with Momcilo Krajisnik at Karadzic's house in Pale (from interview with Colum Murphy, spokesperson for Carl Bilt, BiHTV News Summary 27 May, 1997 and BBC Summary of World Broadcasts, June 21, 1997). In August of 1997, met with reporter at his office at the Famous truck factory in Pale (*Esquire*,

Name (Ethnicity) Where Crimes Committed	Town/Country/Entity	Whereabouts
Radovan Karadzic (cont.)		December, 1997). May have left Pale. House empty during April 1998 SFOR exercises, but wife seen in Pale bakery at that time (Agence-France Presse, April 18, 1998).
13) Dusan Knezevic (Bosnian Serb) Keraterm	Nenanja Vlatkovic Street, Sipovo, Republika Srpska	Unemployed and living in Nenanja Vlatkovic Street in Sipovo. Reportedly obese (Human Rights Watch source, December 1996; international monitor in Sipovo, July, 1997).
14) Dragan Kondic (Bosnian Serb) Keraterm	Prijedor, Republika Srpska	Said to have connections with special police in Ljubija. Hangs out almost every night at "The Pink" bar in Prijedor (SFOR Wanted poster, January 21, 1997).
15) Milojica Kos (Bosnian Serb) Omarska	Omarska, Republika Srpska	His brother Zeljko Kos owns the "Europa" restaurant in Omarska, across the street from the Omarska camp buildings; Milojica Kos is frequently at the restaurant. Otherwise, he is keeping a low profile in Omarska (*Christian Science Monitor*, November 28, 1996).

Name (Ethnicity) Where Crimes Committed	Town/Country/Entity	Whereabouts
16) Radomir Kovac (Bosnian Serb) Foca/Srbinje	Foca/Srbinje, Republika Srpska	A journalist said at the IFOR press briefing on November 19, 1996, that Kovac was still working for the Foca/Srbinje police. IPTF spokesman Alexander Ivanko replied, "I heard these reports. We can't confirm them. We have to take [Bosnian Serb Interior] Minister Kijac at his word, and he says nobody who has been indicted is working as a policman in his letter to Peter Fitzgerald, so for the time being we'll take him at his word."
17) Goran Lajic (Bosnian Serb) Keraterm	Bulevar Revolucije, Banja Luka Republika Srpska	Living on Bulevar Revolucije in Banja Luka (SFOR Wanted poster, January 21, 1997).
18) Zoran Marinic (Bosnian Croat) Lasva Valley	Busovaca, Federation of B-H	Living in Buscova, Federation of B-H Croat controlled town (SFOR Wanted poster, January 21, 1997).

Name (Ethnicity) Where Crimes Committed	Town/Country/Entity	Whereabouts
19) Milan Martic (Croatian Serb) Zagreb rocket attack	Ulica Milosa Oblica 88, Banja Luka, Republika Srpska	"[H]is place of residence has been precisely located . . ." (Telegraf [Belgrade], Feb. 28, 1996). Believed living in Banja Luka (London Press Association, March 8, 1996). Said to have regular meetings with Plavsic, et al. Attended a public event near Banja Luka in July also attended by IFOR personnel (Human Rights Watch press release, November 8, 1996). Seen in Banja Luka on Nov. 5, 1996. Lives less than 100 meters from IFOR civilian affairs center in Banja Luka (Human Rights Watch press release, November 8, 1996). Gave a videotape interview from his office in Banja Luka (*ABC World News Tonight*, November 26, 1996). Milan Martic lives at Ulica Milosa Oblica 88. (Mario Dederichs in The Associated Press, May 25,1997). The London *Times* interviewed Milan Martic in June 1997. His house is within walking distance of the International Police Task Force building, the regional office of the High Representative, and other international agencies. There are 5,000 British SFOR soldiers five miles away (London *Times*, June 10, 1997).

Name (Ethnicity) Where Crimes Committed	Town/Country/Entity	Whereabouts
20) Zeljko Meakic [also spelled "Mejakic"] (Bosnian Serb) Omarska **Indicted for genocide**	Omarska, Republika, Srpska	Deputy commander of Omarska police station (*Boston Globe*, Oct. 31, 1996, page A6). Put on leave (*ABC World News Tonight*, November 26, 1996). On duty as recently as October 20, 1996 (*Christian Science Monitor,* November 28, 1996).
21) Slobodan Miljkovic (Bosnian Serb) Bosanski Samac	Kragujevac, FRY	Kragujevac is 60 miles southeast of Belgrade (*Time* Magazine, May 13, 1996).
22) Ratko Mladic (Bosnian Serb) Sarajevo and Srebrenica **indicted for genocide**	Han Pijesak, Republika Srpska Belgrade, FRY	Lives inside his headquarters (numerous sources). Maintains an apartment in Belgrade. General Mladic lives in the bunkered command center Crna Rijeka in the mountains of Han Pijesak (Mario Dederichs, The Associated Press, May 25, 1997). Was to travel to Belgrade to attend his son's wedding sometime in June. Seen in Montenegro and Serbia on several occasions (Bosnian Serb media and *Extra* Magazine in Agence France Presse, June 16, 1997).

Name (Ethnicity) Where Crimes Committed	Town/Country/Entity	Whereabouts
23) Mile Mrksic (Yugoslav Serb) Vukovar	Banja Luka, Republika Srpska	General in the JNA at the time of Vukovar takeover; then went to work for the Krajina Serbs. Reported to have been in Banja Luka (*New York Times*, January 5, 1996). Later reported to have retired and now living a solitary life in Belgrade (*Vreme*, April 6, 1996).
24) Dragan Nikolic (Bosnian Serb) Susica	Vlasenica, Republika Srpska	Either in the Republika Srpska army or the Republika Srpska civilian government (Reuters, February 16, 1996).
25) Milan Pavlic (Bosnian Serb) Omarska	Petrov Gaj, Republika Srpska	Reportedly living in Petrov Gaj, near Omarska (Human Rights Watch source, December 1996).
26) Dragoljub Prcac (Bosnian Serb) Omarska	Prijedor, Republika Srpska	Unemployed and reportedly living in Omarska with his wife and two children (SFOR Wanted poster, January 21, 1997).
27) Drazenko Predojevic (Bosnian Serb) Omarska	Prijedor, Republika Srpska	Unemployed and reportedly living in Prijedor, where he tends his family's livestock (SFOR Wanted poster, January 21, 1997).
28) Miroslav Radic (Yugoslav Serb) Vukovar	In the Serbian "provinces"	Operates a private company in the "provinces" of Serbia (*Vreme*, April 6, 1996).

Name (Ethnicity) Where Crimes Committed	Town/Country/Entity	Whereabouts
29) Ivica Rajic (Bosnian Croat) Stupni Do	Split, Croatia?	Lived in a Croatian-government owned hotel, believed to be the Zagreb Hotel, but has since reportedly left Split (Globus [Zagreb]; reported by Reuters, October 23 and 24, 1996).
30) Dusko Sikirica (Bosnian Serb), Keraterm **Indicted for genocide**	Prijedor, Republika Srpska	Tried to get on the ballot for municipal elections. OSCE spotted it and stopped him. OSCE should know his address (SFOR Wanted poster; *Stern* Magazine, July, 1997).
31) Blagoje Simic (Bosnian Serb)	Bosanski Samac, Republika Srpska	Highest-ranking public official in Bosanski Samac, with an office in the town hall (*Boston Globe*, November 1, 1996, page A1).
32) Veselin Sljivancanin (Yugoslav Serb)	Belgrade, FRY	Reportedly had falling out with his superior, Gen. Milan MRKSIC, also indicted for Vukovar (*New York Times*, January 5, 1996). Promoted to full colonel and transferred to Belgrade (Agence France-Presse, February 16, 1996). Now head of the Center of Advanced Military Schools in Belgrade (Svijet [Sarajevo], Apri 25, 1996). Also referred to as an instructor at the Center of Advanced Military Schools in Belgrade (*Vreme*, April 6, 1996). Living in Belgrade.

Name (Ethnicity) Where Crimes Committed	Town/Country/Entity	Whereabouts
33) Radovan Stankovic	Foca/Srbinje	Working in the Republika Srpska police in Foca/Srbinje as of August, 1996, according to IPTF spokesman Alexander Ivanko. In August, Stankovic walked into IPTF police station near Sarajevo, but IPTF did not recognize his name. Local police stopped him, asked to see his driver's license, recognized his name, ordered him to come to a police station, whereupon he fled—later to file a complaint with the IPTF alleging that the Bosnian police fired shots at his car (Reuters, November 8, 1996). In August, 1996, Stankovic filed a complaint against the Bosnian police at an IPTF office. "After being embarrassed by the fact that journalists discovered five others indicted on war-crime charges in the Serbian police force, U.N. officials reacted by forbidding their monitors to discuss the Stankovic case with reporters" (*New York Times,* November 9, 1996).
34) Nedjeljko Timarac (Bosnian Serb), Keraterm	Prijedor, Republika Srpska	Works at Prijedor police station (Reuters, October 29, 1996). Put on leave (*ABC World News Tonight*, November 26, 1996).

NAME (ETHNICITY) WHERE CRIMES COMMITTED	TOWN/COUNTRY/ENTITY	WHEREABOUTS
35) Stevan Todorovic (Bosnian Serb) Bosanski Samac	Donja Slatina, Republika Srpska	Deputy of the local office of Republika Srpska state security in Bosanski Samac; works the night shift (7 P.M.–7 A.M.) (*Boston Globe*, November 1, 1996, page A1). Lives in the village of Donja Slatina, a 3 minute, 30 second drive from American-staffed NATO base of Camp Colt, with 1,000 soldiers. His commuter route is routinely traveled by NATO patrols (*Boston Globe*, November 1, 1996, page A1).
36) Zoran Vukovic (Bosnian Serb) Foca/Srbinje	Prijedor, Republika Srpska	Living in Prijedor (SFOR Wanted poster, January 21, 1997).
37) Dragan Zelenovic (Bosnian Serb) Foca/Srbinje	Foca/Srbinje, Republika Srpska	A journalist said at the IFOR for the Foca/Srbinje police. IPTF spokesman Alexander Ivanko replied, "I heard these reports. We can't confirm them. We have to take [Bosnian Serb Interior] Minister Kijac at his word, and he says nobody who has been indicted is working as a policeman in his letter to Peter Fitzgerald, so for the time being we'll take him at his word."

Source: Coalition For International Justice http://www.wcw.org/wcw/, last updated: April 16, 1998.

About the Background Papers Authors

Bringing War Criminals to Justice: Obligations, Options, Recommendations

Marshall Freeman Harris is vice president of Freedom House, a Washington, D.C.-based organization dedicated to promoting democracy and liberty throughout the world. As a U.S. Foreign Service officer, he served for eight years in overseas missions in Britain, Bulgaria, and Macedonia and in Washington as special assistant in the office of Secretary of State James Baker. In 1993, he resigned from the State Department in protest against U.S. inaction in Bosnia. He was a founder of the Action Council for Peace in the Balkans and, in 1995, cofounded the Balkan Institute. He served as the institute's executive director until joining Freedom House in 1997. His op-ed articles and other commentary on Balkan and European security issues appear frequently in national newspapers and other publications.

R. Bruce Hitchner is director of The University of Dayton Center for International Programs and professor of ancient history and archaeology. He received his A.M. from the University of Chicago and Ph.D. from the University of Michigan. In 1994, he was elected by-fellow at Churchill College, Cambridge University. He is the recipient of grants and fellowships from the Fulbright Commission, the British Academy, the National Geographic Society, the National Endowment for the Humanities, the French Ministry of Culture, and the United States Information Agency, and he is the author of numerous publications on Roman history and archaeology. He organized the Dayton Peace Accords Revisited Symposium in Dayton in 1996, the workshop on war crimes funded by the Packard Foundation that culminated in the publication of the report "Bringing War Criminals to Justice," and the Dayton Peace Accords Revisited Forum in 1997.

Michael P. Scharf is professor of international law and director of the Center for International Law and Policy at the New England School of Law. He holds a J.D. from Duke University School of Law and served as judicial clerk to Judge Gerald B. Tjoflat of the U.S. Court of Appeals for the Eleventh Circuit before joining the Office of the Legal Adviser of the U.S. Department of State in 1989. While at the State Department, he served as attorney adviser for United Nations affairs and as a member of the U.S. delegations to the UN General Assembly and Human Rights Commission. In 1993, he received the State Department's Meritorious Honor Award "in recognition of superb performance and exemplary leadership in support of U.S. policy initiatives regarding the former Yugoslavia." Since leaving the State Department, he has authored two dozen articles and four books, including the Pulitzer Prize-nominated *Balkan Justice*. During the first trial before the International Criminal Tribunal for the former Yugoslavia, he served as a frequent expert commentator on *Court TV*.

Paul R. Williams is a senior associate with the Carnegie Endowment for International Peace, where he directs the Public International Law and Policy Program. He is also executive director of the Public International Law and Policy Group, which provides pro bono legal assistance to developing states and states in transition. In addition, he holds a joint appointment as assistant professor of law and international relations at American University's Washington College of Law and School of International Service, where he directs the J.D./M.A. joint degree program. During the course of his legal practice, he has served as legal adviser to the Bosnian delegation during the Dayton peace negotiations, advised the president of Estonia on territorial negotiations with Russia, advised the president of Macedonia on matters relating to state sovereignty and its various disputes with Greece, advised the president of Bosnia on implementation of the Dayton Peace Accords, and established a program to provide legal assistance to the International Criminal Tribunal for the former Yugoslavia.

Responsibilities of States Participating in Multilateral Operations with Respect to Persons Indicted for War Crimes

Diane F. Orentlicher is professor of law at the Washington College of Law, American University, Washington, D.C., where she has taught since 1992. She is also director of the law school's War Crimes Research Office, which undertakes legal analysis in support of the Office of the Prosecutor of the International War Crimes Tribunals for the former Yugoslavia and Rwanda. She has taught courses on international law and policy at Oxford University and the law schools of Harvard, Yale, and Columbia Universities. She has undertaken numerous field investigations on behalf of the Lawyers Committee for Human Rights, Human Rights Watch, the International Human Rights Law Group, the United Nations Human Rights Centre, and the International Criminal Tribunal for the former Yugoslavia. She has degrees from Yale University (B.A.) and Columbia Law School (J.D.), where she served as an editor of the *Columbia Law Review.*